REBEL SUMMER

CINDY STEEL

This is a work of fiction. Names, characters, places, and incidents either are the product of the author's imagination or are used fictitiously. Any resemblance to actual persons, living or dead, events, or locales is entirely coincidental.

Copyright © 2024 by Cindy Steel

All rights reserved.

No part of this book may be reproduced in any form or by any electronic or mechanical means, including information storage and retrieval systems, without written permission from the author, except for the use of brief quotations in a book review.

Cover Design by Melody Jeffries

www.cindysteel.com

ALSO BY CINDY STEEL

Pride and Pranks Series

A Christmas Spark

That Fine Line

Stranded Ranch

Double or Nothing

Christmas Escape Series

Faking Christmas

The One Series

The One with the Kiss Cam

TRIGGER WARNING

Though this book is a lighthearted and comedic closed door romance, there are a few heavier themes woven throughout. Namely—parental manipulation, narcissism, sibling abandonment, and a brief scene of an attempted sexual assault. These topics are handled with as much care as possible, but please consider this knowledge before you proceed.
Thank you!

To James,
The best qualities of my fictional
male heroes are always inspired by you.

WELCOME TO SUNSET HARBOR

Sunset Harbor is a fictional island set off the west coast of Florida. Each book in the Falling for Summer series is set in this dreamy town and uses crossover characters and events, creating fun connections throughout the series. Though each book is a standalone novel, be sure to read all seven novels so you can fully experience the magic of Sunset Harbor!

PROLOGUE

Where it began
Day 47

The palm trees above my head swayed in the breeze, causing an eerie sound as I sat in the pitch black, wondering what to do next. I had just left a ribbon-cutting ceremony at the island's nature preserve. My golf cart made it halfway home before coming to a sputtering halt, leaving me stranded on the side of the road. I tried both of my parents' numbers again before chucking the phone into my purse. Apparently, they cared more about whatever bigwig they were trying to impress tonight than accepting a phone call from their only daughter.

Volleyball practice started at 5:30 the next morning, and my dad hadn't been anywhere near ready to leave his precious event, hence me skipping out on my own. I contemplated walking home, but I had worn a dress and the highest heels in my mom's closet and couldn't fathom covering the distance. A flash of headlights turned the corner, coming my way. My initial instinct was to hide, but there was a good chance on this tiny island that I knew whoever it was. I stepped out of the golf cart and waited until the fast-approaching cart came to a screeching stop beside me.

I definitely should have hid.

Dax Miller peered over at me through the open doorway of

the cart, his eyes slightly wild. He glanced behind him before calling over to me.

"You broke down?"

"Battery died. I'll just call Cat."

My unfortunate biology partner—no, that didn't sound right...the biology partner I was unfortunate enough to have wasn't someone I was about to step into a vehicle with. If I couldn't trust him to operate a scalpel properly, there was no way I would trust him to take me home.

"It's almost eleven. Just get in." He seemed distracted, obsessively checking every direction. I was distracted by his distraction and absolutely *not* by the manly jawline or the dark rumpled hair that gave the unruly moron a certain boyish charm. My feet stayed firmly planted on the blacktop.

"You gotta move faster if you want a ride, Books."

"I don't." I smiled at him.

To his credit—and he didn't have much credit with me—a look of hesitation passed over his face. "I can't leave you here in the dark."

"Nothing ever happens on this island."

His eyebrows rose. "You sure about that?"

The warm island breeze lifted the curls at the nape of my neck. The trees rustled above me. I glanced around the darkened road, trying hard to look like I wasn't nervous at all to be stranded. It was a small island—less than two thousand people. I'd be fine. I didn't need Dax's help. He jolted his cart onward a few paces, testing me, and my feet lurched forward after him.

"Come on," he said.

"Fine. Why are you in such a hurry?" I asked, reluctantly trudging toward him.

"So I can write in my journal before I go to bed," was his obnoxious reply as I slid into the seat beside him.

The golf cart looked fancy—a newer model with plush seats and one I was surprised to see Dax driving. In all actuality, he looked more like a car guy. If the island of Sunset Harbor ever allowed actual cars to be driven on the streets, I'd imagine him in one of those scratched and dented old muscle cars.

"Nice wheels," I said.

The bottom of my sequined dress had barely crossed the threshold before Dax slammed on the gas pedal and peeled out. Obviously, "peeling out" in a golf cart was really more just springing ahead in a quick burst of forward movement.

"What are you doing?!" I asked, grabbing the handrail on the dash in front of me. Though we weren't going fast by a car's standards, there were no doors on this thing, and I was in a slick dress.

Dax didn't say a word as he rounded the bend toward the quiet town square in the center of the four-mile-long island.

"What's going on?" I asked again.

Suddenly, flashes of red, blue, and yellow blazed behind us. A police siren cut through the night. I turned around and stared at the police golf cart with lights strapped on top. I wondered who he was—

I stopped. Turning slowly in my seat, I gave Dax a withering glare.

"Is he chasing you?"

No answer.

"Why is he chasing you?" I demanded.

Dax glanced in the rearview mirror. "I mean...there's not a lot to do here."

Things began slowly ticking into place.

"Is this golf cart *stolen*?!"

To my dismay, Dax laughed off my question.

"Let's just say borrowed."

"Stop right now, and let me out!" Panic surged inside me. I glanced down at the road, now a blur beneath my feet, and considered the physical damage if I were to jump.

"No can do, Books. He'll catch up. Just hang on. I'll outrun him in a sec."

"If you get me in trouble, my dad will kill us both."

"Hey, you got into this cart of your own free will."

"I didn't know it was stolen!" I smacked his arm with my purse.

Dax's hand pressed on the top of my hair, pushing me down in my seat. "Get down, then. Your curly mop's a dead giveaway."

I smoothed down my hair, slinking further into my seat. He took a hard right, down a dark street just past the shops on the town square in the center of the island, causing me to slide against his body. For one blinding moment, it felt like we could be out on a date. An evening ride coming back from watching the sunset while I sweetly laid my head on his shoulder. I righted myself immediately. He was a criminal. Now was not the time to feel attraction.

"Where are we going?" I demanded.

There was a slight pause before he said, "Your house."

My jaw dropped as he turned down my street.

"No! There's a cop back there. I'm not a part of this!"

"Ever heard of being in the wrong place at the wrong time, Ivy Brooks? It's usually pretty normal for politicians."

"Pull over right now!" I yelled, ignoring his crack about my dad.

"If I pull over, he'll see you. If you start running, he'll probably tackle you to the ground."

I squeezed my hands on the handrail. "Dax, I hate your guts. It's official."

He nodded toward my garage. "Get ready to open the door."

"I'm not letting you in."

"Then I'll be parked outside your house when he drives by. You're an accomplice either way. If you hide us both, then you're home free."

His logic was flawed. I knew that, but still, my heart thundered inside my chest when the cart came to a roaring stop on my driveway. I flew from the seat, clutching my shoes in my hands, and stormed toward the doorway leading into the garage. Adrenaline coursing through my veins, I didn't give myself time to think as I pounded on the garage door opener. Dax rolled inside, and I punched the button again. It closed, leaving us in complete darkness.

No more than thirty seconds later, flashing lights lit up the garage, giving me a chance to find my bearings and to see that Dax was now out of the golf cart and striding toward the small windows at the tops of our garage doors.

He found my dad's stepladder and used the extra height to peer out the window.

"Is he coming?" I whispered frantically, making my way closer to him in the dark. If I were caught harboring a fugitive, I would be disowned.

Dax watched out the window for another long moment before he said, "Nah. He's just turning around."

I let out a breath before saying, "I'm going to kill you."

"Where's your sense of adventure?"

"Why do you have a stolen golf cart? Whose is it?" I interrogated, hands at my hips.

Dax had the audacity to laugh even as his eyes trailed briefly down the length of my dress. "Every few months, me and some of the guys...uh...rearrange the golf carts on the island. Move them to different houses. But that's all I should tell you."

"That's *you*?! They've been trying to catch you guys for months. My dad's cart was moved to Larry Donald's house last time. He was ticked."

One side of his mouth pulled into a smile. "Guilty."

Once the policeman had left my driveway, I flipped on the garage light and began nudging Dax toward the contraband golf cart. "Okay, well...bye. This has been fun."

"Same time next week?" he teased, ignoring me to peek out the window again. "We could use another lookout."

With muscles I didn't know I had, I yanked him off the stepladder and pushed him toward the golf cart. "You have to go! My dad will be home any second."

He stopped abruptly, and my body pitched forward, brushing against his shoulder before I pulled back like I'd been burned.

"Wait. The senator?" Dax asked, his tone growing elevated.

"Yes! Bye! I had a terrible time."

"How exciting! Do you think he'll shake my hand?"

I threw every ounce of strength I had against him as talk of my dad created a panic in my chest. "Go! I'm serious."

He turned around to face me, mischief lighting his features. "You know, I've been meaning to mail him a letter about that new water bill."

"No, you haven't!"

"This will be great. It'll save me a stamp."

A laugh bubbled out of me before I could stop it, even as hysteria began to climb up my neck in the form of heated red splotches. Twenty minutes ago, I was leaving a ritzy ribbon-cutting ceremony. Now I was HIDING FROM A COP. Based on my current heart rate, a life of crime was not for me. I looked down to find that Dax's hands were now on mine, counteracting my attempt at shoving him toward the cart.

Suddenly, he stopped resisting my efforts and allowed his arms to go slack, which meant that, without the resistance, I also went slack.

Directly into his warm chest.

My body froze, cocooned against a chest with a heart beating much faster than normal. Or maybe that was mine. Last I checked, we were fighting. We were always fighting. He loved to make me mad, and I loved to put him in his place.

Nestled against his chest was definitely not my place.

Our clenched fingers had yet to uncurl from their fisted embrace. His chest just felt so...warm. A direct contrast to the detached image he presented to the world. He didn't pull away. Instead, it almost felt as though he inched closer.

"You want me to go?" Dax's low voice sent my pulse skyrocketing.

I still hadn't moved away from him. The feeling between us had shifted so quickly my head was having a hard time catching up. This was DAX. The biology partner I detested. The guy barely passing high school. Dax, who made me miserable in class.

He was trouble.

I just...didn't know trouble could have such gentle hands. His fingers released mine to move to my neck, tugging the locks of my hair and coaxing my chin to lift. It was troubling to gaze into murky eyes that enticed and pulled and...convinced. When his darkened gaze lowered to my lips, a shiver nipped my spine. Trouble grew closer until he was a blur of lashes and softness. Troubling lips, brushing ever so—

The side door flung open, slamming against the shelves lining the garage. We both jumped at the sound. Seeing who it was, I pushed myself out of Dax's arms.

My dad stood there with my mom peering around his shoulder. My mom wore a new gown of hunter-green silk she'd bought for the occasion. My dad wore a striking gray suit and green tie to coordinate. They both wore matching expressions of shock that brought the whole ensemble to another level.

The senator's voice wasn't loud in anger, though sometimes I wished it was. To have the tone match the words would have definitely made things less confusing. His voice was soft, but his words were cold like steel. Like the knife I had metaphorically stabbed in his back.

"What is going on here?"

Dax ran a hand through his hair and took another step back.

"I was just taking her home, sir. Her cart ran out of battery."

"In a stolen golf cart?"

We both looked at him in shock while my stomach coiled into knots.

He let out a dry laugh that held no trace of humor. "Francis, from the police department, just called me. Said he chased a stolen golf cart into my garage and thought he saw my daughter inside. But as a favor to me, he said he'd let me check it out first."

"Dax was just..." I floundered for words. For some reason, a protectiveness for Dax surged through my veins, and I wasn't sure what to do with that knowledge. "It was just a prank. They're not really stealing them."

"The second you take a vehicle off of someone's property without them knowing, it's stolen." He scoffed and nodded toward Dax. "Is that what he told you? That he's not really stealing it?"

I glanced at Dax. *Yes, but...*

"It's my fault, sir," Dax said, casually stuffing his hands in his pockets.

My dad's gray eyes narrowed in on Dax. "Oh, I know it is. That's why you're going to leave now, return the golf cart, and stay away from my daughter. You hear me? Unless you prefer that I go to the police."

"Yes, sir." Dax's voice was polite, but his face twisted as though something amused him. He took a seat in the golf cart and turned the key.

My dad brushed past my arm, punching the garage door button. The squeak of the door rising felt like awkward elevator music while we all waited.

"I now know who's involved in these thefts," my dad said, walking alongside Dax as he backed out. "So remember that. If I hear of you doing this again, I *will* be going straight to the police. If Francis is not out there waiting for you right now, consider yourself lucky. Now get off my property."

My dad turned around and strode back to where my mom and I stood. A small smile touched Dax's lips before he threw me a salute and disappeared into the night.

CHAPTER 1

From: drbarbmeadows@email.com
To: ivybrooks1234@email.com
Date: June 6th
Subject: RE: HELP ME PLEASE

Hi Ivy,

It's so nice to hear from you again. I'm proud of you for reaching out. Spending time with a difficult family member can be emotionally complex. It's so important to give yourself grace while creating boundaries for yourself.

I have a few tips I like to give to clients. Obviously, nothing in life goes as smoothly as we'd like, but hopefully, these tricks will help your weekend to go as well as possible.

1. Avoid engaging in unnecessary conversations.

2. If you do have an encounter—keep calm. Breathing exercises can help maintain composure over passive-aggressive remarks or manipulative tactics.

3. Create an exit strategy. Put distance between yourself and the situation.

4. Surround yourself with positive influences.

I hope these tips help you. Feel free to reach out anytime. I love hearing from past clients. My door is always open.

Best,

Dr. Barb Meadows
Licensed Marriage and Family Therapist

I closed my email, checked the time, and slid my phone into the inside pocket of my purse. Four things. That was doable. Easy to remember. Bless your sweet little heart, Dr. Barb.

Drawing in a steady breath of salty ocean air, my gaze skittered across the crowd dressed in suits and silks and sipping champagne, and settled on a man of medium height and unremarkable brown hair talking animatedly in a crowd that hung on his every word. I doubted he even remembered I was here. Clinging to his arm was a brunette beauty named Angela, his new wife of one year.

So far, avoiding conversation had gone swimmingly.

A trail of sweat left its mark down my neck as I drained half a bottle of Coke. For all the money this fancy resort probably made in one night, you'd think they'd be able to afford decent weather—or at least a temperature less muggy.

A warm hand smacked my right shoulder.

"Did you get him?" I asked, turning to smile at my lifelong childhood friend, Cat. The blonde bombshell, who looked absolutely stunning in her blush-pink midi dress, checked her hand before wiping the remnants of the mosquito on her cocktail napkin.

"He's very dead."

"Great. Ten hundred thousand million left to go."

"For a math whiz, your calculation skills are questionable," Cat said, wiping sweat off her forehead with the back of her hand.

"It's a talent." I rubbed at my temples, trying to quiet the uproar inside my head for a moment before glancing around at the wedding party still going strong.

After a staggering number of flight delays and re-routes—thank you, summer storm—I finally made it from Nashville to Florida late this afternoon. I caught the ferry to the island in the nick of time, throwing back a Tylenol and an energy drink.

With ten minutes to spare, I made it to the bride's room at the Belacourt Resort just before the actual ceremony took place. My aunt stuffed me into a bridesmaid's dress much too roomy in the chest before taking a disheartened look at my hair in all its glory. After thirty hours of airports and no sleep, it was a sight to say the least. Within seconds, a gaggle of women I didn't know, bathed in floral perfume and tan lines, went to work giving life back to my limp brown curls and bland complexion.

Once deemed passable, I was hustled from the room to take my place in line to walk down the aisle.

My cousin, Mariah, hadn't grown up on the island, but she had spent many summers here with me and my family. So, when she decided on Sunset Harbor as her preferred wedding venue, nobody blinked an eye. When she called, insisting that I be a bridesmaid, nobody blinked an eye. When she set her wedding date in June on our beautiful but hot and muggy island off the west coast of Florida...well, several of us were blinking our eyes to keep out the sweat—and swatting approximately ten thousand mosquitoes.

Combine all of that with the fact that it was, once again, campaign season with my local senator of a dad, and it was like all the money I'd invested in therapy since leaving the island had gone right out the window.

The twinkle lights at the top deck of the resort shimmered beautifully as I excused myself to grab another Coke, praying this time the caffeine would actually make a difference in my mental state.

"Ivy." My dad, officially on the prowl for votes, grabbed my arm as I passed by and motioned around to the group of partygoers he was standing with. "Friends, this is my daughter, Ivy. She's here visiting for the weekend. She's a mathematics professor at Vanderbilt."

Professor at Vanderbilt. That did sound nice. If I said the words enough times in a row, would it actually happen? Something to think about.

My dad wasn't a tall, imposing man, for as much consternation his presence bestowed upon me. Maybe a few inches taller than my own five foot seven. He kept himself trim for the spotlight and, with the help of hair professionals, had a full head of brown locks. Though, unlike me, he worked hard to keep the curl out. His mid-fifties had been kind to him. Add to that a winning smile that seemed to sparkle in the sunlight, and he was a poster boy for a politician.

Having been well-trained for moments like these my entire life, it was almost comical how I could summon up my beam of a smile toward the men and their wives looking at me curiously.

"Hi! So nice to see you all."

"Vanderbilt?" One of the men chuckled as he leaned across the circle to shake my hand. "No surprise your dad swayed you to Vandy. If you would have talked to me first, I would have put in a good word for you over at Auburn."

My dad's politician laugh was loud and boisterous, like he was telling some great joke at the same time he was selling you the latest and greatest carpet cleaner at your front door. A master salesman. But I could detect the false note in his laughter, and it always surprised me how nobody else seemed to notice.

He put his arm around my shoulder and squeezed me into his side. "I wouldn't let her come back to visit if she came home wearing blue and orange."

The group laughed, and I joined in. Painful memories of my family suddenly becoming the Brady Bunch for these occasions came flying into my mind. Deep breaths. My exit strategy would be employed in T-minus 60 hours.

I could handle it all for one weekend.

"You're a little young to be a professor, right?" A blonde woman in a floral dress standing next to me smiled. "That's impressive."

My dad wouldn't have made this distinction, but I felt it was important. "It's actually a postdoctoral fellowship position, which is mainly a lot of research, but I will be teaching a block class later this summer." I smiled at her and the group. "So, not technically a professor, but I'm hoping to get hired in another year."

Actually, I and the entire country of post-doctorate graduates in mathematics were all hoping for the same thing, but no need to go into the numbers on that.

"She's still teaching the class." My dad shrugged and laughed like my distinction had been unnecessary to voice, and he moved the conversation forward.

"Nice to meet you all," I whispered to the crowd while another man was talking, and I slinked away and out from under my dad's arm. My dad's wife, Angela, attached to his other arm, shot me a timid smile and a wave at my exit. I summoned all the grown-up kindness I could and gave her a nod and a smile.

"I'm so glad you're here," I told Cat, after I made my way back to her. When I raced off to college immediately after high school ten years earlier, Cat, who stayed on the island, was my collateral damage. Our phone calls, text threads and video chats were the lifeblood that got me through years of deadlines, research, dissertations, my parents' divorce, and now...postdocs.

"Yeah, you're lucky I like Mariah or else you'd owe me one."

Whenever my cousin, Mariah, would come to visit, Cat was usually with us too, the three of us inseparable during her stay.

I glanced at Mariah in her white dress and couldn't help but laugh when she stopped mid-conversation with a plastic smile on her face to smash a mosquito on her neck. At least the insects didn't play favorites.

I shifted my weight in my heels. "I need out of these shoes. Want to go walk the beach for a bit?"

"Yes, please," Cat said.

We dropped our shoes by the staircase of the resort leading to a private beach access and began making our way down the torchlit walkway. I stifled a yawn that threatened to overtake my entire face. I hadn't gone with so little sleep since...well, ever. My rabble-rousing college days were spent in the library. But I was determined to spend time with my old friend, and if I had to staple my eyes open to do it, so be it.

"How's the B&B?" I asked. Cat's uncle ran an adorable inn on the island, and Cat was his right hand. The resort was beautiful, but I definitely preferred the cozy feel of the Keene Bed and Breakfast.

She sighed. "It's fine. It's just hard to keep up with all this." She motioned toward the glowing lights of the posh resort behind us. "But we're doing okay, I think."

We walked in a comfortable silence, the crash of the waves from the dark ocean the perfect white noise as we ambled away from the resort lights.

"How are things with the new wife?"

Angela. My dad's wife of one year. A brunette beauty perfectly occupying the space my mom used to fill. My childhood had been complicated enough, dealing with my parents' rocky relationship. I'd actually been grateful for the divorce and my mom moving to Atlanta. The new wife seemed a little quiet and unassuming, but I didn't have anything against her.

"She seems nice," I finally said. "I honestly just feel sorry that she's hitched her wagon to my dad."

"Are they still technically considered newlyweds?" Cat eyed me with a wicked smile.

I moaned. "I'd better not find out, but if I do, I'll be moving to the couch in the basement." My bedroom was much too close to my dad's room for comfort.

"I wish we had an opening at the B&B for you. But we're booked solid for weeks."

I threw her a grateful look. "Thank you. But I need to put in some face time in order to go another two years without seeing him."

"How's your mom liking Atlanta?" she asked.

"Well, since she's currently on a two-month European tour with a couple of recently divorced friends, I think she's loving it."

She smiled, smacking at a mosquito on her leg. "Any guys in Tennessee?"

"It's so weird. I haven't seen one guy there yet."

She laughed and slung her arm through mine as we walked, our feet squishing through the wet sand. "Come on…fess up. Guys love a bookish math nerd."

I barked out a short laugh. "Apparently, men don't love it when you're always researching and writing papers and never spending time with them."

"That *is* weird. Maybe you should spend time researching guys instead of math theories."

"Math is a much less complicated subject," I said lightly.

There were guys in Tennessee. I had told myself that, after I graduated, things would be different. It didn't take me long after graduation to realize that nothing was different. Postdocs, it turned out, were still endless amounts of research and time away from home. I was open to love but hesitant to offer myself to someone who might find me and my inability to commit lacking, like Stephen, who dumped me two months into our budding relationship last year because he was tired of me silencing his calls from the library.

I mean…I do get it, but I wasn't sure what to do about it.

I took a long breath through my nose, feeling the relaxing pull of the beach. The salt in the air and the low hum of waves crashing next to us. I had a lifetime of memories on this beach. This island. It was heaven on earth, and a small part of me resented being so removed from this life. In Tennessee, I hardly had time to notice what was missing, but here... at this moment, the inviting pull of the water and my toes squishing the sand was hard to overlook.

I checked the time on my phone and stopped walking to rummage through my purse.

"What are you doing?" Cat asked.

"Tylenol," came my one-word reply. I didn't know why I bothered; the medicine hadn't even touched the pain so far. Thirty hours without sleep had been the extra-strength Tylenol's downfall.

I fished out the two white pills and, without water, threw them into my mouth and swallowed.

For the last bit of our walk, Cat regaled me with stories of island life, our friends, and the things she was convinced I was missing in landlocked Tennessee. I listened with great interest as long as I could before my movements grew more sluggish, my thoughts more foggy as we trudged up the stairs of the resort.

"Can I take you home?" Cat asked, eyeing me with concern.

"No. I'm fine. It's not that far. Have fun. Go show some poor innocent guy your dance moves," I teased, using the last of my strength to make a bad joke so she'd feel better about letting me go. I didn't need a babysitter. I needed a bed.

It took a few more protests before she finally relented and gave me a hug, promising to see me again before I left, before winding her way through the crowd to chat with more people. One quick glance at the bride and groom swarmed by guests told me it would be at least a twenty-minute wait before I could get close enough for a goodbye hug. I would just text Mariah a honeymoon joke tomorrow. Apparently, I've got big jokester energy when I'm half delirious.

I found my dad speaking to a set of councilmen and their wives, the ever-faithful Angela standing beside him, hanging on his arm.

Senator Clayton Brooks had been running for something my entire life. He'd been a state representative when I was a child before finally winning the local state senator position when I was in high school—a position he's kept rather easily until this summer when, apparently, someone from the mainland had the audacity to run against him.

He was busy talking, and I knew he wouldn't want to be interrupted, so I stood next to Angela and tapped her on the shoulder.

Her eyes grew wide as she took me in, which made me wonder what state of deterioration I was currently at.

"Hey," I said, smiling brightly.

"Are you okay?" she asked, peering closer.

I forced my eyes to go bigger, though I wasn't sure if that helped. "I'm exhausted. Do you mind if I take a golf cart back home?"

Angela looked at her watch and glanced at my dad, still in conversation with...someone. It was amazing how quickly names could slip my mind. It had been too long since I'd been forced to follow my parents around while my dad social-climbed.

"I don't think your dad will want to leave yet."

My limbs now weighed a thousand pounds. I couldn't wait any longer. I'd walk if I had to.

"But we drove here separately, so you could take your dad's cart home, and then he can come home with me."

I threw her a grateful look. "That would be great. Thank you."

"Ang, have you met Mr. McGreggor yet?" my dad broke in, his hand on Angela's back stealing her attention.

My body swayed slightly as I waited through an impatient minute of small talk before Angela could glance my way again. She pulled my dad's keys out of her purse and handed them over. "Here."

"Okay, thanks. See you—" I had almost said I'd see her at home, but I couldn't imagine it ever being her home, so my words drifted awkwardly between us.

She eyed me with concern. "Are you sure you're okay? I can drive you."

"No. I'll be fine. It's not very far."

"Be safe."

I stumbled my way to the valet in front of the resort and waited until he brought me the golf cart. At this point, my eyes almost needed something to prop them open. Did I say goodnight to Mariah? I had been thinking about giving her a hug goodbye. But did I? Maybe I should go tell her to have fun on her honeymoon.

No.

I'll send her a text...someday. Sometime. Tomorrow. Or maybe in September.

It wasn't far. I could drive the distance in my sleep. I opened my eyes as wide as they could go and took a big breath of salty air. I turned the key and started the engine. The low rumble gave me a shot of energy as I pulled out onto the roadway designed for golf carts only. Sometimes it was annoying living on an island where cars were illegal. Most specifically, times where a bridesmaid had done my hair in an amazingly intricate updo, and the wind instantly erased all her effort. It didn't matter, though. I would be dropping onto my bed in seconds. Minutes?

Or...September?

I slapped at my face until my cheeks flushed, only to have my vision go blurry. I blinked several times in a row until my sight cleared. I forced myself to look at my surroundings as I rounded the small bend in the road passing the retirement home where I used to spend time visiting with the residents before I left for bigger and better things. Or, at least…bigger. I wonder if Mrs. Anderson was still there. Or Mrs…uh…Mrs…

The golf cart veered left, and I jerked upward, correcting my course, headed toward the boat repair shop. What was it called now? Sunset Repairs? That was where…never mind. I wondered if he still worked there.

Eh. He was probably sporting an ankle monitor while picking up trash on the side of the road somewhere.

Gooooood riddance.

My head weighed a thousand pounds, which was strange when it was literally filled with cotton. Or…bowling balls.

Have I ever bowled before?

A half mile more. I could do that. Easyyyyy peasy.

Easyyyyyy…

Two more minutes. I could handle two more hours. I mean…minutes. Twoooo minutes.

Just like…

…

…

Just like…

The sharp sound of shattering glass popped my eyes open only to have them shut once more as shards came raining down on my arms. Another loud boom and jolt from the cart forced my eyes to open again, only to see what looked like a million bright-red and black plastic toys raining down on me. They fell in slow motion, hitting the windshield of the cart before scattering onto the floor. The golf cart came to a stop with a dramatic huff in the center of the room.

I looked around in a daze before I began losing the battle with exhaustion. I'd done a bad thing. I could sense it. But I couldn't bring myself to compute much beyond that.

Things were so fuzzy.

I leaned forward, my arms resting on the steering wheel, and finally did the thing I'd been wanting to do all night long. I closed my eyes.

Somewhere in my haze of semi-consciousness, I heard noises. Voices. One voice maybe?

"What the—"

A door banged open from somewhere. Footsteps slapped against the concrete, coming closer. A hand shook my shoulder.

"Hey! Wake up! What happened?"

"Ivy? Ivy Brooks?"

Was that my name? Why did it sound so different?

"Are you drunk?"

I couldn't remember my dreams ever having cursing in them. But this dream definitely did. So much language filtered in and out of my consciousness. I'd never heard of some of these words. It was almost offensive.

It *was* offensive.

I was offended.

This guy would be getting an earful from me whenever I felt like giving it to him. And that voice… I couldn't place it, but it was so familiar to me. Something about frogs?

"Ivy! You've got to wake up. You're bleeding. There's glass everywhere."

This guy can't tell me what to do. I had finally gotten to a place where I could just sleep.

More swearing and loud noises. Something kept poking at my side and on my skin, occasionally sending bolts of sharp pain up my arms. I jerked away, pushing and fighting whatever it was that didn't feel good.

"Ivy. Stop hitt—ouch! Never mind. Go back to sleep."

Then I was flying alongside a delicious-smelling cinnamon Pop-Tart before landing on something soft, and then I was gone again.

CHAPTER 2

Biology Class
Day 2

Five minutes after the tardy bell rang, Dax Miller strolled into biology class, interrupting our teacher, Mr. Gray, in mid-sentence. He wore baggy jeans slung low at the hip, and a tight, black t-shirt. His hair, barely touching the tops of his ears, would almost be sexy, if it wasn't Dax Miller. On a rocker in leather pants on a stage: yes. It would be sexy hair. Biology class: no.

"Thank you for joining us, Dax," Mr. Gray remarked dryly.

"My pleasure, sir." Dax shot him a lazy smile as he made his way toward his usual seat in the back.

"There's been a change in lab partners," Mr. Gray said. "Please take your new seat next to Ivy."

Dax's eyes found mine immediately, and I stiffened in my seat. I hadn't been aware he'd even remembered my name for how little we'd ever interacted. After a moment's hesitation, Dax changed course and moved languidly toward my desk, dropping into his seat with a sigh. Mr. Gray resumed his demonstration, and though I straightened and kept my eyes firmly forward, the picture of a model student, my mind was centered squarely on the body in the seat beside me.

Glancing over, I found that he had turned his head in my direction and was staring at me. Even when I met his gaze, he didn't look away.

Instead, he gave me a smile. The kind of smile that gives the impression that someone is laughing at you. My chin lifted as I looked back toward Mr. Gray. It was another long moment until he finally, blessedly, looked forward.

APPARENTLY, when you wake up in a clinic, confused and having somehow crashed a golf cart into a private business, they send in the big dogs—unless, of course, you're on a tiny island with little to no crime. Then they send in the only cop on the island, who just so happens to be Beau Palmer, an old friend from high school.

Which wasn't mortifying in the least.

Within a half hour of waking, I had been poked, examined, and had blood extracted from my body for testing, all while being accused of being drunk or on something by my sweet father.

Even after I denied all of it.

Instead of asking how I was feeling or telling me how relieved he was that I hadn't been hurt, he'd spent most of the morning pacing the hallway in the clinic on the phone, doing what he called *damage control*.

"I drank a Coke. Ask Cat. I was with her the whole time."

"Then what happened?" Dad asked. "People 'not on something' don't crash into buildings." He held up his fingers in air quotes, causing my jaw to grow rigid.

"What building did I run into?"

"The mechanic's shop. Crashed right through the huge glass entry and smashed into that big spinning Lego car."

Suddenly, a few of the puzzle pieces clicked together. *The mechanic.* The sound of Dax's voice. I leaned my head back onto my pillow. I crashed into Dax Miller's shop. Apparently, he wasn't making license plates in an orange jumpsuit somewhere.

"Remember him?" My dad's piercing gaze locked onto mine.

"The kid with all the tattoos? I'll bet you do. We're going to have to pay out the nose to keep him quiet."

Thankfully, soon after this, Beau the cop knocked on the door and sent my dad and Angela away so he could grab a statement. It took my brain a minute to get used to the idea of seeing Beau dressed as a cop. He was that classic tall, dark-haired guy that most girls on the island had been in love with. And I couldn't blame them. He had a sweet, teasing smile that automatically put a person at ease—unless that person was being officially questioned by Beau the COP. Then it was much more difficult to relax. Between thoughts of Dax Miller and now Beau Palmer, it was like having a high school reunion from my nightmares.

After some small talk, he got down to business, leaning back in his chair. "Okay, I want you to tell me what happened last night in your own words, as far as you can remember everything."

I filled him in on all my flight delays, my headache, and our walk along the beach.

"I was with Cat Keene almost the whole time. She can verify my non-existent alcohol intake." I rubbed at the dull ache at my temples.

"You said you had a headache?" Beau looked down at his notes.

"Yeah."

"Did you take anything for it?"

"Just some Tylenol."

"When did you take the pills?"

I thought for a moment. "When I was on the beach with Cat."

He nodded and scribbled more notes. "Other than the headache and being tired, did you feel off or strange at any other point during the evening?"

The whole night almost seemed a blur now. I had been so

tired. But my limbs had gotten sluggish just after our walk. I remembered wanting to curl up and cry on the stairs leading up to the resort, but in my defense, there were a lot of stairs, so that attitude wasn't necessarily sleep-related.

"When I returned from my walk on the beach. It seemed to get progressively worse from there."

"Then what happened?" he continued, his chin resting in his hand, giving me his full attention.

"Angela gave me the keys to my dad's golf cart, and I started driving to the house. From that point, I just have flashes of random memories." I thought hard but still came up with a fuzzy picture. "I remember hearing a big crash and a loud voice swearing a lot."

A slow smile carved across Beau's face, crinkling the edges of his eyes. "That would be Dax."

"So I gathered."

He was quiet as he finished writing his notes. "So, most of what happened after you entered the golf cart is a blur?"

"Yeah."

More scribbling in his notebook while I sat there feeling like a mouse in a cage while the scientists peered inside. I decided to ask my own questions. "Can *you* tell me what happened after that?"

"Yeah. Dax was working late at the shop, heard the crash, and came running in to see what happened. He called me immediately. Once he saw that your arms had gotten hit with some glass, he removed as much of it as he could with you swiping at him. He got cut a bit himself before he picked you up and moved you to a couch in the waiting room until I got there."

I swallowed as I began to understand the havoc I had caused. It was also strange to think about Dax Miller touching me in that way. I blinked, forcing those thoughts to retreat. "Is he okay?"

"Who?"

"Dax."

"Oh. Yeah. He's fine."

"So, what…happens now?" I asked, playing with a loose string on my blanket.

He met my gaze. "Once we get the blood report, we'll be able to make an official call." He adjusted his position in his chair. "I do need to tell you that I took an inventory of the golf cart you were driving."

"What does that mean?"

"As part of my job, I take everything I found inside and then photograph and document it. We do that so when they tow the vehicle, we have a record of what was inside."

"Is the golf cart totaled?" My dad had bought it last year and would definitely not appreciate his luxury splurge wrecked.

"Not totaled, but it will be in the repair shop for a while. Your dad wants it ferried to the mainland to be worked on."

Of course my dad wouldn't have Dax fix the golf cart.

Why was Beau looking at me like he knew something I didn't? I had nothing to hide. The most incriminating thing I had in my purse was a tampon.

He cleared his throat. "I found Ambien in your purse."

I waited for a beat, confused. "It's a prescription. I got it a few months ago to help me sleep—"

He held up his hands. "It's not a problem that you had it on you. I'm wondering if you could have mixed up the pills."

My gaze settled on him in disbelief while my mind worked back to the evening before on the beach with Cat. It had been dark. I got stomachaches if I took any other type of pain pill except for Tylenol, so that's what I always kept in my purse.

Except…I had taken some Ambien after a bout of stress-induced insomnia claimed my life for a short time when trying to line up a new job for next fall. I remembered bringing them with me on my trip to Atlanta to see my mom. Had I mistakenly left them in my purse? Could I have—?

Beau was watching me carefully as my face, no doubt, left very little by way of mystery. I hid my expression behind my hands and moaned.

It wasn't a freak accident. I didn't faint or pass out for any medical reason I couldn't have foreseen. I drove behind the wheel after taking not one, but two, very high doses of a sleeping pill. The knowledge of this continued to build, until a hundred-pound weight pressed upon my back, threatening to crush me. I could have hurt someone. What if Dax had been in the room when I crashed inside? What if someone had been walking across the street? A child? I wouldn't have seen them. My breath came in and out in short bursts as I tried to make sense of this.

"I'm so sorry. I'm so sorry. I didn't mean to. I—"

Beau held up his hands, probably trying his best to ward off the onslaught of tears we both could feel coming. "I don't think anybody who knows you, Ivy, would ever think you'd do this on purpose. That's what had me so confused. It sounds like it was an accident. Take a breath."

I did what he said, pulling air into my lungs, in and out in a rhythmic pattern.

He continued, "It was a bad thing that happened, but it could have been a lot worse."

I nodded, my head back in my hands, trying to take some comfort in his words and physically stopping myself from replaying worst-case scenarios in my head.

"What happens now?"

He scribbled a few more notes before pulling out an official police notepad and began scratching away at that. "I'm going to write you up a citation and submit this to the prosecutor." He checked his watch. "Judge Baylor's next day on the bench is Tuesday, so we'll hope for a court date then."

"Wait, what?"

He looked up at my tone, a question on his face.

"I thought you said it was an accident," I said, the weight on my back now dropping like lead in my stomach.

"It sounds like it was."

"Why do I have to see the judge?"

"Because you were driving under the influence and crashed into a private business."

"Okay, but it was an accident, and I wasn't drunk." Did it seem like we were circling?

"Once we get the blood test back, confirming you didn't have alcohol in your system, we'll be able to prove that you weren't drunk. But, either way, you were still driving under the influence of medication, and you were obviously impaired. That's still a DUI."

My heart dropped at the sound of those letters. Those three letters were found in newspapers and reports under a mugshot. A DUI was for criminals. Didn't it require criminal *intent*? Drinking and driving was something so black and white to me. A no-brainer. If you wanted to have a few drinks, call a cab or a friend to take you home. The Ambien was a mistake. I thought it was Tylenol. That could happen to anyone. I made a mistake. Do people get in trouble with the police because of *mistakes*?

Pause.

Okay, I could maybe see the issue.

Panic bubbled up and out of my chest in heaves and bobs. I had just wanted to go home and sleep. One tiny bad decision shouldn't have to cost me so much. If I shouted those words loud enough, could I get a re-do on last night?

I couldn't meet with a judge on Tuesday. I was leaving. My exit for this island was set for Monday morning.

"Is there a fine I could pay or something? Just skip the judge. I'm sure he's busy. I'll talk with Dax and pay him for the windows." The thought of talking with Dax gave me minor heart palpitations, but I'd figure it out. Anything to get out of here.

Beau hardly looked at me as he scribbled away, my immediate future currently in his hands.

"There's a good chance the prosecutor will deem the judge non-negotiable," he said with a helpless shrug. "The state of Florida has a no-tolerance policy for DUIs—even if it's not alcohol-related. I'm sorry. It's out of my hands."

"My plane leaves Monday morning at ten."

He stood, handing me the paper. "Your plane will probably still leave at ten. You just won't be on it." The words were soft, and his eyes were apologetic, but his policeman tone held zero room for argument.

I've heard tourists say that being on a small island for periods of time made them feel trapped. Being completely surrounded by a body of water certainly has the potential to mess with someone's mind, but it was a feeling I had never understood. I loved the water. Though my family's property wasn't exactly beachfront, we were close enough that I used to fall asleep to the sound of the ocean through my open window. I *had* felt stifled at times. But that was mostly due to the environment in my own home, not because of the island. And I had never felt trapped.

Until this moment.

"I liked you a lot better when you weren't a cop," I said, flopping back against the pillow, trying to process my new reality.

"I get that a lot." He flashed me a smile brimming with sympathy. "Someone will be in touch, Ivy. But until then, you're not going anywhere."

CHAPTER 3

Biology Class
Day 3

We sat at our table with a dead toad in front of us and the smell of formaldehyde punching at our noses. To the right was a scalpel. Dax sat with his eyes closed, drumming to a song while his fingers rapped against the desk.

"What do you want to do?" I asked, raising my voice so I didn't sound timid. The last thing I wanted to do was sound weak. But my voice came out wobbly, and I immediately hated that it did.

"I don't care."

"Great," I said cheerfully. "I'll sit here and watch while you carve." I inched the scalpel his way, really missing my old lab partner and her fascination with dissection.

A soft laugh came from his lips. "I doubt that."

"Why?"

"Because there's only one person at this table who cares about their grades."

We sized each other up while I desperately tried not to show fear.

"Don't you want to graduate?"

He shrugged. "Makes no difference to me."

"Then why are you here?"

A tiny smirk crossed his face. "I'm bored."

THANKS TO GOOGLE and my fear-induced flying fingers from the hours between two and six am, I now knew that a DUI in Florida could technically be a felony or a misdemeanor. The severity of the sentence depended on past convictions, which, thankfully, I had none. It would most likely be reduced to a misdemeanor, and hopefully, the judge would go easy on me.

Hope filtered throughout my thoughts the rest of the night. Along with the words like: jail, convictions, fines, jail, felony, sentencing, jail, etc.

The cheerful yellow walls of my childhood bedroom mocked me as I woke up. In my teens, I had gone through a photography phase which resulted in frames hung all around the room. Pictures of me and Cat on the volleyball team. Making banners for a pep rally with my friend Jane. Dressed with friends for Powder Puff football my senior year. Smiles and laughter radiated from the pictures, evidence of happy times. Noticeably absent were pictures of my family. Without even realizing it, my room had become an oasis for me growing up.

Good vibes only.

All morning long, my brain scrambled to form a new plan. My exit strategy had been blown to bits, along with Dax's windows.

Dax.

He had also filtered his way through my spiraling thoughts. It wasn't only courtroom dramas and prison jumpsuits keeping me awake well into the morning, but faint flickers of his voice, the feeling of flying, and the press and cradle of his body holding mine. Some things were just vivid enough to be remembered through a hazy fog.

Which meant I now knew two things for certain.

I owed Dax Miller an apology. And I needed to get out of this house before my dad could corner me again.

As fun as it was to spend most of the previous night listening to him make phone calls and excuses to politicians and supporters about his daughter's untimely accident, I wasn't about to subject myself to his contemptuous comments today. I'd find things to do.

Even if that something was apologizing to Dax.

So, when I heard Angela and my dad heading out for their morning run on the beach, I flew to the shower. I washed in record time, coaxed a little gel and direction into my wild curls, and rummaged around for some old clothes in my closet. I slid on a pair of blue chino shorts and a flowy tank top, feeling a little more like myself. A small moment of order and normalcy in my otherwise alternate reality of existence.

The hallway leading down the stairs had been stripped of the family picture frames that used to line the walls. A pang of sadness bolted through me, but I pushed it aside and stepped into the spacious kitchen to find the flip-flops I'd kicked off after getting home from the clinic. My heart sank when the back door suddenly opened, and my dad and Angela stepped inside.

I hadn't been fast enough.

The only thing that slightly gratified me was noting the sweat stains across the senator's chest and armpits while Angela hardly looked winded.

"Hey. How are you feeling?" Angela asked, breezing past me, dotting her glistening neck with a tissue.

How am I feeling?

I currently have a court date to see a judge because I had plowed into a building while under the influence. How did she think I was feeling? But there was only one answer in this house.

"Fine," I said, giving her a smile while tracking my dad's movements toward the kitchen sink.

"Good. I'm going to shower, but stick around and I'll make you some carrot juice and an egg white omelet, if you're interested."

All of that sounded terrible, but I smiled anyway. "I'm going for a walk, but thank you."

"Hold on a minute, Ivy. I need to talk to you," my dad called out before filling his glass with water.

As Angela disappeared upstairs, the life of the entire room went with her. I couldn't avoid this conversation, but I wasn't sure how calm I could be anymore. My dad tipped his head back to drink, the water leaving the cup in slow, steady gulps, packing more tension in the room with each swallow. Though itching to run, my feet were glued to the floor until he neatly placed his cup on the counter and turned toward me.

"Your court date is Tuesday morning at 9 am. My lawyer, Will Frost, is going to represent you."

"Okay. Thanks." I took a few steps toward the doorway before he spoke again.

"Have you thought about how you're going to handle your little indiscretion?" His low Southern drawl showed slightly in his speech.

Even though the way his voice coated the words "little indiscretion" was enough to clench my teeth, I turned and faced him with a neutral expression on my face.

"What?"

"Right now, people just think it was some sort of accident. But if the judge slaps a DUI on your record, it follows you for a long time. It could mess with your job. It will be all over the papers. Online. It could ruin your reputation. And not that you care, but when people find out, it could sure as hell ruin mine."

The twist in my gut made a familiar presence. It was ironic for him to imply that I didn't care. My entire childhood had been seeped in the knowledge that one wrong move on my or my mother's part could ruin my dad's political career. His aspirations had gotten him as far as a local senator. But he was always hopeful for more. Always campaigning, so to speak. I could only imagine how difficult my actions would be to a man who honored his fake image with much more gusto than his real one.

"You'll meet with my lawyer tomorrow to go over some things. Specifically, how to act and what to say. In the meantime, stay away from the mechanic."

"Why?"

"I don't want it looking like you're guilty. We need to keep things quiet—keep you quiet. And hopefully, we can make this all go away. Brookses don't make mistakes."

Aw, the loving family motto of my youth.

"But if we do, we're going to be quiet about it," my dad added. My eyebrows quirked upward. That part was new.

"I'm pretty sure everybody knows what happened by now." Cat and Jane had both called to check on me yesterday, which meant the island gossip mills were already humming. Dax's shop was somewhat of a landmark in town, just off Main Street and up the road from the island ferry, not to mention next door to the worst gossip of all—the Seaside Oasis Retirement Home.

"It doesn't matter what people say today. What the judge says on Tuesday will be what everyone remembers. That will be what gets spread around. You plead not guilty, and that will give us more time to make it all go away."

Not guilty. The words poked at my conscience.

"I did it, though."

His sharp eyes met mine. "What?"

"The DUI. I didn't mean to do it, but it still happened. Shouldn't I have to deal with it?" The contemptuous look on my dad's face sent the tiniest chill down my veins. Then I remembered Dr. Barb and took a deep breath.

He ran his hand through his hair impatiently. "You will be dealing with it. You'll pay for what happened. For the damages.

But it wasn't the kind of DUI that should be on your record. It was an accident. A pill. Not alcohol. You don't want something like that hanging over your head." He folded his arms across his chest, looking at me in a patronizing way. "Do you know how long a DUI stays on your record in the state of Florida?"

I didn't react, but he didn't need me to.

"Seventy-five years. You want that following you around for the rest of your life?"

Or *his* life.

"I know I can make this disappear. But you have to plead not guilty." At my look, he said again, slower, "Because you're *not guilty*."

I didn't know much about the legal process beyond what I'd seen on TV. Maybe pleading a certain way to lessen a sentence or bargain for a deal was normal and not just good TV drama. But there was a thought that persisted uncomfortably in my heart that wouldn't lessen. I *was* guilty. I had done the bad thing. I hadn't meant to. But I did. Should it all go away because my dad wanted to save his reputation?

"I'm going for a walk," I said before making my way to the nearest exit.

My dad grunted something before I closed the front door, the tension in my shoulders lessening almost immediately as I stepped onto the sidewalk.

The warm island breeze and the chirp of the birds only distracted me for a moment. Never far from my mind during my talk with my dad was the very real knowledge that Dax Miller and I were about to collide once more.

It had been ten years. A lot could change for a person in that amount of time. My dad could grow a whole new personality depending on who he was talking to, so...it was definitely possible that Dax had changed. That maybe he wouldn't make my life miserable over this. We weren't teenagers anymore. This accident would be just that...an accident.

Just an itsy-bitsy violation of the law.

My dad's words were a distant memory as I walked toward the town square. And though my hands grew clammy and my movements a bit twitchy at the thought...Dax deserved an apology from me today.

And he would get one.

CHAPTER 4

Biology Class
Day 3

Mr. Gray's voice broke through the classroom. "You should have started your incision from the frog's cloaca to its lower jaw. Consult your instruction card if you need to see exactly where to begin the cut."

A bead of sweat dripped down the side of my face as I grabbed the scalpel, fully prepared to ignore the dolt sitting next to me. I could do this. As soon as I figured out where and what the cloaca was.

I squinted toward the instruction card and placed the scalpel in the correct-ish spot. Dax nonchalantly tapped the desk to the beat of a song playing in his ear, but I felt his gaze. My right leg bounced up and down no matter how much I tried to keep it still.

"Tick-tock," Dax murmured beside me.

I mentally flipped him the bird while my wobbly, scalpel-clutching hand pressed the tip into the frog's skin. Nothing happened. I tried again, this time giving enough pressure to dent the skin.

"Did Ivy Brooks get her last partner to do all her dirty work?" Dax asked, a sudden interest in his voice. "Because that would make my entire day."

"No."

He nodded toward the frog. "Dig into him, then."

His brown eyes were laughing at me. My nostrils flared, and without *giving myself time to think, I jabbed the sharp edge into the frog. The feel of the knife cutting through layers of skin and body parts made me immediately drop the scalpel. I turned toward Dax as my body began dry-heaving in big, jerking motions.*

With great alarm, Dax threw his hands to the table and pushed himself two feet away, the violent scrape of the chair on the hardwood breaking into the low hum of the room.

THE FLORIDIAN SUN warmed my skin as my steps quickened in the direction of Dax's shop. With the entire island being only four miles long, it didn't take long to walk or bike anywhere.

My resolve to walk directly to Dax's shop held firm for an entire block. I arrived at the town square, just down the road from his shop, with startling efficiency. But it was fine. I was going to right a wrong. I just wasn't sure why that tiny moment in my garage with him all those years ago kept playing in my mind. He probably didn't even remember. I certainly never thought about it.

Until…last night.

So it was a little confusing how my mind suddenly seemed to remember *every* detail, down to the way he looked at me right before he—

Hey, look at that!

The Book Isle was open.

With the exception of Sunrise Cafe, my old job and stomping grounds, The Book Isle was my favorite shop in town. I checked my watch. It was only a few minutes after 9. Showing up that early would make me seem eager. I had a conscience that refused to ease up, but that didn't mean I wanted Dax to think I was excited to see him.

I entered the book shop and settled in for a good half-hour browse until I realized that yet another friend from high school, Briggs, worked there now.

"Hey, Ivy. Heard about the crash. How you holding up?" Briggs looked like he belonged in Hollywood. He had that boy-next-door vibe that worked well in his favor. Like now, his sandy-blond hair was curled slightly at the edges, and glasses framed a pair of sweet green eyes.

Why couldn't I have crashed into *his* shop? He would have definitely been a gentleman about the whole thing.

Granted, I still didn't know how Dax would react when I spoke to him, but I definitely didn't think his eyes would be giving off *sweet* vibes.

"I'm okay. Thanks." I smiled at him and attempted a change of subject, a reason for me to linger. "Is Sunny Palmer's new book out yet?"

Briggs was quick to crush my spirits in his shy way, telling me that Sunny's newest book would not be released until later this summer. After some small talk with Briggs and with no other books tempting me to purchase, I stepped out of the store in full adult mode, heading north toward Dax's shop.

Apprehension caused my hands to sweat and my heart to beat like a drum in my ear. The feeling of puke lodged in my gut was a bonus for my efforts. This wasn't a neighbor or friend I had accidentally wronged. Or sweet Briggs from The Book Isle. This was Dax Miller. The guy I'd basically told once to have a nice life amounting to nothing on the island.

Of course, that was after he had accused me of being a fake and caring more for the public opinion than my own. Just like my dad. Coincidentally, Dax had been one of the only people in my life that had seemed unmoved by my dad's politician act.

So, crawling to Dax to thank him for his help as well as apologize for my actions wasn't something I was pushing people out of the way to do.

Even though I was GOING.

The road curved, and I sucked in a breath at my first sight of his building since the accident. Billowing blue tarps, held together by rope, flapped in the breeze while covering the gaping hole in the double-story glass window. I took it all in, unease filling my stomach to the brim.

I had done that. To someone else's property.

Me and my accidental stupidity.

It was nothing but pure willpower forcing my feet to close the distance. A large driveway to the right of the building led to three garage doors—all of which were closed today—and a sidewalk down to Dax's private marina where he stored and fixed boats. I made my way toward the front entrance, grateful to see that the damage had only been to the windows. At least it wouldn't be months of repair to the entire building. Just a quick re-ordering of a humongous custom window set.

Easy peasy.

I opened the door and stepped into a large, empty, two-story room. The glass had been swept away with visible dust streaks on the glossy epoxy-coated concrete floor. In the center of the room were two large garbage cans full of...Lego pieces. A flash of the crash came back to me as I remembered the pounding noise they made raining down onto the golf cart. Realization sunk in. I had destroyed *the Lego car*. A literal town landmark, formerly showcased proudly on one of those fancy slow-rotating display pedestals. A gigantic car almost as large as a real-life Volkswagen Bug, now in shambles.

I cringed, thinking about the poor soul who would have to spend fifteen years of their life putting that back together again.

Against the back wall of the large room, there was a counter with several old barstools. I saw a bell, which I rang hesitantly, after a two-minute internal debate on whether I should just wait to speak with Dax in court, until my conscience won out. The sound of music wafted through the hallway that led toward a shop door with a partial window at the top. After another minute spent gaining courage, I stood and strode toward the closed door.

Woman up, Ivy Brooks. You can do this.

When I opened the door, the soft sound of music suddenly turned loud as I stepped into an uncharted domain.

Though I wasn't sure how I knew it, the song "Old Time Rock & Roll" rang through the speakers. I was decades too young to know it, but the tune seemed to transcend all time and years, giving me the feeling I'd heard this song a thousand times but couldn't place where.

Dust particles filtered the air as I looked around the massive room. In front of one garage door was a boat sitting on a trailer. Every other spare inch in the shop was cluttered with lawn mowers, weed eaters, trimmers, and golf carts.

I inched my way into the room, if only to give my body a job that didn't include dancing to oldies music in a shop I wasn't sure I'd be welcome in. But there was something off with this version of the song. A voice. A voice that got decidedly louder as the chorus picked up again.

But the part that drew my attention was the feet and legs sticking out from under a golf cart. It almost seemed strange, seeing a golf cart where a car usually would be, but that was Sunset Harbor for you.

Dax's voice noticeably waned through the next verse, still making noises along with the tune but in a much more distracted way, like he was tightening a bolt at the same time. Hearing his voice without him knowing felt intimate. Too intimate. Dax had always been a wild card. I had no idea how this little chat would go. I was trying to get the courage to alert him of my presence when he suddenly rolled out from under the cart.

Our eyes met instantly. Though, to my slight disappointment, he didn't startle at my appearance. Instead, he sat up, his dark gaze swallowing me up in one big gulp. My skin came alive with goosebumps as he bent forward, propping his arms on his knees. His eyes drifted briefly down my flowy tank top and blue shorts, landing at the bandages on my arm before returning to my face—at least, I assumed. I was occupied elsewhere.

He was shirtless.

So…

That's where I was.

He leaned over and picked up his dusty phone from the floor, and soon, the music blaring from the speakers in all four corners of the shop was turned down to a normal level.

And then he spoke, erasing ten years between us with his words.

"Look who's back in town, gracing us all with her superior and, might I add, explosive presence."

It's amazing what the brain can hold onto throughout a decade. In reality, though, my body sighed with relief at his words. The tone felt right. He'd be annoying, for sure, but we'd be fine. I deserved that, and I would graciously let him get it all off his chest.

"Yeah. Hi, Dax."

He stood and sauntered toward me. To my surprise, he kept coming closer, and when he held out a greasy hand toward me, I stared, frozen, until he used the back of it to nudge my arm, gently pushing me away from his bench.

"I wouldn't lean against that bench in those clothes."

I stepped away, still unable to say much as I soaked him in. Experience with Dax had taught me to be prepared, and if I had to give a bodily description to a detective someday, I'd say he was pushing six foot two, had grease all over his…neck and chest area, which was highlighted by glistening sweat, and he had definitely filled out since I'd seen him last. My eyes raked over what I could see of his tattoos spanning the width of his shoulders. An outline of an old car was what I made out before I forced my gaze to move farther north.

"Please tell me you didn't drive here." He reached for a towel stuck in the waistband of his jeans and began wiping the grime off his chest and hands.

I followed his movement with fascination until I closed my gawking mouth and focused on an interesting set of wrenches lined up on a pegboard above the bench.

"I walked."

He nodded, throwing the towel down on one of his workbenches surrounding the perimeter of his shop. "You alright?"

His voice seemed lower to me, more manly than I remembered. It sent chills down my spine and had me imagining cozy snuggles by the fire—before I reminded myself that I was currently on a very hot island in the middle of summer, and stamped that stupid fire out.

"Yeah. I'm good. Just a few cuts and scrapes, but you already know about those." I raised my arms briefly, in case he was interested, but other than a quick glance, he didn't seem to be. Were his eyelashes always that long?

Nope. Stop it.

Pull yourself together, Ivy Brooks.

Just because I felt bad about destroying half of his shop didn't mean I should let my brain turn him into some sort of person I ogled. Save that for the women who LIVED HERE.

Also the women who didn't...you know...break his building.

Dax seemed to be waiting for something—which was my cue.

I flung my hand back toward the doorway I'd entered. "I tried ringing the bell, but you didn't hear me. So I came to find you." By nature, apologies weren't a strong suit of mine, so to ease myself in, I attempted the old trick of forcing him to apologize for something first.

"It's Sunday. The shop is closed."

"Oh." I deflated.

Dax folded his arms, leaned against his bench and considered me, a self-satisfied look on his face. The kind of look that told me he knew exactly how hard this little chat was going to be for me. For the record, I would give him my apology. I would. He deserved it.

I was just warming up.

"So, it looks like I'll have to add breaking and entering to your list of crimes," he said.

I smiled sweetly. "The door was open."

"The whole front side of the building is open." His tone didn't sound angry. It was more matter-of-fact, with a slight, gleaming-eyed edge to it.

"Yeah..." I trailed off, attempting to gather words. "Anyway. About that. I'm really sorry I ran into your building."

Dax blinked. Several beats passed before a slow smile crossed his face. And then he laughed, rubbing his forehead while he did so. I stood there with shifting feet, hating every miserable second.

"Thanks, Books," he said once he finally got a hold of himself. I stilled at the use of his old nickname, and once again, a wave of problematic familiarity came crashing over me. When I began to turn away from him, he held his hand out. "Wait."

I turned back to look at him.

He stayed still, almost like he was waiting for something to happen. My eyes narrowed warily.

"Yeah, I think I feel a tear welling up." He leaned closer, pointing to his eye. "This eye. Do you see anything?"

I leaned forward to swat him across his stomach while he laughed again and began rummaging through a toolbox. I froze, shocked at my boldness. I hadn't seen this guy in ten years, then I destroy half of his shop, and now I was basically throwing myself at his half-naked body. The way he went about unfazed was a definite red flag. The feeling between us like I'd just seen him a week ago wasn't lost on me.

But it certainly wasn't welcome. Time to move this along.

"Anyway, I really am sorry. Truly."

He made a noise but didn't actually acknowledge me before reaching deeper into his toolbox.

"I feel terrible," I tried again. Still no reaction.

My fingers curled into fists. Here I was, basically groveling at this man's feet, and he couldn't even give me the decency of eye contact. But I wasn't going to get annoyed. I took a deep, calming breath—the soothing kind I would write to Dr. Barb about.

"Can I help you find something?" I asked sweetly.

He pulled out a tool and inspected it, wiping some grease off with the towel before looking at me, the glint in his eyes telling me he knew exactly what he was doing.

"No. I'm good. Thanks, though."

My gaze drifted across his arms, landing on the tangle of ink dressing his shoulders. The casual, deliberate way he pushed my buttons came flying back to my remembrance. I was suddenly aware of why I had been so nervous to speak to Dax. It wasn't that I was scared to talk to him. It was the way he made me feel.

This weekend was an anomaly. A crazy shift in the universe. So him making it seem like this was something he knew would happen one day had me clenching my fists into balls. It was like being on the second day of my period and someone next to me chomping on the crunchiest vegetable in the world.

Annoying.

But not today. I wouldn't let him push me that far, which meant I needed to wrap this up. I had said my first apology. And I still had one more.

Also, he needed some clothes.

"Oh, are you looking for your shirt?" I looked around the room, found what I sought, and grabbed the crumpled t-shirt from the floor, shaking the dust off before holding it out to him. "It's right here." I smiled at him, friendly-like, as if to say *let's put our differences aside and forget about me smashing into your building*.

He eyed the shirt like taking it would give me too much

satisfaction, then just stood there and looked at me while I awkwardly continued to hold it out. I shook it at him.

"Come on," I said, like he was a cat I was trying to convince to eat.

He leaned against the workbench, his ankles and arms folded, taking me in with definite joyous undertones.

"Why do you need me to wear it?"

"I just think you would feel better wearing the shirt while I'm here. While we talk business."

Oh, I don't know, Dax, maybe because it's the professional *thing to do.*

I had no business telling this man what to wear. I knew this. Yet the deliberate way he was trying to trigger me was…triggering.

He spread his arms out wide and looked around. "This *is* my business. That you broke into, I might add. So no, I won't be putting on a shirt. But I'm sorry if it's distracting for you."

I was in the process of begging the flush rising on my cheeks to disappear when he leaned toward me, flashing a brief grin and adding, "Man, it's good to see you."

I pretended to brush a speck of dirt off my sleeve. "Listen, I know you're enjoying all of this—"

"Am I?" he asked.

My gaze narrowed. "You know you are."

"Just tell me one thing…what does Karma feel like?"

"Dax!" I drew in a breath, physically stopping myself from punching his arm. My hand slapping against what I could only describe as warm, solid rock definitely wouldn't help anything.

He moved toward the golf cart while he flipped to a specific song he wanted. He was clearly dismissing me, but I wasn't finished. Not even the song "Witchy Woman" would get me to leave.

Also, these songs…what year was this?

"Listen, Dax," I began, raising my voice louder to be heard

over the music. To my surprise he turned to face me. It took an immense force of willpower, but my gaze locked onto his, ignoring the temptation to peek downward to the land of muscles and abs.

"I also wanted to tell you thanks for your help the other night. And for calling Beau."

He studied me for a long moment. "You're welcome."

It was the humor lurking on his face that transported me back to high school biology class, watching a troubled, dark-haired boy attempt to hold back his sly smiles. Though, there was something more settled about this manly version of Dax, his body still held tight with hard edges and a touch of defiance.

Before I could say anything else, Dax motioned me toward the door. "Well, let me see you out. You probably need to get some beauty sleep for your upcoming mug shot." The look I gave him did nothing to quell the growing smile on his face. Since I said what I had come here to say, there was no other option than to follow him out of the shop and into the lobby.

Motioning toward the garbage cans full of Lego pieces, I said, "Good thing that was just a fake car, right? Pretty sure I wouldn't be able to afford a real version if I had totaled it."

"You're looking at a beloved landmark for Sunset Harbor tourism."

I huffed out a laugh before giving him my best patronizing smile. "I'm sorry I knocked over your Legos."

I metaphorically patted myself on the back. I'd given three apologies, not just two. Not a bad day's work, given how terrified I was to come here.

He blinked before peering into my eyes, as though he were checking my sincerity and finding it lacking. To be fair, I hadn't been serious. I found the Lego car to be quite dumb.

"Good luck in court, Books," he said in a voice that sent a nervous thrill racing down my spine. He held the front door open for me. "Maybe I'll see you around."

CHAPTER 5

Biology Class
Day 3

"Everything alright over there, Ivy and Dax?" Mr. Gray asked.

I looked at Dax, who was staring at me, his too-cool-for-school persona looking a bit disheveled, before I glanced toward my teacher, wincing inside at his obvious disappointment.

"We're good," I said, trying to sound chipper. "Just had a scalpel malfunction."

I turned my attention back to my desk, feeling the weight of this entire dumb class all on my shoulders.

"A scalpel malfunction," the idiot beside me repeated in my ears. "That's a generous interpretation."

Suddenly, I had him. I knew I did. If we were playing poker, he had tell—a crack in his exterior. Though it felt like an angle my dad would try...desperate times and all that. I needed an A in this class, and Dax needed his butt handed to him.

I angled my body toward his. "Hey, Dax," I whispered.

He moved closer, his arms leaning on the desk, feigning great interest in what I had to say. "Yeah?"

"Pick up that scalpel and start dissecting that frog right now, or I promise that next time I will throw up, and I know just where to aim."

"I could just leave now." His eyebrows raised.

"You could," I stated, my voice low and controlled. "But then, for the rest of your life, you'd remember how dumb you were to let twelve years of school go to waste instead of just sticking it out for a few more months, putting in a little effort, and getting your freaking diploma."

The air between us came to a sudden halt. I sat, inwardly gaping at what I'd just said to Dax Miller. I waited, with bated breath to see how he would react.

After a long moment, the sides of his mouth lifted, and he eventually moved to pick up the shiny instrument. With long fingers, stained with marks of grease, he brought the frog closer.

Dax's brow furrowed as he paused and leaned closer, peering at something on the lifeless body.

"Gross. This one's still juicy."

"What? He shouldn't be." I cautiously leaned closer.

He waited until I had my head at just the right distance before he inserted his scalpel at just the right angle and with just the right amount of pressure to send a squirt of frog juices in a perfect line through the air and directly onto my cheek.

I SAT in the courtroom with my foot twitching uncontrollably. Next to me, the foot of my dad's attorney was not moving at all. Will Frost sat cool as a cucumber, every strand of gray hair perfectly in place, a placid smile, and his long fingers sitting atop his slightly rounded stomach. A direct contrast to my shallow breathing and torn fingernails. The whole walk to the courthouse had been surreal. It felt like I was watching somebody else's life implode.

My friend, Jane, had lent me an outfit. The clothes in my overnight bag had been severely lacking in *courtroom chic*. The flowy floral dress from Jane looked fashionable and gorgeous on her, but it didn't feel like me, which had me fighting the urge to fidget even more than I already was.

My dad had a meeting on the mainland today, which thankfully explained his absence this morning. He'd been very present yesterday, however, when we'd spent an hour with Mr. Frost, going over the plan for court. What to say. What *not* to say. And all of it in direct contrast to the feelings in my gut.

Beau, the cop, was now sitting behind me, looking dashing in his blue uniform. He shook my hand and gave me a friendly smile.

My attorney leaned toward me, whispering with minty-fresh breath, "Remember, after you tell the judge your plea, let me do the talking. He'll set another court date, and then the meeting should adjourn. Next time we meet, we'll have everything in place to get the charges severely reduced or dropped entirely."

He oozed confidence, reminding me so much of my dad it was hard not to cringe.

His mouth kept moving, but my unfortunate attention was pulled behind me by the entrance of one Dax Miller—in a blue button-up shirt and khaki pants, I might add. He was in clothes that covered his body and pants that didn't have grease stains. That warranted a second look. Even his hair was…styled, in a sexy-actor-on-the-big-screen-winning-over-the-jury type of way.

He wasn't supposed to be here. My attorney specifically said that this was a case brought against me by the state. Not Dax. So why was he here?

"Hey, man," Dax said to Beau as he stood, and they did a weird hand-slap-shake thing. I tried to ignore it, but it was hard to not see it all out of the corner of my eye, even while looking at my lawyer spouting words at me. I wanted to give him my full concentration, but there was too much happening behind me.

"You see that game the other night?" Beau mumbled to Dax, and I wanted to cry in annoyance. Why was he here?

"Had it on at the shop."

I knew that the reason I was sitting in court was my own fault, but somehow it felt very unprofessional to have the guy whose shop I accidentally smashed into be friends with the cop who had given my citation. They could at least keep it under wraps in the courtroom. My lawyer's attention gravitated to something on his phone, and I turned back around in my seat. But their words kept finding me.

"How's the shop? That tarp hanging in there okay with all the wind we've been getting?"

"Barely. It's almost a full-time job keeping it secure."

"How are you holding up?"

"I actually spend a lot of nights crying myself to sleep. Tears. Tissues. Everything."

I scoffed out loud but refused to turn around.

"The Lego car?"

"The Lego car," Dax agreed solemnly.

"It's a crying shame," Beau remarked.

"What if I had been standing in front of those windows? She would have plowed over me like a lawnmower."

"You're too pretty for that," Beau said.

"That's what I thought."

Even as I shook my head, a smile itched to escape, though I held it in. *That* was why he was here. Dax would never pass up a front-row seat to my utter humiliation.

I turned around to meet two guys both holding back smiles at the same time. They had clearly been awaiting my reaction. Using a few specific words, I told them exactly where they both could go, resulting in laughs from both of them.

"Did you hear that language? It's no wonder she ended up here," Dax said to Beau.

"Did you brush off the old courtroom outfit from your days as a juvenile delinquent?" I asked Dax pleasantly now that I had his attention.

"You know what's good about being a juvenile delinquent?"

I leaned forward, pretending great interest. "What's that?"

"A squeaky-clean record as an adult. I don't know if you'll be able to say the same after this."

"I highly doubt you have a squeaky-clean anything."

Ew. That sounded much better in my head. Now I had to watch Beau laugh and a smile crawl across Dax's face.

"I haven't had any complaints," he said.

Thankfully, a loud voice told the courtroom to stand.

"Good luck," he whispered to me. "I'd better go to my side of the court." Then, he meandered toward the chairs behind the prosecuting attorney.

"You need to stand up," my lawyer instructed. I yanked my eyes off Dax and stood as a door in the front opened, and the Honorable Judge Henry Baylor strode into the room. He sat on his chair and motioned for us to sit down with a wave of his big paw. I straightened in my seat. I had never seen him in his official black robe. He used to be a regular at Sunrise Cafe when I was in high school. He'd been enthusiastic about the cafe food, and we'd grown a friendly rapport. He was a kind man, I knew that for certain. But he also could be a bit...eccentric. Like... some days for breakfast he would order a waffle with a side of cheeseburger.

Soo...here goes nothing.

"Take your seats," Mr. Baylor said. He straightened some papers at his desk before looking up and meeting my gaze with his curious eyes.

"I was surprised to see your name on the list, Ms. Brooks. Quite the lead foot you have."

Shame filled my entire body to the point that I wanted nothing more than to melt into the floor.

"Yes, Your Honor. Sorry about...this. I— It was an accident."

"Stop talking," my attorney whispered in my ear. I took a breath as my hands grew jittery. Already, I had forgotten all the details of how I was supposed to act in court.

Judge Baylor's focus moved over to where Dax was sitting, his low drawl as much of a character trait as the twinkle in his eye. "I see we have Mr. Miller here today. Have you been keeping out of trouble?"

"Trying my best, Your Honor." Dax nodded toward me. "It found me, though."

Judge Baylor wheezed a laugh, his shoulders shaking merrily. "I'd say." He nodded toward Beau and the two attorneys in the room before he sighed.

"Let's get to it, then." He cleared his throat and looked at me. "For the record, is your name Caroline Ivy Brooks?"

Okay, right out of the gate with my grandmother's name. "Yes, Your Honor."

"You are being charged with driving under the influence on the evening of Friday, June 7th. How do you plead?"

At my hesitation, my attorney gave me an expectant look. The not-so-friendly pep talk from my dad at breakfast this morning ran quickly through my mind. I had a job and research lined up in Tennessee that I needed to be back for. Staying on the island was simply not an option. I'd worked too hard to gain my independence only to be sucked back into my dad's orbit. He couldn't play mental games with me in Nashville. At least, not as easily. Besides, I couldn't afford to stay in town for the court dates required if I were to plead not guilty.

I had been driving under the influence, no matter how innocently it had happened. It was my fault. Pleading guilty was the honorable thing to do, and could my public saint of a father really dispute that? And if it so happened that I got to pay a quick fine for being willing to make things right and fast-track my buns out of Sunset Harbor, so be it.

"Ms. Brooks?" the judge asked again, giving me the nudge I needed to state my case.

"Guilty, Your Honor."

There was a gaping pause in the courtroom. Will Frost turned his head sharply at my statement, but I ignored him, focusing on Judge Baylor. The judge's brows raised slightly, and I shifted in my seat as his gaze focused on me.

"Guilty," he repeated.

"Yes," I said, the end of my sentence coming out like a question. Across the aisle, I could feel Dax's gaze on me, but I kept my focus trained forward.

"I see. Do you currently reside in Sunset Harbor, Ms. Brooks?"

"No."

"Where do you live?"

"Nashville."

"And what do you do in Nashville?"

I hesitated before phrasing this next part very carefully. "I've been working at Vanderbilt University."

"A professor?"

"I'm working on a postdoctorate, Your Honor. But I hope to be a professor soon."

His eyes were twinkly as he gave a low whistle. "I always knew you'd do good things." He sobered for a second. "You know, except for this."

A soft snort came from Dax's direction. I lifted my chin a fraction but gave him no mind.

"What are your summers like, with your university?" he asked me.

"Mainly filled with research. Later this summer, I'm set to teach a class."

He nodded thoughtfully. "I see. Later, you say?"

It was his piercing stare and his weighted words that suddenly brought me up short. I couldn't put my exact finger on what he wanted from me, but I instinctively knew that it might be in my best interest to be extremely busy this coming summer.

"The class starts at the beginning of August, but I need to be

—" He held up his hand to stop my onslaught, but I was half panicking at this point. "Mr. Baylor, I—"

"Your Honor," my attorney hissed in my ear, though he rested his head in his hands next to me.

"Your Honor," I added in a rush, "I have some money in savings. I'm happy to pay for all the damage." I shot a side glance to find Dax watching me, leaning forward in his seat with his arms folded casually across his stomach and a somewhat curious expression on his face. "I feel terrible about Da—Mr. Miller's shop. I'm happy to make everything right. So just let me know how much to pay, and I—"

"Ms. Brooks," Judge Baylor's soft drawl broke into my furious onslaught. "Thank you. I have no doubt we will make it right. It's just deciding…how, exactly." He looked at Dax. "Mr. Miller, how are you doing over there?"

"I'm good, Judge." Dax gave the judge an easy smile. "How's that golf cart holding up?"

"It's been running fine, thanks to you."

It was that exact moment—watching Dax and Judge Baylor with their easy rapport together, probably from Dax's past misdemeanors, that I knew my summer was about to blow up in my face.

Judge Baylor tapped his chin for a long moment. "You know. We're all here right now. Let's figure this out. This isn't usually how it's done, but it is my courtroom."

"Mr. Miller, beyond the cost of the windows, was there any other damage to the structure of the building? Marks on the floor, damage to the back wall? Any landscaping ruined?"

"There was no damage to the actual structure of the building. Just the windows. Insurance will take care of that, so we should be good there." I breathed a bit easier. So far, Dax didn't seem to be throwing me under the bus, which meant I should probably be wary.

"Now, I'm going to ask about the thing that has me, and I'm

sure most of the town, concerned. The Lego car. How can we make it right?"

All my do-gooder attitude went completely out the window as I gaped at the judge who was looking toward Dax with a definite twinkle in his eyes. I threw Dax a pleading look, but he kept his gaze averted.

"That's what has me most concerned as well, Your Honor. All the pieces survived, but the structure was completely destroyed."

Really? *Most concerned?* Half of his building was wrapped in a tarp.

"How many hours do you think were spent on the initial construction of the car?" Judge Baylor asked.

"My brother and I worked on it for a few hours after school for probably a year. Two hundred hours' worth of time, I'd guess." With that statement, Dax glanced at me, and there was a definite gleam hidden in his eyes behind the fake Boy Scout persona he seemed to have donned for today's court date.

"Judge Baylor," I began, my hand at my heart. "I'm happy to pay to fix whatever damage I caused," I said, panic raising my voice all while my attorney shook his head, hardly sparing me a glance. "As for the Lego car, I can hire somebody to rebuild it. I'm guessing Orlando has guys that could do it in their sleep."

The Legoland guys would take a credit card, right?

"With all due respect, Your Honor," Dax began, standing up and clutching his chest with one hand. "Maybe Ms. Brooks is used to just flinging money around to cover up her mistakes, but money can't replace what was lost. Not in this case."

My body tightened as I stared at him.

"Where's the line? How is she supposed to learn her lesson if she just writes a check anytime she makes a mistake?"

To my utter horror, Judge Baylor began nodding in agreement.

"I mean," Dax drawled on while I dug my nails into the

armrest, "how is she ever going to learn to never drink and drive again if we just let her write a check and be on her way? The way she lost control—"

"I wasn't drinking!" I stood up, my hands at my waist.

"Shhhh," my lawyer whispered furiously, hopelessly mortified because his lady doth protest too much.

"You *were* under the influence, Ms. Brooks," the judge said.

"Right. Yes. But it *was* an accident," I protested.

"I, for one, believe the children in this good town would feel safer if—"

"Mr. Miller?"

Dax paused in his stride. "Yes, sir?"

"Sit down."

"Yes, sir."

Dax sat down and shot me a glance so brimming with mischief my stomach tightened with nerves. He was playing me. Playing the judge. Playing everybody. Getting his reactions. This wasn't about the car. It couldn't be. This was about him wanting nothing more than to mess with me.

The next few minutes were spent watching a ping pong match go down in the courtroom between both attorneys. Realizing he didn't have much choice but to go along with my plea, Mr. Frost began arguing back and forth between the prosecuting attorney about negligence versus recklessness. How it was my first and only offense. I sat back in my chair while the scene played out around me, unable to do anything but watch with growing unease.

Mr. Frost elbowed me lightly in the arm. When I glanced at him, he nodded toward the judge. "He's talking to you."

My attention shot back to the judge to find that yes, he had indeed been talking to me. "Sorry, Your Honor. What was that?"

Judge Baylor closed his eyes briefly before saying, "Wasn't it you who worked in the cafe when you lived here? Back in high school, right? I think I remember you. You were a good waitress."

I was confused, and also slightly flattered he remembered, but I tried not to show it as I answered him. "Yes. That was me. I worked there for three years."

He nodded, and I wondered if that was just small talk, like how he and Dax had chatted about his golf cart. It had been ten years since I hung up my apron at the cafe. I was surprised he remembered.

He cleared his throat. "Well, I think I may have the solution for our predicament."

Predicament? As long as I was willing to fork out the check, it seemed like there didn't have to be a predicament at all, but I knew better than to say that out loud. Instead, I kept my gaze focused on Judge Baylor and any emotions off of my face.

"For your information," he began, looking at me, "Harold and Judy, the owners of the Sunrise Cafe here in town, have had to take a significant amount of time off due to Harold receiving cancer treatments off the island. My wife received word from Judy the other day that they'll be detained for a couple of months. They might be in and out, but the cafe is in need of some help, and we as a community are determined to keep them up and running."

My mind reeled at this information. Harold and Judy were basically my second parents all through high school. Harold, the sweet man who used to quiz me on math problems and showed up to my volleyball games, was fighting cancer.

"Ms. Brooks, I mentioned the cafe because I'm hopeful that, while you are here rebuilding what you've broken, you'll also give some of your time to help at the cafe. Since you're already somewhat familiar with how the restaurant runs, I can't help but think it would be a great way to give back to the community you've wronged. Is this something you are able to do?"

I swallowed and nodded, my brain having a hard time registering everything he was saying before he spoke again—leveling me completely.

"So, with that in mind, Ms. Brooks, in regard to your charge of driving under the influence in the town of Sunset Harbor, I sentence you to ninety days in jail. But I will suspend all ninety days and put you on probation for twelve months. I also impose a fine to the court for the cost of $500. You will serve two hundred hours of community service, to be performed within the next seven weeks. All two hundred hours will go toward helping Mr. Miller rebuild his Lego car and whatever else his business stands in need of. Since this is your first offense in the courts, Ms. Brooks, I will withhold adjudication."

I stared at the judge in growing trepidation, a hand over my mouth.

"Adjudication?" I whispered frantically to my attorney. "What does that mean?"

"He'll remove the charge from your record after you pay your fines and serve your hours," he whispered back. "That's very generous."

I sat back in my chair. Two hundred hours of community service.

To Dax Miller.

The judge went on about how teaching a lesson to the community in times like these was important. Getting our hands dirty to fix what we had broken was a trait this nation was losing a generation at a time.

Not on Judge Baylor's watch.

"I'm aware this is an unusual sentence, Ms. Brooks." The judge's kind eyes peered out of his spectacles. "Do you have any questions for me?"

Questions? Sure. I had questions. But none that he could answer.

Judge Baylor had a standing golf tee time once a week with my dad. He was one of many in the community who only knew the politician side of Senator Brooks. The side that could charm, and schmooze, and golf with the best of them. The side that showed up to funerals of people he had barely tolerated while pretending to grieve and spouting flowery things to all. The side that cut ribbons, made deals, shook hands, and said all the right things. The side that would never forgive me if I were to ask the judge how he expected me to live in my dad's home for seven weeks.

Brookses don't make mistakes.

"Ms. Brooks? Any questions?" the kind voice of the judge sentencing me to the worst possible punishment for a crime I didn't mean to commit asked again.

This time, I smiled bright and channeled my dad. "No, Your Honor. I'm happy to serve my time. I'm grateful for the opportunity to right what I accidentally wronged." There we go. All things considered, dear old dad would have to be proud of that answer.

Did I look at Dax Miller after I said that?

Nope.

"Alright, then." There was a squeak of movement in Judge Baylor's chair as he adjusted his position. "Your service hours start tomorrow. I'll let you and Mr. Miller work out the details. And I will inform the cafe they now have some extra help they can count on." He gave me a broad smile before smacking his gavel.

Court adjourned. My life upended. For a long moment, I sat there, soaking it all in. To re-cap, I could have had jail time but instead got community service for a crime I hadn't meant to commit but did. Judge Baylor called Dax Miller a good man. I was now a...criminal...I guess? And I was left wondering what planet I had accidentally landed on from my hellish plane ride three days earlier.

After shaking hands with my lawyer and thanking Beau for... being here, I guess...I fumbled with my purse while Dax sauntered my way. I was tempted to take off toward the front doors, but I knew I'd have to face him eventually.

Like…tomorrow.

"Well, that was entertaining, Caroline."

I folded my arms and leveled him with a warning stare. "It's Ivy."

"I was reminded how fun it is to watch you under pressure," he said, folding his arms across his chest.

"Yeah, and thank you so much for making sure I couldn't just pay you and leave."

"I thought we could build a legacy of togetherness."

It was the way he so casually used part of my dad's campaign slogan against me that had me turning my annoyance into a smile that didn't reach my eyes. I would be here for seven weeks. The worst had already happened. His words couldn't touch me now.

"Did you get that out of your system?"

He shrugged. "I wouldn't say that. What time are you coming to work?"

I leaned over to adjust the back strap of my sandal, feigning an attitude of nonchalance. "I'll see if I can do a morning shift at the cafe and come to your place in the afternoon."

He shoved his hands into his pockets. "You know, I'm kind of excited you'll be back at the cafe again. I haven't had a mediocre cup of coffee for about ten years now."

My hands found my hips. "First of all, I made good coffee. Second, I will buy you your own coffee machine if it means you'll stay out of the cafe while I work there."

He made a face. "No can do, Books. I'm incredibly lazy about making coffee. See you tomorrow," he said before striding toward the front door, leaving me wishing my cousin had chosen anywhere else on this planet to have gotten married.

CHAPTER 6

Biology Class
Day 4

"You can't just threaten to throw up on me every time you don't want to get your hands dirty, Books."

"It's Brooks," I said.

"I know. But you look like the sort of person who makes friends with her books. It just fits."

"You act like that's an insult."

He smiled at that, but I refused to be affected by the sight. I had bigger fish to fry, namely the small pig not staring back at me—because it was dead and without a clue that we were about to violate its pink, wrinkly little body. "I do all the writing and our reports. You hate doing that and now you don't have to. It is more than fair."

"I just think my conscience won't be able to rest knowing that I'm doing all the dirty work, and you're only writing stuff down."

"You can't just pull out words like 'conscience' whenever you want to win an argument. I stayed up until nine the other night, working on our report, okay? I'm doing loads more work than you."

He dropped his mouth open in shock, one hand on his cheek. "Nine?!"

I brandished the scalpel in the air in front of him, speaking slowly to the growing gleam in his eye. "Shut. Up."

T-minus 50 days to exit
Dax hours remaining: 200

I WALKED HOME from the courthouse in a bewildered daze. My phone, however, was very on top of things. After silencing three calls from the senator, I made two of my own. One to my neighbor back in Nashville to see about watering my plants, and one to my professor over my postdoc position later this summer. I hadn't been looking forward to that phone call, with good reason.

"You have to stay for the summer?" came the voice I had been dreading speaking to since the verdict. Kathleen was one of the department heads for mathematics at Vanderbilt. She was firm, knew her stuff, drank eight cups of coffee a day, and frequently made decisions affecting her students' lives based on her caffeine consumption. I'd seen many students leave her class in tears. I could only pray her veins were buzzing this morning.

"It's a big misunderstanding, and I've been court-ordered to stay here for seven weeks to do some community service. I'll be back in plenty of time to teach my class, but I won't be able to help with the research I had agreed to do over the summer." At her demand, I told her the basics of my sad story.

"Huh," she said again, the line going silent. I heard the sound of shuffling papers. "Part of your postdoc required research this summer. You won't be able to do that?"

"It's not likely," I said. If I were only working at Dax's, I might have been able to squeeze in some research, but working at the cafe as well put a major dent in my plans.

"Let me think about a few things, and I'll get back to you."

I stifled my groan and said thank you before hanging up. I wasn't sure what I wanted her to do. Call Judge Baylor, guns blazing, and force him to reconsider his punishment? The thought immediately filled me with warring guilt. I wanted to make things right. I did feel horrible about what happened. Not to mention mortified. But couldn't I feel horrible *and* write a check at the same time?

Instead of going home to where my dad could find me, my feet took me on a pathway to the beach instead. There was a public access point a few streets over that led to the side of a beach that wasn't great for families and swimming. The water was too choppy, which meant that it was a great place to sit and watch the waves and seagulls while trying to make sense of my life.

The beach was nearly empty. Every once in a while, I'd see someone running or taking a walk, but otherwise, the wind and the muggy afternoon air seemed to be enough to give me what I was craving.

The quiet. No islander judgment. And no Dax Miller.

After ten minutes, my life was still as confusing as ever, which was why, when Cat's name came up on my phone, I answered.

"You're here for the whole summer?" Cat's voice squealed into the phone after I relayed my afternoon in court.

"For seven weeks."

I put her on speaker, lay down on the sand, and filled her in on all the details. *Almost* all the details. For whatever reason, I had no desire to talk about Dax any more than I had to. And it had nothing to do with the fact that I knew Cat had thought Dax was cute for many years, even with my strong objections. Lots of things could be cute but still annoying.

Like cats.

"I hate how easy it's all been for you. I've been trying to get Dax to notice me for years. And then you come back into town for a weekend, and bam, one criminal charge later, you get to hang out with him nonstop for two months?"

Despite myself, I laughed. "You can have him. In fact, you can take over my service hours. I'll run the inn with your uncle."

Suddenly, that thought sounded so appealing. "Please, can we switch?"

She scoffed into the phone. "Dax would never let you get away with that. I have to know, did you guys bring up *the garage* while *in* a garage?"

"Why do you have a freakishly good memory?"

"From the second I heard it was his garage you smashed into, I haven't been able to stop thinking about the irony."

Despite myself, I laughed. "Shut up."

"Was it weird seeing him after so long?"

"He was exactly like the Dax I remembered from biology." Minus the muscles, the array of tattoos, and the overall manliness of his features, but she didn't need to know that.

"So he's flirtatious under the guise of not caring?"

I needed to shut this down quick.

"Why are you asking me? You should know him better than I do. You stayed on the island after high school." I tucked my long skirt underneath my legs as another gust of wind threatened to expose me to the elements.

She made a noise like I was crazy. "I only admire from a distance, like a proper low-threat stalker, thank you very much. If he actually spoke to me, I'd probably faint."

I huffed out a laugh before changing the subject. "Anyway, how's the B&B? Got any rooms available for me for the summer?"

"I'm so sorry. I wish we did, but we're booked solid for the next few weeks. There might be something available after that, though. Do you want to just stay with me?"

"Thanks, but I'll be alright. Let me know if a room opens up." Crashing at a friend's house was tempting, but I couldn't bear the thought of inconveniencing anybody because of my stupidity. I wanted my own space, but if that couldn't happen, this would be great motivation to get me back to Nashville in seven weeks.

If not sooner.

The truth in the words of a t-shirt in one of the town square tourist shops hit me like a ton of bricks.

Life is a beach.

THE SILVERWARE CLANKED on the dishes later that night as I moved the cauliflower rice and roasted chicken around on my plate. I sat at the kitchen table my parents had bought after my mom complained that our previous table wasn't large enough to throw dinner parties. Now, in a twist of irony, my dad's new wife was the one hosting events at the house.

Bless her heart, Angela had been attempting small talk all evening, chattering endlessly about things normal families would probably discuss at the dinner table. She brought up the abnormal heat and the wind the island had been getting. She talked about the new community pool hopefully going in over the summer and how nice that would be for all the kids on the island. She chatted about the farmers market and how she couldn't wait to go back again this Saturday to get some of the goat milk lotion that had made such a difference for her skin.

But there was a storm brewing at our table. My dad had been given time to absorb what I had told him about my morning in court and hadn't said a word to me since. But with each impatient bite of his food and every grunt given in reply to Angela's chatter, a budding hurricane grew in the space between us—a tension I remembered well throughout my life.

I wanted to balk at the feeling. Push it away. I wasn't a little girl anymore. I had spent my entire life attempting to prove myself worthy to someone who had never deemed me as such. I graduated at the top of every class and graduated with honors in every degree I attained afterward, but I couldn't shake the feeling that I was still nothing but a disappointment to him.

It was almost a relief when he wiped his mouth with his napkin and spoke.

"Even with your blatant disregard for everything my attorney and I told you to say, I'm still going to try to keep this out of the press. But I do know there are people just itching to spread the news that Clayton Brooks's daughter is here serving a community sentence."

Deep breaths. Remain calm.

Swallowing, I said, "I don't think there'll be that much gossip. Everyone will know it was an accident."

My dad stared at me incredulously—like I was missing something so completely obvious. "They'll know that my daughter pleaded guilty to a DUI. And that's all they'll have to know."

"Didn't Larry Donalds get a DUI for driving the golf cart drunk on the beach last year?" Angela asked, her timid voice attempting to cheerfully dislodge us. A piece of my heart softened at her attempt.

"Well, Larry isn't running the biggest campaign of his life at the moment. And it's all going to be ruined because my daughter came home for the weekend."

Obviously, Dr. Barb didn't have an egotistic politician for a father. The way he could so casually destroy me in one sentence or less was a work of art. I forced myself to speak.

"Dad, it's a local senator election. You're not running for president. I'm not going to jail. I think you'll be fine." My body tensed after I spoke the words, as though I were bracing myself for something coming. There were two parts of my personality at war with each other: the part that cowered under my dad's disappointment and the part that was trying to never let myself feel that way again.

He stared at me, betrayal written all over his face. His words were a careful mix of control and seething anger. "Now, I'm a senator. But what if I do run for president one day? Everything we do in this family is monitored. You think I'm causing all of this fuss for myself? It's to keep all of us safe. If you don't think everything you've done isn't going to be found out by reporters, you're grossly naive. Which makes this whole thing beyond maddening. You pleaded guilty to a DUI, instead of fighting something I know I could have fixed."

"I was guilty, Dad."

He banged his hand on the table, causing the dishes to jump along with me and Angela. For all his anger, he didn't yell. He hissed and seethed like a snake, but never yelled.

"I golf with the judge, for Pete's sake. You weren't drinking. It was just a completely idiotic..." He looked like he wanted to say a lot of words just then but reined it all in and, through gritted teeth, ended on, "...mistake."

Mistake.

My body tensed. There was that word again. It always seemed to find me. My dad had the tone down perfectly, with the hiss of the *S* and just the right inflection of speech to punch the gut. Suddenly, memories of being a child and crying under my covers came rushing back over me. It was amazing how one small word could set me back a decade or two of mental and emotional growth.

"The judge told me if I do my hours, then it will be removed from my record. So, it will be fixed."

"Well, how nice of the judge," Angela's voice rang between us. She jumped up, bumping the table as she did so. "Who wants dessert? I bought an angel food cake, and I've got some sliced strawberries and sugar-free whipped cream, if anybody wants some." She didn't wait for our answer and scampered into the kitchen. I took a bite of dry chicken and swallowed.

"Ivy. One more thing."

My eyes left my plate of half-eaten food to meet his. For a split second, hope pierced my heart. Maybe now he'd tell me how glad he was that I hadn't gotten hurt. How, when he heard about the crash, his first concern had been for my safety. It was pathetic, really, how even after years of therapy, I still found myself aching for the one thing I never got from him.

But like always, love was nowhere to be found.

"Not counting your DUI that I now have fighting against me, you hanging around that boy was the worst thing the judge could have done to me. We both know your history."

That boy.

I blinked back the hot splash of emotion in my eyes. "There is no history. That was nothing. I haven't spoken to him in ten years."

He shrugged. "Maybe not. But I remember what I saw. And just so you don't forget, people don't change that much. He's trouble. Always has been. So you remember that."

All the words I wanted to say swirled around in my head, taunting me, but I wasn't fast enough to catch them.

And he wasn't finished.

Leaning across his plate, he waited until I looked at him. "I live here. Not you. Your last name is mine. I gave it to you. You'd better start earning it."

We both startled when Angela brought our plates of fat-free cake and set them in front of us, all while humming a tune I didn't recognize.

My dad picked up his fork and took a bite of cake, relaying one last parting shot as he did so. "You do your hours, and then get out of that shop. You hear me?" He didn't wait for me to respond. Instead, he turned to his new bride and gave her a smile, "The cake is good. Thank you, honey."

Case closed. Conversation over.

Message received.

CHAPTER 7

Biology Class
Day 7

"I have a question for you," I whispered to Dax, a grave look on my face. Mr. Gray's lecture was particularly dry today, and I needed something to keep me awake.

Dax looked over at me, slouched in his chair, with his eyebrows raised in question.

I pursed my lips. "It's important."

He didn't say anything, but his gaze never left mine.

"Why did..." I broke off and blew out a breath, rubbing my hands against my shorts.

I began again. "Why did—"

His lips parted ever so slightly, and I thought I detected a hint of concern on his face, but I probably imagined it. I went in for the kill.

"Why did the DNA cross the road?"

Dax shook his head slightly before looking back to Mr. Gray.

I couldn't contain my glee, so I didn't try. "Any guesses?"

He refused to look at me.

I leaned closer. "To get to the other strand."

Dax leaned forward and put his face in his hands.

. . .

It turned out that the cafe, though grateful for the help, needed a day or two to rotate me into their schedule. Unfortunately, that brought me to Dax's place first.

I arrived after lunch wearing an old volleyball t-shirt and cutoff shorts. Even though my hours were going to be tight, a full day of Legos was something a girl needed to ease into. I gave the two black garbage cans of Legos the side-eye as I made my way toward the doorway leading into Dax's garage.

When I stepped inside, Larry Donalds, the town leech I remembered from my youth, was sprawled onto a barstool, talking loud enough over Dax's music that the retirement home next door could probably hear him. Whatever story he was telling required arms flying and spittle spewing. Ultimately, Larry was harmless, if a little annoying. He never seemed to go to work anywhere and had a knack for always being where you didn't want him.

My entrance hadn't been discovered yet, so I stood watching the scene, unable to resist the opportunity to observe Dax in his natural habitat. While Larry droned on, Dax bent over the underside of a lawnmower with tools in his hands. With Dax's obvious disinterest and Larry's oblivious nature, it became clear to me that he hadn't been invited into this space.

"How can you listen to Bob Dylan?" Larry asked when his story was over. "It sounds like he's sick and he's spewing it out all over the world."

There was a long pause before Dax said, "I'm going to have to charge you extra for that, Larry."

Larry's big boisterous laugh seemed to shake the walls as he stood up, groaning as he did so. "Well, guess I'd better get home and see what the missus has cooking for me."

"Is your missus the Sunrise Cafe?" Dax asked, his voice sounding almost bored. Larry had to be pushing fifty and was as single as they come.

"I hear the cafe is getting some new scenery. The senator's daughter?"

Annoyance burned in my chest at Larry's mention of me. I waited for Dax to tell him I would be arriving any minute, but he didn't.

"And she's closer to my age than the rest of 'em. I checked. Maybe I'll be getting hitched sooner than I thought."

"Yeah, but she'd have to wake up to your ugly face every morning," Dax said. "That might be a deal breaker."

Another exuberant laugh from Larry, but he didn't leave. Dax noticed as well. "Alright, get out of here, Larry. I've got work to do."

Before I could change course or hide, Larry turned toward the door and spotted me, eyeing me with pleasure.

"Well, there she is now. You're a sight for sore eyes, darlin'."

Dax looked over at the mention of me, but I kept my focus on Larry, smiling politely instead of snarling at this man who was always very vocal about supporting my dad. "Hi, Larry."

He ambled closer to me. "Well, if you're not at the cafe now, maybe it's a TV dinner kind of night."

I sidestepped him, putting a small distance between us. Larry had no clue about the ick vibe he gave off. He probably wouldn't believe anyone who tried to tell him.

"I can't wait to run into your dad and mess with him over all this DUI stuff. What great timing." He shook his head in laughter. "How long you back in town for, honey?"

Dax stood and ambled closer, clasping Larry on the shoulder and propelling him to the door leading out of the garage. "Time to go, Larry. Your leaf blower is on the list. I'll have it finished in a couple weeks."

While Dax walked Larry out, I took in all the details of the drafty room that smelled like dust and oil. The floor looked like it hadn't been swept in months, but overall, I was mildly surprised at the organization. The shop floor was a disaster, littered with motors, lawnmowers, leaf blowers, chainsaws… along with a boat on a trailer, but his tools were hung and organized on shelves and pegboards throughout the room. I glanced at the large clock on the wall made from boat propellers. Two hundred hours seemed a bit excessive when I had only been here two minutes and was already itching to leave.

Voices from the other room came closer, and for a second, I wondered if Larry was coming back. To my surprise, Beau Palmer and another guy close to my age wearing a suit stepped into the room.

"Hey there, Lead Foot!" Beau greeted me, his uniform looking freshly pressed and a teasing smile on his face.

"Oh, are we friends now, Officer?" I folded my arms across my chest.

"Are you still mad about the citation?"

I shot him a look while he laughed and held up his hands. "Friends don't let friends plow into their *other* friend's shop and not get a citation."

Despite myself, I laughed and shook my head.

Beau grinned before asking, "Do you know Phoenix? He moved here after you left, but he comes around every now and then."

"Hi." I smiled and waved at the dark-haired man in a suit. This mix of friends seemed to cover all the bases: a mechanic, a cop, and some sort of businessman, by the looks of it.

"That still looks bad," Phoenix said to Dax, pointing toward the room where the tarp flapped obnoxiously, a reminder to the entire town what I had done.

"How did you not get hurt?" Phoenix asked me, his dark gaze incredulous.

"Ivy can thank the roof of the golf cart for her life," Beau said, plopping down onto the stool Larry had last occupied. For a second, I wondered if I should offer to disinfect it for him before dismissing the thought. "And her hero, Dax Miller." Beau leaned toward Dax and roughly squeezed his shoulders.

Dax shot me a look, amusement lining his features. "If I had to have someone smash into my building while under the influence, I would have hand-picked Ivy out of a crowd."

I glared at Dax while the guys laughed and looked like they would have kept talking along that line, but Dax shifted the conversation, looking toward Beau.

"Any cats that needed saving from a tree today, Officer?"

"Not today," Beau said, tilting the barstool against the wall. "I spent most of my time trying to convince an old woman to not harass the staff in the retirement home."

"Who?" I asked.

"Her name is Virginia. She's sassy, mean, and has a massive crush on the boat mechanic next door." Beau nodded toward Dax.

"Can I file a complaint for harassment too?" Dax asked, bending to clean out the underside of a lawnmower. "She's made me blush twice already today."

"Gotta keep the goods hidden, Dax. You're driving the elderly wild."

At my confused face, Beau filled me in. "He goes around with his shirt off all morning, fixing boats out in the marina, and the old ladies can't get enough."

"It's hot," Dax protested, a light flush crawling up his neck.

"They think *you're* hot," Beau said.

"Their eyesight must be going too, huh?" I said, while Beau and Phoenix laughed.

"Have you clocked in yet, Books?" Dax asked, for the sheer pleasure of annoying me.

"Where would you suggest I do that?"

He motioned toward a calendar pinned on the wall to the side of me. One glance told me exactly what I needed to know.

The calendar was dated August 1967 and showcased a voluptuous blonde in a mini skirt and red-and-white polka dot shirt.

"Are you serious? Why is it set on August?"

He shrugged. "I think she was Keith's favorite."

My heart grew heavy at that. Keith McMannus owned the repair shop when I was a kid and had been a beloved member of the island. His sudden passing a few years ago had rocked the whole town.

"The days of the week won't line up."

"Won't matter. Just write it on the same date."

"Doesn't the judge need something more official?"

He shrugged. "He just gets a report from me when you're done."

I tapped the calendar with my finger. "I'd hate to ruin such an heirloom. How about I keep track on my phone."

He shook his head. "I want it on the calendar. I'd hate for you to cheat me out of what you owe."

"You're worried about *me* cheating?" I asked incredulously as several memories of him attempting to cheat off my test in our biology class came flying back to me.

As if remembering the same thing, a smile lifted the corners of his mouth. "I wouldn't have thought you'd have a DUI on your record, but you just never know about people these days."

Before I could respond, he laughed and pointed toward something behind me. "There's a pen on that bench. Mark the time you arrive and the time you clock out each day. Beau, come help me for a sec."

Beau wandered over to Dax, holding the riding mower steady while Dax set the engine into place. Under lowered lashes, I couldn't help but watch. His hands moved fluidly from one part to the next, deft and capable and basically...it was startling how attractive a man that knows his way around tools could be. Let me be clear, it wasn't Dax that was attractive. It was the *idea* of him.

"Why is it always me? Phoenix is sitting right there too," Beau complained, taking great care not to get any grease or grass clippings on his uniform.

"He looks too pretty in that suit," Dax said.

"I do look pretty in this suit," Phoenix confirmed, helping himself to a Coke from Dax's mini fridge under the counter.

"You need to hire some help," Beau complained, as the motor was set, and the boys stood tall once more.

"Why, when I have you two over here every day, stealing my food? It's the least you can do."

"We come for the music of our forefathers," Phoenix said dryly as The Beatles played in the background.

"We're going to grab some lunch. You in?" Beau asked Dax.

He hesitated a moment, tightening something on the lawn mower. "Nah. I'm good."

Deciding I should move my focus somewhere else, I scratched my initials on the calendar along with the time and tossed the pen back onto the counter.

I turned to Dax. "Where do I start? The Legos?"

Dax stood, brushing the grass off of his hands. "We'll get to that soon enough, but since I've got you here, I thought you could do a few other things first."

My body tensed, immediately wary, a new energy suddenly buzzing around the room. "Like what?"

"I've got a bathroom here that—" he began.

My eyes widened. "No."

"I try to clean it every so often, but I just don't have the time." He motioned around the room filled with machines.

"No," I said again. "I'm terrified of what 'every so often' means to you."

The straight face he tried to keep intact faltered a bit at that. "I haven't had any complaints lately. But—" he motioned toward Beau and Phoenix—"this place is like an airport with people coming in and out all day. If you were to clean it, it would really help me out."

"That's not what the judge sent me here to do."

A smile crossed his face then. Whatever his trap was, I had walked right into it.

"I believe the judge said that you're required to give me two hundred hours to help rebuild the Lego car and..." He paused for effect before adding, "...whatever else my business needs. And right now, it really needs the bathroom cleaned."

I immediately looked at Beau, who was now scratching his neck and motioning for Phoenix to stand up.

"Well, we'd better get going."

"Wait!" I called. "Beau, is that true?" My time in the courtroom was blurry, to say the least.

Beau shot Dax an annoyed look. "That's what you were asking me to look up the record for?"

Dax smiled.

Beau sighed and looked at me. "It's true. It was specifically for the Legos, but Judge Baylor also added that it could be for other things in the business too." He gave Dax a look before turning his attention back to me. "But if the *other things* part gets out of hand, come talk to me."

Beau and Phoenix left after giving me words of encouragement and looks to Dax that I wasn't sure how to decipher. Dax very obviously wanted me to hate the very idea of this. And... honestly...I did. But he would never know. So when he handed me the bucket of cleaning supplies, I took it with a smile.

Except, Dax smiled too, motioning with his hands. "It's just around the corner."

Using all my willpower, I kept a smile pasted on my face before disappearing into the public bathroom of a very manly repair shop.

A small unisex room with one toilet and a pedestal sink greeted me. Nothing fancy.

It also wasn't…terrible.

In all actuality, it seemed like it had been cleaned somewhat recently. There were still streaks on the mirror. I wasn't about to entertain the thought that Dax Miller might have cleaned the bathroom in his shop before he made me do it, but I did wonder if his mother might have secretly done it on a visit to her son. That seemed like a motherly thing to do.

Clean bathroom or not, I did, however, milk a bit of time. There was only so much I could do to get back at Dax, so of course, I cleaned like a sloth. I could play games too.

A knock pounded on my door. "Get out of there, Books. I know what you're doing."

"I'm not done yet," I said, leaning back against the wall, languidly reading a book on my phone that I'd started on my plane ride.

"The longer you take in there, the worse it will be out here."

"Worse? I'm having a great time!" I lied.

"Good to know."

I forced myself to pretend to read for two more minutes—on principle.

Flinging the bathroom door open, I stepped out, peeling the rubber gloves off my hands, and looked at Dax, who was sorting through papers on the counter. Invoices, it looked like.

"You know what I decided in there?"

In an obnoxious power move, he waited five seconds before he answered, pretending to look busy scratching on the paper. "Not sure. Larry says that's where he does his best thinking, though."

"Ew."

Though he wasn't looking my way, his grin was enough to devastate me, but I rallied quickly. "You don't scare me. So let's do this. Throw me your worst right now so you can get it all out of your system."

"Worst? I was being nice starting you in the bathroom."

"Come on, what's next? Do you need me to Clorox the blood off all your chainsaws?"

The puff of laughter escaping his lips felt like a double win.

"I wouldn't trust you with an assignment of that scope, but I'm touched to know you'd do something like that for me."

There was an exhilaration between us as we each played our own version of tug of war, something so reminiscent of the past I couldn't help but feel energized. I had forgotten what it felt like to be around someone I could tell exactly what I was thinking. And he was just obstinate enough to like it.

Eventually, he stood and walked toward a storage closet on the other side of the room. Was it me, or did he have a bounce in his step?

He pulled out a large book that looked like a parts catalog and leafed through it for a moment. Under the guise of nonchalant glances and boredom, I allowed myself a moment to soak him in. He wore a pair of jeans and a black tank top. His dark hair was messy and disorderly. It was nothing special. The best thing he wore was the smirk across his face, and I would never admit that in a million years. So it didn't make sense how the overall appearance of this man striding toward me had me tucking my wayward curls shyly behind my ear as he grew closer.

"This way, Books," he said, brushing past me to fling open the doorway into the hall before leading me into the main lobby of the shop, where the noisy tarp flapped against the breeze. It was only noon, but with the tarp blocking most of the light, it felt much later than that. Dax stopped at the first black garbage bin of Legos.

"Holy crap," I whispered, caught at an unguarded moment, once again taking in the sheer number of Legos in the garbage cans.

"I feel like now is the time to tell you that I've never played with Legos before," I said.

"I guess now is as good a day as any to fix the travesty that is your life."

I looked at him, my arms out wide. "Where do I even start?"

With great aplomb, Dax handed me the book he'd brought in from the other room. I turned it around to read the cover, only to discover that it was the guidebook for the Lego car.

It was the size of a phone book. An old school one. The hefty brick-sized ones you used to get in the mail before that thing called the internet was invented.

"One piece at a time, Books. Be sure to follow the directions to the letter. You'd hate to have to restart halfway through. Good luck to you." He began making his way back toward the garage when my voice called out in a panic, "Wait! Where are you going?"

"Back to work."

"I thought you were going to help me."

He raised an eyebrow. "What made you think that?"

"I don't know what I'm doing. And you..."—I motioned toward the Legos with my hands—"must love Legos."

He smiled, a wolf on the scent. "I do love Legos. But some of us don't have the luxury of playing all day."

"Dax!" I yelped when he started moving again. "What do I do?" I hated that my voice was laced in panic, but I couldn't help it. My brain was shutting down. The sheer number of Legos would be overwhelming to even the biggest Lego enthusiast, not to mention someone who had never really done them before.

Though I could have imagined it, a faint shadow of compassion crossed his face as he took me in, probably looking like Albert Einstein in a panic, hair and eyes wild in frantic alarm.

"If it were me, I'd dump the Legos out and start organizing them by type before you crack that book open. Or else you'll be searching for each piece for days."

He took his leave, calling out his final parting shot before he left the room.

"Don't forget to clock out when you're finished."

After a moment, I dumped a pile of Legos onto the ground and began looking for similar shapes. I suppose little boys everywhere might be jealous of an assignment like this, but other than the fact that I did feel bad about destroying it, being locked away by myself to build a Lego car of this magnitude felt like the worst kind of torture.

CHAPTER 8

Biology Class
Day 9

"What are your plans after graduation?" I asked Dax, trying hard to be so pleasant and friendly that he wouldn't overthink the fact that he was the one holding the scalpel.

"Not much."

"What does that mean?"

He leaned forward to stare into the rodent's underbelly. "Get over here, you gotta see this."

I leaned forward, plugging my nose with two fingers and keeping my eyes closed firmly. "What is it?"

He laughed lowly, a deep, breathy sound that sent a small ray of light into my belly. It always happened like that when he laughed. Though I hated my reaction to it, there I was, trying not to smile.

"Open your eyes, or I'll bring him to meet you."

I jerked back, eyes open and fully aware of the grin on his face before it disappeared.

"If you're not careful, I'll tell everyone exactly how many teeth you have," I said.

His brow furrowed. "You've counted my teeth?"

"No. It just means that I've seen your smile and probably nobody else ever has."

"*Why didn't you just say that, then? Why be the creepy teeth girl?*"

Blushing hotly, I smacked him across the stomach, annoyingly elated when he laughed again.

T-minus 49 days to exit
Dax hours remaining: 195

FOR THE MOST PART, waitressing felt like riding a bike—same old drill, getting coffee, taking orders, and giving the cook a hard time. It was fun seeing my old friend, Marco. He'd been the head cook at Sunrise Cafe for as long as I could remember, and during peak tourist season, he was the reason we had lines out the door. My new manager, Jean, seemed nice enough. It did take me some time to get back into the groove of customer service, but navigating the rush of the breakfast crowds, endless dietary restrictions, and strange food orders was preferable to getting teased mercilessly about my sentencing from all the old cafe regulars.

Despite the senator's best efforts, the entire town knew every detail of the crash. The first few days with my apron strings tied went something like this:

"I heard you were back in town, Ivy." Then another patron replied, "Everybody heard that. The shatter of glass woke my dog up, and he wouldn't stop barking all night."

"What did your dad think about your DUI?" That one was from Larry.

Or my personal favorite, when a particularly rowdy group began banging their hands on their tables, demanding, "Justice for the Lego car!"

But the real kicker was when a sweet little old lady with big eyes and thick glasses, who had been a community staple my entire life, asked in her crackly voice, "Are you sure the judge was in his right mind making you work with that dark-haired, tattooed boy at a time like this? You, of all people, getting a DUI? I don't think he's the right influence for you, dearie."

All of this I bore with a smile and a laugh.

And then, the inevitable happened.

On my fifth day working the early shift at the cafe, at precisely ten in the morning, Dax Miller walked into the restaurant and sat down at a table near the door. He looked casual in a dirty, white t-shirt and tousled hair. Maybe a smudge of grease on one cheek, but really, who was looking that close?

Though I could feel the heat from his gaze following me, I ignored him. I wasn't his waitress. He was in Sorel's section, a young girl with red hair and cheeks full of freckles, who was about to be a senior in high school.

Over the past few days of working for him, Dax had made me clean his bathroom, sweep his floors, and call customers before sending me into the Lego torture chamber by myself each night. I knew it was all part of my sentence, but I was off his clock at the moment. He was in my house now.

So, I proceeded to chat with my tables, perhaps laughing a little too loudly at jokes while taking credit cards before hiding in the kitchen and helping Marco plate food.

Ignoring him like a boss.

I was leaning against the counter in the middle of a riveting discussion with Marco about the best way to cook a hamburger when Sorel came to find me.

"There's a guy here who wants his coffee from you."

"What?"

"The hot mechanic guy. He wants a cup of coffee, but he says he wants it mediocre, and you're the only one who can do that." She made a face, looking slightly horrified before adding, "He told me to say that word for word."

Marco started laughing until I hit him in the arm and turned back to Sorel. "Tell him I'm not his waitress, so I can't do it."

"I did. But he insisted, and Jean told me to come and get you."

"Go on," Marco said, motioning me toward the door. "Give that hot mechanic what he wants."

I groaned loudly before stalking out of the kitchen and grabbing the pot of coffee. I walked toward Dax, who was awaiting my presence with growing eagerness.

Without a word, I stared him down while filling his mug before stepping back to watch him take his first sip. Streaks of a cozy yellow light filtering in through the windows made the scene look like Dax was some tortured artist taking a drink of his coffee. It wasn't attractive. He has too many plans to annoy me for him to be attractive. The second I realized I was twirling a runaway strand of curly hair spilling out of my loose bun, I stopped immediately.

He let out a big sigh and set his mug down with a satisfied clink. "That's the stuff I've been missing. Perfectly average."

"It's very rude for me to take over someone else's table, so next time you come in, you get who you get."

"They don't do it right."

I leaned closer, setting my hand on his table. "I grabbed the coffee pot and dumped it directly into your cup. I promise, any one of us can do it exactly the same."

"It just hits different coming from you." He leaned back in his seat. "Speaking of...I'd like to order some food."

"I'll go get Sorel."

"Can't I just tell you real quick?"

"I'm not your waitress."

"I'm sure you know what to do with my order, though, right?" His face shined with barely bridled delight.

I took a step closer to him, lowering my voice so the other decent human patrons of the cafe wouldn't hear me. "You want me touching your food?"

"No." He shook his head emphatically. "I want Marco touching my food. I want you to bring it to me."

"Okay, but it sure would be a shame to have one of my long hairs you used to find so annoying end up on your plate." I smiled sweetly at him. His eyes drifted upward as he considered my wayward curls.

"Eh, I'm willing to risk it."

I sidled up to him. "Good to know. What can I get for you then? Gator and eggs?"

"I've got a busy day, so I'd like you to keep the coffee coming. Just you, though. And I'd like some bacon, scrambled eggs, and hash browns."

"Great," I said. I couldn't blame him for his order. The cafe was famous for its all-day breakfast as well as its selection of homemade syrups.

Before I could turn and leave, he added, "Oh, and could you put a little cheese on top of those eggs?"

"Sure." I made to turn around, but his voice stopped me —again.

"And can I get some toast?"

Slight pause while I inhaled a deep breath. "Yeah."

He waited two beats before adding, "Are you going to ask me what kind?"

Dax had a death wish. So it was strange the way my body went into a chokehold to hide the smile suddenly wanting to escape my lips. If I broke, that meant he won, and I couldn't allow that.

With the fakest of fake smiles on my face, I asked pleasantly, "What kind would you like?"

"White. Light on the butter."

"Light on butter," I repeated softly, pretending to write on an imaginary pad of paper.

His face cracked as a smile broke, and for a second, I could only stare at him, helpless as the lines on his face morphed into something...kind of sweet when he looked at me.

I refrained from adding any hair to his food—but just barely. I was still new at this job, and I didn't want it to get back to the judge that my behavior was a problem. My behavior was *never* the problem. That was what hurt so badly about this arrangement. Even though I wasn't going to add it to his food, I very much enjoyed the idea that he might not know that.

With a grand flourish, I set his breakfast before him on the table.

"I hope you enjoy all the parts of your food."

A satisfied feeling settled over me as I watched him double-check his plate before taking the first bite.

Once Dax left, the cafe became much more relaxed. Near the end of my shift, Cat, Jane, and another friend, Holland, came in and sat at one of my tables in the back. My friends were each striking beauties. So much so that if I hadn't had a lifetime of memories with two of them, I would have probably felt self-conscious in their presence.

"Hey, girls," I said, glancing around the cafe to make sure it was slow enough before I nudged Cat over and sat down next to her.

"Busy today?" Jane asked, flipping her long brown hair over her shoulder. She wore the same floral dress she had lent me for my court date. It *did* look better on her. She was pure sunshine and the corals and sunset yellows from the dress amplified that fact.

"It was. I'm glad you guys came after the rush so I could chat."

"Can you take a break *after* you put in an order for us?" Cat grinned over at me, her blonde hair tied up with a ribbon. I groaned good-naturedly but stood up. "Cheeseburger?" I confirmed.

"Yup," Cat said, "and tell Marco not to skimp on the fries this time."

"Same for me," Jane said.

"Pancakes for me, " Holland supplied with a smile across her heart shaped face. Holland was an island transplant after I'd left. She had grown close to Cat in my absence and though I'd only met her a handful of times, she was funny and insightful and seemed to fit in but not completely take my place with my friends, which I appreciated.

I put their orders in, along with a cheeseburger and side salad for me, before telling Jean I was officially taking my lunch break. She waved me off, and I moved to sit back down with the girls.

Cat was eyeing me with interest. "How are things with Dax?"

I snorted, playing with the sugar packets on the table. "He was here earlier for the sole purpose of making me serve him food, if that tells you anything."

My two friends shared a look. "I think that tells us a lot, actually," Jane said, smiling before taking a sip of the water I'd brought her.

"I've never seen him in here before," Cat said, folding her arms on the table.

"And she would know." Jane smirked, while Cat kicked her under the table.

"If I don't murder him before the summer is over, he should consider himself lucky," I said.

"He's been a saint for a long time." Cat quipped, grinning at me. "I'd hate for you to be a bad influence on him."

I threw a packet at her face while she laughed.

"How is it there? Do you guys talk a lot?" Holland asked, running a hand through her blonde hair.

"I don't see him much, to be honest. After he makes me sweep his floor or clean his bathroom, I go to work in the lobby, and he's in his garage. It's usually just me and Sunny Palmer's audiobooks keeping me company."

To be honest, I had a hard time concentrating on the books while I was there. I loved Sunny's romances, but then I'd hear a tool fall to the ground one wall over, and my mind would...wander.

"If you hate the Legos, I say you just force Dax to let you help him," Jane said, a smile curling her lips. "Can you imagine, you and Dax underneath a golf cart, changing the oil."

"Pretty sure that's not where you change the oil," I said, blowing the wrapper of a straw onto her face.

"Yes," Cat added, leaning forward excitedly. "You and Dax underneath the golf cart, fixing...something...on one of those roller scooter things. Every time you go to move or hand him a tool, you keep running into his muscles."

Despite myself, I laughed and kicked her under the table.

"Okay, subject change," Jane said, probably eyeing my heated cheeks. "Jean told me she was going to put you in charge of the farmers market booth for the cafe, the week after the Fourth of July. Is that still okay? Can I put your name down?"

Jane worked in the mayor's office on the island and was over most of the town events.

"Yeah. That should work," I said.

"It's pretty easy. Jean usually bakes up some pies and breads to sell. You just sit there and look pretty, taking money."

"Oh. Then that shouldn't be a problem at all," I said, posing with my chin in my hands.

The girls laughed as Jean brought our food to the table. In between bites of cheeseburgers, the conversation moved to the Fourth of July bash coming up in a couple weeks.

I was grateful the conversation had moved on. The girls were crazy. Dax didn't have any interest in me beyond inducing torture and revenge. Our relationship was a court-ordered business deal with a side of annoying each other for pleasure.

Was I attracted to Dax Miller? Sure. What red-blooded female wouldn't be? The guy could fix anything with or without a shirt and had muscles built from physical labor.

The attraction couldn't be stopped.

It was science.

But that didn't mean I would be acting on or even acknowledging that fact. I guess there was something the senator and I agreed on...Dax *was* trouble. Trouble I needed to stay far, far away from.

You know, as best as I could while being legally required to see him all summer.

CHAPTER 9

Biology Class
Day 11

"Alright, there is now a line on this desk. If your hair crosses it one more time, I'm chopping it off."

I gave him an annoyed look, pulling my curly brown hair onto my shoulder, away from Dax. I didn't say anything, just continued to read over the worksheet we'd been given.

"Gross. It's everywhere. You're shedding like a cat."

I looked over at him, unable to help the laugh that came out from seeing his disgusted face dry-heaving while scraping long brown curls off his desk.

"Sorry," I said in a sweet enough tone that Dax looked at me with a wary expression.

For good reason. I just had a great idea.

T-minus 46 days to exit
Dax hours remaining: 176

THE SENATOR
> How many hours do you have left at the mechanic?

> ???
>
> Ivy. Answer me.

> ME
> 176

> THE SENATOR
> You've only worked twenty four hours? You've been here for a week. How is that possible?

> ME
> I'm working at the cafe too.

> THE SENATOR
> That's on a volunteer basis. You need to cut your hours back there and wrap it up with the mechanic.
>
> Ivy?
>
> ???

> ME
> I'm on track to be finished in plenty of time. Leave it alone.

"I'M DYING," I said dramatically, bursting into Dax's shop a few days later, flinging the top half of my body onto his work bench. I eyed the bag of Sun Chips on the counter and snuck my hand inside for a quick dip.

"I saw that." Dax finished changing out the battery on a golf cart before wiping his hands on a towel.

"I can't do this anymore," I moaned.

"What? Eat my chips?" He made his way toward me, taking a few swigs of a Coke sitting on the counter. I watched his Adam's apple do its thing while the liquid slid down his throat before flicking my eyes away.

"The Legos. I hate it so much. Why can't I pay someone to do it?"

"Sorry, Books. If it's any consolation, I'm having lots more fun this way."

I glanced around his space, seeing another stack of invoices yet to be filled out. "Do you want me to do some of these while you work? You can just tell me what you did."

Dax pointed at himself. "Did you just offer to help me?"

"I'd rather do this than Legos. That's how low I've sunk in my life."

He debated for a moment until a hint of humanity showed on his face. "Alright. Don't get used to such a cushy job, though."

I pulled the top invoice and read the name Dax had scrawled on top. "Matt Hall. Are you done with his lawnmower?"

Dax climbed on top of the fishing boat he had sitting on a trailer on the far side of the garage. "I just finished. Put on there that I cleaned the mower and replaced the motor." He paused while I wrote. "One hour of service time. And then add a line for parts ordered, and I'll find the invoice for it later."

I wrote down everything he said before moving on to the next invoice. We did this for a while—working rather seamlessly, I might add—until the pile was finished. Dax had moved from one project to the next, cleaning, bolting, removing, and all with a level of care I wouldn't have expected of him.

"Quite the stall tactics you have, Books. But since it still benefits me, I'll let it slide."

I couldn't see his smile because he slid under a golf cart, but I could feel it in the air.

Out of things to do, I sighed and began making my way toward the torture chamber when Dax's voice rang out like a beacon in the dark.

"If you're still desperate for a break, I was going to run to my house and grab some tools I left there." He slid out from the golf cart and stood, pulling a set of keys from his pocket. He dangled them toward me. "I'll *allow* you to go as long as you can confirm you haven't taken anything today."

Like a cat to a bowl of cream, I moved toward him. "You'd trust me to go into your house?"

"No, but I know where you live."

"You do?"

The words were out before I thought them through. Of course he knew.

His eyebrows raised slightly. "Are you on something now?"

My cheeks grew slightly heated against my will, while he laughed. For the first time since I'd been back in his orbit, he'd brought up the night in the garage, shedding light on something we'd hidden away, and now I didn't know what to do with my hands.

"Tell me you didn't forget about your *first* brush with the law."

"I was an innocent bystander." The heat from my cheeks began spreading outward to my neck, and I wasn't sure how to stop it.

He folded his arms, enjoying himself. "That first dabble into a life of crime is always a special moment. If only we'd known what it would lead to one day."

Our gaze held, and something flashed across his face. My mind brimmed with the memories I thought I had squashed years ago. I took a step back and held out my hand for the keys.

He brought them closer, almost within reach, before he yanked them back before I could snatch them. "It's the door on the right side of the house. You are to enter the premises and grab the red toolbox sitting on my table. Do not touch anything else. No trying on my clothes. No collecting locks of my hair. No going through my underwear drawer."

I put a finger up to my cheek. "I hope I can remember all that."

"Books..." he said, his voice low with warning. He held the keys out of my reach as I tried to grab them again. My hand landed on his chest, using him to steady me as I yanked them out of his hand.

Dancing away, I reveled in my newfound advantage. "I noticed you're almost out of chips. Do you have any at home I could grab for you?"

He rolled his eyes, but I detected the humor. "Bottom cupboard to the right of the fridge. Grab the chips, grab the tools, then come right back."

"I'll try to remember all of that."

"The brake is on the left. The gas is on the right," he called out, sounding more cheerful than usual.

Fifteen minutes later, armed with chips and a toolbox, I slammed the door open into his garage once more. Dax looked up at the sound. I could only stare at him, my mind a whirl of possibilities. It was amazing what a person could learn about someone in such a short period of time.

I had to figure out the best way to play the game. Straightforward wouldn't work. If Dax knew how much I wanted it, he'd never let me have it. If it was even something possible to have.

Feigning a calm I didn't feel, I strode farther into the room and placed the toolbox and the chips on the counter. The chips were half gone, the hazards of eating my emotions during the ride back.

"What's wrong?" Dax asked, eyeing me up and down before sitting down on his roller.

"When did your house get turned into a duplex?" I asked him, casually taking a sip of his Coke he'd left on the counter.

He moved back under the golf cart, a tool in hand. "Keith helped me do it about five years ago."

"It didn't used to be a duplex, though. Right?"

"Nope."

I inched closer. "Is anybody living there right now?"

"Nope. I'm planning to repaint and tile the bathroom this summer." His voice sounded strange, like he was feeding me a line.

"In all your free time?"

"Yup."

I stood, biting my thumbnail, waiting until he rolled back out from under the cart and stood up. I tried not to show him all my cards, but it was probably difficult with the near feral look in my eyes.

"What's with the weird—"

"So, are you, like...looking for someone to rent it? Or help you with painting or something?" My finger reached up to twirl a loose curl before I shoved my hands in my pockets.

Light dawned in his eyes. "Oh... You got something you want to ask me, Books?"

"I mean, if you needed a part-time renter, I could...help you out." I wanted it so badly I was almost bursting out of my skin. The tension between my dad and me in my childhood home was at an all-time high. My exit plan had been blown to bits by my sentencing, but maybe some form of escape was still possible. "In exchange, I could paint it for you or retile..." My voice drifted off on the last one.

Dax leaned forward with great interest.

"Retile it? Really? I'd love to know what experience the senator's daughter has in tiling floors."

"Okay, maybe not tiling, but I'm an excellent painter," I began.

Side note: I was not any sort of painter.

"I'll wash the windows. I'll be the best tenant you've ever had." I leaned forward, my hands in praying position.

He considered me, which lulled me into a false sense of security. "Why do you want it so bad?"

I thought about not answering. I didn't want to say why, but

I didn't think Dax would accept any answer but the truth. And I think he already knew.

"I'm currently living with my dad. It's a campaign year, and his daughter just got a DUI. Everything about him is toxic to me. It would just be for the six weeks I have left here."

Dax eyed me for a long moment before he spoke. "I originally changed the home into a duplex so I could rent half the space out and not have a mortgage. I had a renter there for about a year, but it turned out I forgot one important thing."

"What?" I asked.

"I don't really like people all that much."

There was a beat of time when I didn't know what to say before a small laugh broke free.

Folding my arms across my chest, I asked, "How long have you been telling people you're going to repaint and retile that apartment?"

He mirrored my stance, arms folded and a smile playing at his lips. "About three years."

I nodded, resigned to my fate that was the senator's house. "Okay. I get it." I moved toward the lobby, feeling awkward at his admission and unsure of what to say next.

"Fifty hours."

I stopped and looked at him in confusion.

"What?"

"Fifty hours for six weeks."

My mouth dropped open as I caught his meaning. "Fifty?"

"Fifty hours, *extra*. On top of the two hundred." He motioned toward the lobby. "At your snail's pace, there's no way you'll get the Legos done in two hundred. If you want to be my neighbor, it'll cost you in time."

"That's twenty-five percent extra work," I protested.

"It's simple supply and demand, Books."

I could only stand there with my gaping mouth, trying to think.

"Unless you'd rather stay with—"

"Ten."

The smile was across his face before I could prepare myself for it. I tamped down the flutters swirling in my stomach.

"Fifty," he said again.

"Fifteen."

"Fifty."

I shot him an exasperated look. "Fifty is too much. I have to be done by the end of July. I'll help you paint. And retile."

"It's a brand-new remodel," Dax admitted with a sheepish laugh. "Completely furnished. It doesn't actually need any of those things."

"What? So you've been sitting with it empty and ready to go for three years?" I asked incredulously.

"Three quiet years with no dogs tearing up my yard and no obnoxious neighbors."

"I don't have dogs. And I'll be super quiet."

He stared at me for a long moment, his face calculating. "If you want to cut a deal, I'm going to need you to prove your extensive tool knowledge."

"What?" The teasing gleam in his eyes filled me with both hope and dread.

"If you show me exactly how to use a…" he thought for a moment, "torque wrench, I'll give it to you for forty."

My body stilled. "A torque wrench?"

A wolf on the scent, he visibly panicked. "No, I meant a—"

"Nope! You said it!" I took off running toward his workbench where his tools were spread out across a pegboard. I raked my eyes over the tools before grabbing what I was looking for and began walking him through all the steps of using it.

I'd like to thank a broken down car in a sleepy Tennessee town and a sweet old mechanic thinking I cared to know about the tools he was using for that tidbit of knowledge.

"Alright. Double or nothing," Dax tried, unsuccessfully attempting to hold back a smile.

"Nope. That's what you get for being a jerk who assumes girls don't know tools."

He folded his arms across his chest. "I don't think that about every girl. Just you. But I stand corrected."

"Forty hours?" I held my hand out expectantly.

"Forty hours, Books." His hand grasped mine to shake it and I had to keep myself from squealing. We had laid down our weapons momentarily to strike a deal. A deal that suddenly filled my mind with all kinds of exciting possibilities.

"I didn't know we could bargain for hours. Are there other things I can do to lessen my sentence? Should I demonstrate using a hammer, for five hours?"

"No more bargaining," he said, turning away from me.

"Come on!" I pressed again. "Just a few things. To give me life. And to help you out."

"You're good at wasting time, I'll give you that," Dax mumbled. "And distracting me."

A warm glow burned in my belly at the way he looked at me just then, an expression on his face so much like the old Dax I remembered in high school. I immediately braced myself.

"You want me to think of some things you can do in exchange for hours?" he asked.

The way he said the words *some things* brought a chill right to my bones.

I held my hands out in protest. "Nothing crazy. Fun. Or even just extra work that doesn't involve me being stuck in that room for hours on end."

"Fun..." He trailed off, rubbing his face.

"Why are you looking at me like it's Christmas morning?"

"I might be starting to catch your vision, Books. You got yourself a deal."

CHAPTER 10

Biology Class
Day 12

"Books."

I looked over to see Dax glaring at me. He had pulled out his seat but hadn't sat down yet. I glanced at the chair he was indicating and saw the huge hairball I had grown and rolled myself sitting on the seat.

"Yes?"

"Is that yours?"

"It's on your seat. Maybe it's a present."

He placed his hand on the desk, leaning in closer to me, and whispered, "You don't want to play these kinds of games with me. I don't lose."

"I'm not scared of you."

He stared at me for a long, dangerous moment before he leaned over and blew the hairball off his seat. His legs sprawled out in front of him as he sat down, his shoulder brushing against mine ever so lightly.

A wave of chills puckered my skin.

The bad kind. Not the good kind of chills.

He made the pretense of looking at Mr. Gray as he spoke to the class, even going so far as to fold his arms and look every bit like he was paying attention. Then his arm pressed against mine a fraction of an inch more.

I wasn't going to move. That meant he would win. So we stayed like that, glued together until the end of class.

Mr. Gray was wrapping up when Dax looked over at me. I looked at him. *His eyes swept lazily down our arms and back at me, leaving a trail of goosebumps flooding my skin.*

Ah, crap.

That was the good kind.

"Let me think," Dax began loudly as he leaned against the workbench. "What *fun* things could I make Ivy Brooks do that would be better than fixing my Lego car?"

I folded my arms, waiting for him to continue, a touch of unease growing in my belly. His tone didn't sound like a man who was about to cater to my very specific whim. Dax didn't cater to anybody.

"Let's see what I remember about you. I know you used to like reading textbooks, but I don't have any of those, unless you count the Lego guidebook." His hopeful gaze was shut down with my annoyed look.

"Sunset Harbor doesn't have a Key Club, or Beach Club, or some sort of Happy Smiles Club for you to be president of, so that wouldn't work."

"There's no such thing as that club," I interjected.

He went on, unfazed and enjoying himself. "I would have you join the Beach Clean-up Club, but you're probably already a member."

I was. At least, I used to be. But he didn't need to know that.

"I've done stuff, okay?" I broke in, my hands across my chest. I wasn't completely sure why I felt like I needed to prove this to Dax. Because I didn't.

"Let's hear it, then."

"No. You'll just make fun of me."

"Tell me you didn't TP a house."

I scoffed. "It wasn't just once; it was several times. And we never got caught."

His mouth dropped open. "Our part-time rent-a-cop didn't catch you hooligans?"

I shot him an irritated look.

"What's another thing?" he asked, sitting on the counter, facing me. "You've got me curious now."

I shouldn't tell Dax anything when he was just going to use it against me, but for a small moment, this was reminiscent of what I felt like sitting next to him in biology all those years ago.

Completely off balance.

A thrill for a girl whose life had always been so measured and calculated. If I got these grades and took these classes, I'd get into this college. If I smiled and shook hands and perfected the art of small talk, my dad wouldn't be embarrassed of me. If I got a doctorate and taught at the highest level possible, my dad would have something to brag about at parties. A structured life of cause and effect.

Dax always surprised me. So much of our time and conversations had been burned into my memories because they were never what I expected. *He* was never what I expected. Just when I had him pegged as lazy, he'd pick up the scalpel. When I thought he didn't care about biology, he'd point out something that he thought was interesting. Just when I thought he was turning a corner, he was in the principal's office for setting off the fire alarms. He lived his life by his own set of rules, and that fascinated me.

"Me and some friends sometimes put bags of goldfish on porches. Then we'd ring the doorbell and run away."

His eyes furrowed. "Like the crackers? For kids?"

"No, like a bag with water in it and a goldfish swimming around inside."

Confusion etched his brow. "Why?"

"For that reaction right there." I smiled, pointing at him.

He brandished a reluctant smile. "I don't think you're going to be able to handle what I've got for you."

"I already crashed into a building, so take it down a few notches from that."

I could almost feel the wheels turning inside his head as he strode to the counter. He took a large invoice pad and ripped the last blank page out. He grabbed a pen and started writing.

Unfortunately for him, he also left his phone unattended on the counter. While I was waiting there, bored, I added a few songs to his playlist while he was none the wiser.

"Okay," Dax began, turning to face me. "Let's not get confused. I want the Lego car finished, but if you've got a hankering for a good time, who am I to stop you? There are a few things I'd be willing to trade hours, for the simple pleasure of watching you do them."

I attempted to peer over his muscled shoulder to determine my fate.

"Number one…get a tattoo. Fifty hours."

"What?!" I pulled his arm, trying to grab the paper, but he moved it just out of my reach.

"You're always looking at mine. Thought you must be thinking about it."

"That's permanent. That should be all the hours."

"Good point. Better make sure I put that in the contract…" He trailed off, writing something while he muttered the word *permanent* under his breath. He looked at me. "I'd hate for you to just get a stick-on for my lack of detail."

I had the strongest urge to laugh, even as exasperation vibrated off me. "I'm not getting a tattoo."

"Great. You can keep the fifty hours and get working on my car."

"Tattoos aren't a big deal. It doesn't mean anything if I get one. Nobody will care. So why don't you pick something else?"

Please pick something else.

Dax smiled. "I know that." He pointed toward the garage door. "Most people out there know that." He leaned closer to me, peering deep into my eyes. "But I think, just like the senator, you have an image you like to portray. Nice and buttoned up. And I think letting people see you with a tattoo might be the hardest thing of all."

I didn't say anything. I also couldn't look directly at him.

He leaned back against the counter, getting comfortable with the pen and paper in his hand.

"Number two. Tag a building." Dax immediately began laughing after he said the words.

"Tag a *what*? What does that even mean?"

"Tag a building. I'm sure a rebel like you keeps a few cans of spray paint on hand."

This list of Dax's was full of crap. I knew that now. He and I both knew I wasn't going to do either of these things. Legos were in my future, and my hope was dashed.

"And the grand finale—my personal favorite. Drive a car around the entire island. One hundred hours."

I scoffed. "There are no cars on the island."

He raised his eyebrows. "That's not true."

I thought for a minute. It was very illegal to have a car on this island. There wasn't even a way to get one here unless you ferried it on. There wasn't exactly a way to do that without being seen. There were only two authorized motor vehicles allowed on the island that were bigger than a golf cart.

"You mean the ambulance? So I have to *steal* the ambulance and ride it around the island?"

"Or the fire truck. You can take your pick."

"Why don't you give me something I can actually do on your stupid list?"

"With an attitude like that, you'll never accomplish anything."

He tacked the paper up underneath the old pinup calendar and turned to me, a look of triumph on his face.

"Sorry, Books. If you can't handle any of these worthwhile

pursuits, you'll just have to…I don't know…" He broke off, waiting until he had my complete attention, and then said loudly and with much emphasis, "BUILD MY LEGO CAR."

I lifted my hands up in the air as if to strangle him. The frustration inside of me warred with the pleasure radiating up my spine at making him laugh.

Off balance.

"Get back to work, Books. I can't believe I let you stay clocked in for all of this."

I headed toward the door, feeling a reluctance to leave that surprised me. Before I got to the door, he called out, "I would love to see you with a tattoo, though."

I slammed the door to the sound of his deep chuckle.

CHAPTER 11

Biology Class
Day 14

"Are you planning on eating those chips right next to me this entire class?" Dax asked.

"I didn't have time to eat," I said, sneaking another bite of Sun Chips. Certainly not the healthiest lunch ever, but the package boasted 100% whole grain, so there was that.

"Why?"

"Because I was planning the pep rally during lunch. I have volleyball right after this. I'm going to pass out if I don't eat something." I looked at him and slid my backpack between us, a family-size bag of chips taking up the entire space. "Do you want some? It won't be as noisy if we're both chewing."

A look of amusement crossed Dax's face before he wiped it away.

"Was that a smile?"

"Nope."

"It was."

He slouched in his seat, scrolling through songs on his phone, signaling the end of our conversation.

"Dax smiled," I sang my words, moving in as close to him as I dared. "Again."

Dax covered his mouth with his hand and looked forward, attempting to block what I could only imagine was another smile.

T-minus 45 days to exit
Dax hours remaining: 210

A PERSON CAN BE a lot of things in their life. For instance, I was always the type to do my homework within the first ten minutes of being home from school. My mom used to call me studious. So, I went about the world, taking great pains to be studious. In reality, I just didn't want my parents to have one more thing to fight about. Bed made? Yes, sir. A on that paper? Of course. In our family, we had to be good enough for bragging rights at parties, and I held that mantle very seriously.

So, when I found myself lying point blank to my dad's face, it threw me for a loop. I had never thought of myself as a liar. I never really even considered lying, because lying was bad. And Ivy Brooks was not bad.

But after my dad's warning, I couldn't exactly tell him that his recently convicted daughter was going to practically be living with the one man he had warned me against. Obviously with a very important wall between our living spaces, but still. My dad certainly wouldn't see it that way. So I told him I was staying with Cat for the rest of the summer to give him and Angela some space. To be fair, he seemed equally relieved to be rid of me.

The next morning, before work at the cafe, I packed a bag with old clothes from my closet that weren't too out of date. Thankfully, beach and island clothes didn't change much in ten years. Chino shorts were still flattering for an upscale look, cut-off shorts were still in, and flip-flops were still a way of life. I threw yesterday's hair up in a ponytail, said goodbye to them both, and stepped out of the door toward freedom.

After my shift at the cafe, I worked on the Lego car for an hour before I got antsy and told Dax I needed to move in. He handed me a key and even offered to drive me up, which was surprising of him, but I declined. I only had one bag and a set of sheets I had bought at the market. I had a hard time believing my luck. On the island, it was notoriously difficult to find housing. Resort and inn stays cost families an arm and a leg, and here I was, being handed a place to stay virtually for free. Though, not because Dax was any sort of saint. He had squeezed forty more hours out of me for this tiny bit of space. It had to be worth it.

Please let it be worth it.

The salty ocean breeze tickled the hair on the nape of my neck as I picked my way toward the duplex, really hoping I didn't see my dad's golf cart on the road. If he were to find me, I wasn't sure what explanation I could give him.

At the far edge of a subdivision, on the north end of the island, a small dirt road led me to a house on a secluded piece of land. The kind of house that looked like a small child's drawing– a box shape with a triangle on top. Except, this house was divided from the tip of the roof, down the center, with a door on each side.

For a long moment, I stood, taking in my reality. My very tiny reality. It was one thing to imagine living near a person, but it was different when you realized *this* was basically like pitching two tents right up against each other. The walls would definitely not be thick enough to suit me. For the first time, I questioned the sanity of my quick decision to stay here.

But then I remembered who my dad was, and I got over it pretty quickly.

Exit strategy and all that.

I put the key in the lock and opened the green door on the left, bracing myself for something awful to pop out or the place to be in shambles. I reached inside and flipped on a light.

To my utter relief, a welcoming scene met my gaze.

The door opened to a living room big enough for a loveseat and a TV. Cabinets and a tiny island lined one side of the space, just past the living room, while a miniature set of stairs led toward a loft. On the opposite side of the kitchen was another door underneath the stairs, most likely a bathroom. Past the kitchen, at the back of the house, was a bedroom.

I stepped inside and closed the door, then sunk onto the couch with a happy sigh because, for the first time since I'd been back on the island, I could almost feel the tension with my dad dissipating. His eyes, constantly watching and remarking and critiquing, weren't in this space and they never would be.

There wasn't much to unpack. The apartment was fully furnished, thank goodness, including a special welcome bag of my favorite brand of Sun Chips and a Coke, which made me smile.

I heard Dax arrive at his apartment next door later that night. If I hadn't noticed his door slam shut, or the opening and closing of his refrigerator, or the shower turning on, the blatant knocking against my wall would have eventually garnered my attention.

A MOMENT LATER, I received a text.

DAX
Everything good?

ME
Great. It's hard to stay annoyed with you when you leave me a welcome basket.

DAX
You probably would have stolen that stuff from me anyway.

ME
> Thank you, Dax. I appreciate you letting me stay.

DAX
> Sure. What did your dad say?

ME
> Um

DAX
> You didn't tell him you were here?

ME
> He might possibly think I'm staying at Cat's house.

DAX
> Why didn't you just stay there?

ME
> I didn't want to impose.

DAX
> Interesting. I feel very imposed upon.

ME
> You don't count. This is a business deal. I'm paying with hours.

DAX
> Whatever helps you sleep at night.

ME
> I think I'll sleep great.

DAX
> I think we need a secret knock. Me and my brother used to have one. It came in handy.

ME
> For what?

I LAUGHED to myself and tossed my phone on the coffee table before flopping myself down on the couch. The rest of my evening was spent lounging in that exact position, mindlessly watching TV and feeling more alive than I had in years. Even watching TV felt foreign. I was now determined to make the best of this summer on the island. Cat had already informed me of the pick-up volleyball games that happened once a week on the beach, not to mention that the Fourth of July was coming up. I hadn't had the luxury of a summer break in nearly six years, and I was planning to take full advantage—in between working double-time to pay Dax back for the extra hours, of course.

Court sentencing or no, this summer was looking up for Ivy Brooks.

Two days.

That was how long we lasted getting along in our shared space.

It was the music that finally did it. For all his talk about noisy neighbors, Dax was sure generous with the volume button in his own home. But more than that, I felt like he was only doing it to get under my skin. Actually, I *knew* he was.

And still...it broke me.

It was 6 am on Wednesday when the whiny, soulful cry of Bob Dylan filtered through my walls. How did I know it was Bob Dylan? I held my phone up next to the wall and used an app to identify the song. I tried banging on the wall above my headboard, which did absolutely nothing. When I heard his shower turn on, I stumbled into the bathroom and cranked my faucet as hot as it would go. A minute or two later, steam began to cloud the bathroom and I heard something akin to a yelp from next door followed by three loud raps on the wall. I pushed away thoughts of Dax in the shower but did have a case of the giggles off and on for the next five minutes while I made myself a cup of coffee.

Then the music was turned up even louder—with singing.

I attempted a few deep breaths. I was desperately trying to avoid conflict with him, but today was supposed to be a relaxing morning for me. The cafe had scheduled me for a day off, and I had planned to sleep in and then take a walk on the beach.

But the music.

I couldn't read. I couldn't sleep. I couldn't listen to an audiobook. I couldn't THINK about anything but my growing disdain for my new neighbor.

So, like the reasonable adult I was, I calmly walked

(stormed) across our shared porch and banged on his door—but only because he probably wouldn't hear a normal knock.

To my dismay, his door opened right away. Even the way he opened his door was smooth and casual. Smooth like the bare chest he currently wore with not a care in the world. Did I allow my gaze to trail downward?

Just a little bit. On accident.

The smile he gave me was almost like he'd been expecting me, which scrolled my annoyance factor up from a casual nine out of ten to a one hundred out of ten.

"Hey, Books. You miss me?"

"Your music is too loud."

He feigned an innocent expression. "Really?"

"Turn it down, or I'll do my worst."

He looked interested. "What's your worst?"

I thought for a moment. "Bubble-gum pop music from the 1980s, turned up to volume ten."

"*Volume ten?*" he mouthed incredulously, holding up all his fingers.

"Look at you go. First try and you got the right number of fingers up."

"You think I can't handle bubble-gum pop?"

"You couldn't handle any of the N'SYNC songs I added to your playlist."

He leaned closer to me, his amused eyes intent on mine. "Trust me, Books, I can handle a lot of things."

I swallowed. Absolutely not appreciating the inappropriate flutterings in my stomach at his words.

"Alright," I began, clearing my throat. "Maybe we do need your secret knock thing."

"Really?"

"Yeah. This will save me some trips over here."

"Why do you assume you're going to be coming to me?" He pointed to himself in mock disbelief.

I motioned to where I was standing. "Because you're always the one causing trouble."

His easy smile brandished before me like a weapon. "I do think it's worth mentioning that, of the two of us, there's only one person court-ordered to be here this summer."

I picked an imaginary hair off my shirt. "The less I have to see your face outside of my appointed hours is probably for the best."

"The life of a felon on parole," he sighed.

"Probation."

"Ah, my bad."

At the exasperated shake of my head, I was rewarded—nay, punished—with another grin.

"I think we need to establish what happens if someone breaks the rules," I said, folding my arms across my chest.

"I think they should get spanked." He tucked his hands inside his pockets and leaned casually against the doorframe like he was the main character from a Sunny Palmer book.

I forced myself to skip over the imagery his comment brought to mind. "I'll be calling Beau."

"Interesting. So you'll be calling one of my good friends to tell on me?"

"I'm guessing he'd be more than happy to get you in trouble."

He smiled at that. "You're probably right. What's our code?"

"Let's see if I can cover all my bases with Dax Miller."

I started to say more before his eyes snapped to mine. "Wait. I'm suddenly interested in baseball. What bases will we be covering?"

I ignored him and held up a finger. "One knock means, *turn it down*." I added one more finger to the bunch. "Two knocks means, TURN IT OFF RIGHT NOW. Three knocks means, *I'm being murdered. Get over here*."

There was a beat of questionable silence between us. Dax scratched his face.

"Wait. Let me make sure I understand," he said, holding up a hand. "You are in the process of getting murdered, and you will somehow extract yourself before proceeding to the wall to give three distinct taps?"

"Yup," I said, folding my arms.

"What's the knock for, *I'm hungry, do you have any food?*"

I smiled brightly. "There's actually no knock for that. It's just this." At the sight of my middle finger, an impish grin crept onto his face, and something inside of me did a little flip.

"I think this summer might be the best I've had in a long time," he said, smiling at me.

"Don't mess with me, Dax. And turn your music down."

"Good to see you too, Books."

With that, he closed the door in my face.

CHAPTER 12

Biology Class
Day 16

"How come you never smile at me in the cafe? You smile at everyone else but me. It can't be good business to glare at your most dependable customers," Dax whispered in the middle of Mr. Gray's lecture.

I kept my gaze forward, silently begging him to stop talking to me while Mr. Gray was teaching. It was so rude. But he kept at it, simply to annoy me.

"I smile when you leave."

I felt his interested gaze on me. "Love seeing me walk away, huh?"

My face fell. "Ugh."

"You walked right into that."

"I know. Shut up."

T-minus 42 days to exit
Dax hours remaining: 195

THE SENATOR
I need a favor.

THE SENATOR

Do you remember Bob Peterson? He's been a big supporter the past ten years.

ME

What?

ME

Kind of.

THE SENATOR

Since the DUI, he has dropped his support for my campaign. Which is pretty disappointing because he was a huge donor.

THE TONE of a text could make or break a conversation. With my friends, I used a plethora of emojis, smiley faces, and exclamation points so as not to confuse the meaning behind my words. My dad needed no such frills. His words came out over text with the same biting edge they'd have if we were speaking in person. So, in response, mine did as well. In my heart of hearts, I knew the Petersons dropping support was probably not completely my fault, but the implication still stung.

ME

Sorry to hear that.

THE SENATOR

An acquaintance of mine and his son, Brent and Lucas Forester, will be coming into town this weekend to meet me and learn about my politics. If they like what I have to say, they could be a huge donor. Bigger than the Petersons.

> **ME**
> Okay.

> **THE SENATOR**
> I'll be locked up in meetings with Brent on Saturday night, but I want you to take his son, Lucas, out for dinner and a tour of the island while we're busy. Can you do that for me?

> **ME**
> I was going to work at the garage this weekend.

> **THE SENATOR**
> Surely you can spare a few hours for this. I feel like it's the least you can do.

"Order up, Ivy!" Marco called from behind the industrial stove, jolting me from my phone.

"Be right there," I called, from my quiet corner of the cafe kitchen.

It was easier to say yes. It wasn't a big deal. The tour around the island would take thirty minutes, and I had to eat anyway. One hour and then I could get back to work at Dax's shop.

> **ME**
> Fine. I can do that.

> **THE SENATOR**
> Great. Be at the house at 6pm. Dress nice. He's going to rent a golf cart from the resort and pick you up. I don't want to risk you driving.

I SWIPED out of his text thread and slid the phone in my pocket, shaking my hands as if to rid myself of his messages.

"You alright, Ivy?" Marco asked as I picked up my serving tray and began loading it with an order of pancakes and fish tacos. His dark eyes searched mine with concern, and I wondered what expression I showed on my face.

With some effort, I schooled the anguish into a smile. "I'm okay. Just tired today."

According to the look on Marco's glistening face over a stovetop of burgers, he didn't believe me. But soon, we were both too engrossed in the lunch rush to give it any more attention. The cafe had needed me for the whole day today, which consequently left me itching to get to Dax's.

To take out my frustration while sweeping his floors.

Even when Dax texted me later that afternoon, I was still only excited to go…sweep his floors.

DAX
Will you bring me a burger and fries on your way here tonight? I'm starving.

ME
That's going to cost you.

DAX
I'll pay you when you get here.

ME
Not in money. Two hours.

DAX
If you want to add two hours onto your time, that's your business.

ME
No. Two hours OFF what I owe you. Since bargaining is a thing between us now.

DAX
One.

ME
TWO. And I won't make you pay for it.

DAX
ONE and I will pay for it.

ME
Fine.

I WAS ALMOST to the end of my shift when my phone buzzed again in my pocket.

DAX
I'm dying. Where are you?

ME
Such a baby. I'm almost done.

DAX
Are you bringing a Coke?

ME
That will definitely cost you extra. One whole hour.

DAX
Never mind. Just the burger and fries. And you.

TROUBLE.

He didn't mean it how it sounded. I had seen Dax text in the shop plenty of times before. Usually with his hands full carrying batteries or tools or placing motors while tapping on his phone one-handed. There couldn't be much thought into his communication, so the way my stomach dipped and rolled like a drop on a rollercoaster at his last two words was troubling. To say the least.

"With a smile like that, you must be talking to some cute guy," Marco said, trying to peer over my shoulder at the phone.

"Hey!" I jumped and pushed him away.

"Who is it?" He laughed at my reaction. "Hopefully somebody different than earlier."

I slid the phone in my back pocket while I attempted to stave off the sudden rush of blood to my cheeks. "None of your business."

He held up a large bag brimming with burgers and fries in one hand and a large Coke in the other.

"'Cause this looks like more food than one person could eat."

I shrugged, slipping on my purse before taking the bag. "I think you're grossly underestimating how much I can eat. Did you put in extra fries?"

"And sautéed peppers on both burgers. If it's a date, you owe me details."

"Not a date," I said, sneaking a fry. "But thanks."

I beelined it out of there, but not before Marco called out one more thing. "I know where you go after the cafe. Remember that!"

WITH MY ARMS full of greasy food, I entered the lobby of Dax's shop. I skittered my way past the small conglomeration of Legos, casually glancing down at my pathetic construction, when I stopped short. The small ball of Legos definitely looked different than it did when I left last night. Setting my bags and drink on the floor, I grabbed the guidebook and opened it.

I burst through Dax's garage door, holding the burgers and Coke in one arm and the guidebook in another. "Alright, fess up! I was not on page fifty-two when I left! You can't—" I stopped short when three heads flung in my direction at my brazen entrance.

My eyes first went to Dax, wearing his standard black tank top and jeans and standing next to a golf cart with the seat up and a large battery in his hand. A man and woman in their late fifties, dressed like tourists, stood nearby.

"Sorry. I didn't know anyone was here," I said, immediately feeling out of place.

"Books, do you know my parents? Mark and Trudy Miller. Mom and Dad, this is Ivy Brooks." He nodded toward the woman wearing knee-length white shorts and a coral blouse with blonde hair cut in a stylish bob. Was this a joke? She looked like she was on her way to dancing lessons at the resort. Cheerful and bright with such a…sunny disposition. My eyes darted curiously to take in the man with his khaki shorts and sea-green shirt covered in palm trees, like he was ready to hit the golf course at any moment.

"The senator's daughter?" Trudy's delicate eyebrows arched curiously.

"That's me." I set the bag and drink on the counter before moving to shake their hands.

"Oh. You're here…to fix the Lego car?" Trudy asked, her gaze sweeping over the cafe take-out bag and back to me.

Dax sauntered over, poking through the bag of fried foods. "Is this all for me?"

"Half of it's mine. I didn't eat lunch."

"Oh, well, we can go so you two can eat your dinner," Trudy said, glancing between us.

I pretended to look busy leafing through the calendar to

clock in while Dax wrapped things up with his parents. I thought about taking my food and leaving, but his parents stood in front of the bag from the restaurant, and I didn't want to interrupt again.

Dax never stopped moving while talking with his parents. His hands traveled in and out of his pockets before he'd fold his arms across his chest, just to repeat it all over again. He was never unkind. He just seemed…uncomfortable. Like he was forcing himself to chat with them.

"So you're coming to my birthday barbecue, then?" Trudy asked, a hopeful lilt in her voice as she looked up at her son.

"Trent's coming?"

"Yes, he'll be here after the Fourth," she answered.

Dax hesitated, and I watched in confusion. If I had parents that sweet, I'd be using every excuse in the book to spend time with them.

"It is my birthday," Trudy reminded her son, with a teasing jab to his ribs.

Dax smiled, resigned. "I'll be there."

They were almost out the door when Trudy stopped and turned back to me. "You're welcome to come too, Ivy. The more the merrier."

It took some willpower not to widen my eyes in shock. Instead, I gave the polite response when someone gets a pity invite. "Oh, thank you. I'll take a look at my schedule."

"Okay, bye now." She blew a kiss to Dax.

"Enjoy your dinner," Mark said, with an eyebrow raised toward Dax.

When they were gone, Dax looked over at me with a knowing expression on his face, which had my defensive nerves kicking up a notch.

"I'm not eating in here with you. I was just coming to clock in and drop off your food. I didn't know your parents were here."

He huffed out a laugh while he pulled out a hamburger from the bag and sat down on a barstool. And because I was still lingering and watching him with a fascination that should be illegal, he kicked out the other stool with his foot and motioned for me to sit down.

"Just eat here."

Tentatively, I sat down on the stool next to him. This should be fine. I served him enough at the cafe. Though, sitting next to him alone in his quiet shop while Billy Joel serenaded us with "Piano Man" didn't feel quite the same as at the cafe.

"Your parents seem nice," I ventured.

He hesitated before taking a bite. "Yup. They're very nice."

Seemingly oblivious, he turned back to his burger, effectively shutting down this line of inquiry. I wasn't in a position to judge so completely, but in a way, it felt similar to how I acted with my own dad. But unlike the senator, his mom had seemed overjoyed to be talking with her son. Still, there had clearly been a distance between them.

I made a note to tell Dr. Barb I would be after her job if this whole mathematician thing didn't work out.

"Is that a Coke?" Dax asked as he watched me take a sip.

"Yeah, too bad you didn't spring for one too."

He smiled and went back to his food.

I took a bite of my burger, and for a moment I gave my thanks and appreciation to the all-American diet. I'd lived over a week with my dad and Angela, and she had no appreciation for such exquisite cuisine.

"Why do you listen to this music?" I asked Dax as the chorus of "Piano Man" picked up.

He listened for a moment before saying. "Because it's the best. You're embarrassing yourself, Books."

"You're a disgrace to our generation."

"Our generation is the disgrace."

"How'd you get into it?" I asked, pointing toward the

speakers in the corner of the room as I dunked a few fries in ketchup.

"It's good," he said simply.

"Yeah, well, my dad thinks '80s rock is the best because it's the music he grew up listening to. That makes more sense than this. Do your parents love it or something?"

"Probably."

We were silent for a few moments.

"Is it a big deal?" I asked when I couldn't take it any longer.

"Huh?" He turned to me.

"Why can't you tell me where you started to like it? You're the only person our age that I know of who listens to this stuff."

"Why do you want to know so bad?"

I lifted my hands. "It's just conversation. Never mind. I forgot what talking to you feels like."

"Like what?" He seemed genuinely curious.

"Like a never-ending circle that gets us both nowhere."

"Maybe you're just nosy."

"I don't need your life history. Just normal stuff. Stuff you'd tell a fr—" My eyes shot to his in panic before I went a different direction. "Stuff you'd tell people you work with."

He pretended to think. "Alright. How about this for convo? How's your dad handling your public misconduct?"

I refused to let him see that he had lobbed a direct hit. Instead, I reached over, grabbed the crisp, icy Coke, and took a long luxurious sip. Sighing dramatically, I put the drink back in its place. "He's probably handling it the same way your parents handled their own son's misdemeanors. Or were they felonies?" I put a finger to my cheek. "I can't quite remember."

"There goes Ivy Brooks, swooping in with her own dodge." He said the words like a sports announcer on TV.

Before I could gather my wits and wound him with a zinger, he asked, "Can you even admit that you did something wrong?"

My mouth opened before closing again. "Yes. I messed up. I

took the wrong pill. In the dark." A stretch of silence grew between us as we sat. Unable to stand it anymore, I added, "But it was still an accident."

He snorted. "The chickens getting loose in the school hallway was an accident too. So far, it feels like we're pretty even."

I shook my head. "I didn't know it was a sleeping pill. You can't possibly tell me that this was even close to the "accidental chickens" or putting the principal's motorcycle on top of the school."

"I mean...it's not as funny."

"Why did you do all that stuff?"

He shrugged. "Why were you on the student council? Why were you in every club the school offered?"

"Because it looked good on resumes and college applications."

"Well, I already had a job I loved. I wasn't planning on going to college. And I already lived on an island. Where was I going to go from there? I was already living the dream."

I was in Mr. Gray's class all over again, sitting next to a boy so guarded in everything he did and didn't say. From what I could tell, he worked in this shop every day of his life. He had friends, but they were always coming to him. Even his parents came to him.

He was a puzzle of heat and ice. And I was one of those kids who used to do puzzles to the sound of an educational TV show in the background.

He motioned to my feet. "You dropped your napkin."

Confused, I looked down, realizing a second too late what his plans were, but he had already reached over me and grabbed the Coke. He took a long swig before placing the drink down on his other side, away from me.

"I'll get it back," I said, picking up my hamburger again.

"Looking forward to it."

A strange thrill rose in me at his words, though I didn't allow myself to linger there. Instead, I stuffed my face with another bite of meat and cheese. We ate in silence for a while, picking at our dwindling pack of fries.

Then, in a moment of perfect delight, a song I'd been waiting to hear for days finally made the cut.

The bold intro to the song "You Give Love a Bad Name" by Bon Jovi blasted through the speakers.

Dax froze. "What the—"

He grabbed his phone on the counter, ready to turn it off, when I tugged at his arm.

"No, please! I love this song. Can we just listen to it once?"

He gave me a pained expression, but once he saw I was in earnest, he set his phone back down.

"The eighties," he said. "Looks like you're a disgrace too, Books."

I smiled sheepishly, my legs moving to the beat. "Maybe."

We sat listening for a long moment, and I attempted to keep my hands busy eating fries until I couldn't help it any longer and busted out an amazing air guitar solo during the chorus. Dax leaned forward, his head in his hands, pretending embarrassment, but I saw him hide a smile.

When the song ended and "Desperado" by the Eagles took its rightful place in the speakers, Dax nudged me. "Why do you like that song?"

I was coming down from the high that song always gave me, and it took a moment to formulate my words. It didn't make sense at the same time that it made perfect sense.

"It's one of the few good memories I have with my dad." I adjusted my position in the seat. "I think I was seven or eight, and he had just gotten elected to be a state rep. It was after we all found out, and this song came on, and my dad picked me up, and we danced around the kitchen to it. We were both laughing." I paused and bit back a smile. Even now, the memory still made me feel happy. "Anyway, even though I know it wasn't real, I still love this song."

"Why wasn't it real?" His low voice covered me like a warm blanket.

A surprising wetness burned in my eyes before I blinked it back. I would crash into another building before I cried talking about this with him.

"Because it wasn't me that made him happy. It was still something selfish. I was just the person closest to him after he won. But still, it's ..." I broke off and turned away, attempting to be casual while hiding the tears that were forming.

I didn't fool Dax, but he didn't bring attention to my emotions. Instead, he sighed.

"Alright, Books. I have to defend my honor. What's your question? You get one."

I sucked in a breath, waiting for him to tell me he was joking. But other than standing up to throw our wrappers in the garbage, he seemed to be waiting for me to ask him something.

"Tick-tock, Caroline. Some of us have work to do."

I had so many questions for him. One wouldn't begin to satisfy the curiosity, so I had to choose carefully. He was already rummaging through his tools. Now wasn't the time for deep and introspective. He'd find a way to brush me off.

"Alright, how did you get into seventies music?"

His hand paused slightly before grabbing a wrench hanging on his pegboard.

"Keith always had it playing in the shop."

A sad smile came to my face when I thought of the sweet mechanic. He always remembered my name and would have candy for me and my friends in his pocket. Whether I was five or seventeen, I never walked away from him without a butterscotch candy in my hand. The entire town had mourned the loss of Keith to a heart attack three years back.

"Yeah. He was the best."

"He was." Dax's gaze wandered to the boat he probably wished he was fixing right now, but he stayed where he was. "We got to be pretty close when I worked here in high school." Dax ran his hand through his hair. "He was...one of the reasons I graduated high school."

"Why?" I asked.

"There was one time in our junior year when Beau and I broke down one of the ferries 'cause we were trying to get out of going to school. Remember that?"

"Yeah. I remember the other ferry showed up ten minutes later. We still had to go to school, and you guys got in big trouble."

Dax laughed. "Yeah, we didn't think that one through too well. Anyway, Keith found out and told me he wasn't going to teach me skills like that if I was going to abuse them." A soft smile touched Dax's lips before he continued. "He told me I'd always have a job with him, but I had to graduate high school first."

Dax looked like he was about done talking when he must have remembered the original question. "Anyway, he loved this music. He always had it playing in here. It took a while before I started liking it. Not every song from that decade was a hit, but I have my favorites."

He had gathered his tools and was about to get back to work, but I wanted more. Always.

"You play it because it reminds you of him?"

He waited a beat. "Maybe a little."

"Thanks for telling me that." I gave him a proud smile, to which he rolled his eyes.

"Get to work, Books," he said, striding toward a riding lawn-mower, but not before I caught his lips turning up in a grin.

Later that night, my walls shook as a long knock sounded above my headboard.

Confused, I lay there and listened intently. It wasn't a

random pattern. It felt calculated. If he was doing this to annoy me, he was in big trouble. We had a code. I grabbed my phone.

ME
Are you dying? That was three big knocks in a row.

DAX
It's your goodnight song.

ME
What is it?

DAX
Can't tell you.

ME
Can't tell me, or you can't spell it?

DAX
I was going to give you two hours if you figured it out, but after that comment, just one.

ME
Do it again.

DAX
Sorry, Books. I only play once a night.

ME
You're annoying.

DAX
Sweet dreams.

CHAPTER 13

*Biology Class
Day 18*

"So, you and Mr. Class President himself, huh?"

I froze, not wanting to discuss anything regarding guys I was seeing with Dax.

"We're just going to the dance."

"Aren't you, like, the class manager-secretary-cheerleader or something like that?"

I gave him a look. "I'm the class Vice President."

His eyebrows raised in excited shock, mocking me. "Maybe one day you'll have little politician babies."

I pushed against his arm and scooted my chair up to the desk, intent on ignoring him. For some reason, Dax was bent on unnerving me at every turn, and I wouldn't allow it.

"Will you guys talk about politics and the weather the whole time you're together, or do you think you'll branch out into the stock market or global warming?"

"Look at all those big words you're using."

"I'm not wrong, though," he said, smiling like a cat toying with a mouse.

"No, you aren't wrong. You even used the words in just the right context."

"Shut up, Books."

"You're not wearing that." My dad's eyes trailed down my clothes, from my cutoff shorts to an old school volleyball t-shirt rolled at the sleeves, before giving me a look of disgust from his place at the kitchen table.

"Hey, Dad. Nice to see you too."

"Hi. Go change."

Earlier that day, I had finished my morning shift at the cafe and let Cat and Jane convince me to skip out on Legos and hit up the farmers market and the beach. I couldn't really say no without it seeming like I wanted to hang out with Dax. But as it turned out, a few hours at the beach, recharging under the warm island sun, did wonders for my outlook on life. Of course, now that I was about to be a high-class babysitter for a politician, showing up smelling like sunscreen and contentment wouldn't be tolerated.

I raised my hands. "I don't have clothes here."

"Well, you can't wear that. Go put on the bridesmaid's dress from Mariah's wedding. You need something nice."

Mariah's dress had been beautiful, but my boobs could not pull it off. It left too many gaps where there shouldn't be gappage. Not to mention, there were probably still glass shards stuck in the fabric.

"It doesn't fit. I'm just taking him to Beach Break, right? I'll be way overdressed."

"I don't care." My dad's tone became clipped. "You are representing me, and the Foresters are here to potentially donate a lot of money. If they like what I'm about and they like the island, it could be tens of thousands of dollars for my campaign. So, yes, you can put on something nice for your date."

"It's not a date," I seethed.

"She can search through my closet," Angela said, striding in from the kitchen, her brown hair tied up in a high ponytail, looking impossibly beautiful in joggers and a fitted t-shirt.

Dad looked at me and nodded toward Angela. "See?"

My chest grew tight, and any coherent words seemed to vanish from my head. I knew he would win. He always won. I had already agreed to this date. Angela and I shuffled through her closet, but nothing would fit. She was at least a size smaller than me, and her boobs were a couple sizes larger. The bridesmaid's dress was my best option.

I flung my closet open and pulled out the blue dress. The soft silk felt good on my skin, though I'd never admit that to my dad. I added a few more curls in my hair, taming the sun-ripened mane into something soft and presentable before applying some of Angela's blush and mascara and walking back downstairs. My dad wore gray suit pants with a white shirt and tie and was leaving to meet Mr. Forester at the resort.

"Thank you. You look nice." My heart stalled at his compliment while my body filled with reluctant warmth at his words.

But alas, he wasn't finished.

"Ivy. I can't have you screwing this up. You need to be nice and charming. No alcohol and no sleeping pills." He opened the garage door, sending one more icy blast over his shoulder as he crossed the threshold. "I can't afford to lose another sponsor."

The door slammed shut.

Another sponsor.

It was the way he would build me up only to slam me down. Casually throwing out knives instead of words, always insinuating that I was the problem. Never yelling or shouting. His words were quiet. Controlled. Matter of fact. It was soft how he bit and quiet how he shattered.

But he couldn't break me anymore. I wasn't going to let him. The second his golf cart was out of sight, I ran back upstairs and changed into my ratty shorts and old t-shirt that smelled like coconut sunscreen.

When I passed by the kitchen, Angela gave a quiet gasp as she took in my new outfit.

"I don't think your dad will—"

"It's fine," I cut her off and moved into the family room at the front of the house to wait. It would be fine. He wouldn't know I was wearing this. I wasn't coming back to the house. I was planning to have Lucas drop me off at the duplex.

A moment later, I sat across from the faux fireplace, waiting for my date to show up. My attention drifted toward the fake fireplace. My mom had been big into interior design, and she loved to comment on how it centered the room. More than that, it provided a mantel for our family's trophy pictures in various frames. And suddenly, our fake mantel became filled with images designed to impress. The pictures looked different now with my mom gone, but there were still moments I recognized from my childhood.

There was a younger version of my dad dressed in his usual suit and tie with a wide grin on his face shaking the hand of the governor of Florida as a state representative years ago. There was me in a cap and gown, graduating with my doctorate. But it was the picture of my dad and me smiling on our vacation to Myrtle Beach years ago that held my gaze. I had been in middle school at the time. My mom had orchestrated the photo, telling us to awkwardly press our cheeks together while the sun lit the backdrop behind us. A gust of wind had blown sand in my eyes seconds before the shot. But the picture had been great of my dad, so my mom paid someone to photoshop a happier face onto mine—one where it didn't look like I had been crying and wiping at my eyes. Only the photoshopped edges didn't quite line up. And my dad's eyes didn't quite shine.

My mom had been the first to shatter the illusion of our family by leaving. Her departure and request for divorce had shocked the island. My dad had been in a horrible mood for an entire year after that. It felt strange to be here without her, to have another woman occupy her space, but our broken family seemed more authentic than the image we'd shown the island when my mom was still here.

The doorbell rang, and I opened the door to a medium-built body and a good-looking face with a smooth smile. He was over-dressed in slacks and a white shirt and tie, and upon seeing me, he stepped back to linger appreciatively at my tanned, bare legs.

"Hi," I said, feeling relief when his eyes finally met mine.

"Hey there." His voice was low with a deep Southern drawl.

"I'm Ivy." I held out my hand, which he held, not shook, in a way that sent my skin crawling.

"Lucas Forester, nice to meet you. I heard you're going to take care of me tonight."

Ew.

I pulled my hand from his and smiled tightly. "I've been assigned to show you the island and take you out to dinner."

"My kind of woman." He smiled and stepped aside, his arm sweeping toward the driveway. "Shall we?"

I closed the door and stepped in front of him on the small sidewalk leading to his parked golf cart. A quick glance over my shoulder told me he was indeed checking me out from behind. Perhaps I should have gone with the plunging neckline of the dress.

"You driving or me, darlin'?"

"It's *Ivy*," I told him again. "And you can drive."

I spent the next half hour politely pumping him with useless information about the island. To be fair, I did make an attempt at being charming. I pointed out the nature preserve, our beautiful town square, my own Sunrise Cafe, mentioning that it was a local favorite and home of the famous Gator n' Eggs breakfast platter. I channeled my dad's salesmanship and became an expert at flourishing statements with very little substance. The more I spoke, the less he attempted to speak, which suited me fine. A few minutes into our drive, my phone buzzed in my purse on my lap, and I snuck a peek.

> **DAX**
> Where you at, Books?

> **ME**
> On a date.

> **DAX**
> Larry finally convinced you?

I SMILED and glanced up to see Lucas watching me.

"That a boyfriend?" Lucas asked, nodding toward my phone.

"Sorry. No. I was supposed to be somewhere tonight, but I forgot to let them know I wouldn't make it. I'm almost finished."

"Do what you gotta do."

I picked up my phone once more, angling away slightly so Lucas couldn't glance down and see what I was typing.

> **ME**
> I wish. A politician's son needed a babysitter tonight.

> **DAX**
> You wish it was Larry? I'll be sure to pass that on.

> **ME**
> Maybe we can double with you and your old lady friend next door.

A SMILE TUGGED at my lips as I pressed send before Lucas cleared his throat, and I immediately remembered myself. I put the phone back in my purse and forced a smile at him.

"All done. Thanks."

I was in the middle of telling him how the island was founded when Lucas held up a hand and stopped me.

"Listen, we're both here because of our dads, right? You don't have to tell me all this. I get the same tour everywhere I go. I think we can just hang out and go to dinner without all the fuss."

I looked at him in a form of shock. Maybe I had misjudged him.

I sunk into my seat, lifted my legs so they lounged on the dashboard in front of me, and sighed. "I'd love that."

With a lingering scan of my legs, which I immediately set back on the floor, he smiled and said, "Great. Now where's this bar at?"

"YOU DON'T HAVE to walk me up," I said, sliding out of the golf cart when we arrived at the duplex.

"I'm a gentleman, though. That's what we do."

I seethed out a silent breath of protest as he slid from the cart—alarmed when he slipped the keys into his pocket. He wasn't coming in. I would murder him well before he entered my apartment. Earlier, once we'd arrived at the bar, he had relaxed too completely, revealing an arrogant, spoiled man, telling me all about the places he'd been wined and dined by hungry politicians—and their daughters. I only saw him have one drink, but it had been enough to loosen his tongue. The ride home was enough to loosen his hands.

I didn't slow my walk to wait for him and practically ran up the steps. When I arrived at my door, the keys fell from my jittery hands, hitting the ground with a clank. Swearing under my breath, I reached down and grabbed them, shoving the key into my door handle before I felt his body behind me and his hands on my shoulders, turning me around.

"What's the rush?"

"I think we're done here."

"It's early. I figured we could watch a movie or something." His fingers lingered at my shoulders before trailing down my arms.

Instinctively, I moved backward, but the door blocked my escape. I reached for the doorknob behind me when he stepped forward, trapping me against the door. He laughed and crowded me further.

"Get the hell away from me," I spat, panic boiling as I pushed against him. He hardly moved. I raised my leg to knee him in the groin, but he inched closer, blocking the movement of my legs.

His laugh was dry, with a teasing lilt at the end, as though we were wrestling for fun. "If you're going to kick at me, I think I'll stay right here."

It was his strength against mine that startled me the most. I tried again to push him away, but my legs and hands were pinned.

"Easy, girl. I'm not going to hurt you. I just want a little kiss. You were cool at dinner. I thought you'd be more fun than this."

If I had been coming off as a *fun* person on this date, he had completely misread all the *get me out of here* signals I had been throwing him all night.

He adjusted his footing, which, for a moment, caught him slightly off balance. I threw my weight into him, feeling gratified as I watched him flail backward. Before I could take a step, though, he was back, pressing into me.

"Get off me!" Alarm spread like wildfire through my veins as he leaned close, his breath hot and wet against my ear.

"If my dad and I have a nice time on this island"—he stopped, taking a second to pin himself against me even tighter—"then my dad is going to give your dad a lot of money." He nipped my ear, sending chills rolling down my spine. "I don't know about you, but I haven't really had that nice of a time yet."

All of a sudden, two hands attached to a pair of arms, one of which sported a car tattoo I'd grown quite fond of, grabbed the back of Lucas's shoulders and yanked him away from me. I sucked in a breath as I watched in relief as Dax chucked Lucas down the three stairs leading up to our shared house. Lucas's body slammed against the wood handrail before he landed in a clumsy heap at the bottom of the stairs. With dark eyes pulsing with anger, Dax strode back over, bending down to look at me.

"You okay?"

I nodded, glancing past his shoulder at Lucas attempting to stand, yelling expletives as he did so. He narrowed in on Dax as he charged up the stairs. Dax turned around, blocking me and the unruly punch thrown his way. He attempted to push and redirect Lucas back down the stairs, when Lucas jerked out from under Dax's grip, attempting another wild punch. I saw the moment Dax's patience was spent, and he sent a blow to Lucas's face that had him clutching his nose and stumbling off the porch.

"What the hell is wrong with you?!" Lucas shouted, turning to yell at Dax now that there was space between them.

"You want me to come and show you?" Dax yelled back, taking two steps toward the stairs.

Lucas blanched before striding toward his golf cart and shouting one last parting shot my way. "Your dad can kiss his money goodbye!"

He slid inside and glowered, flipping us off with both of his middle fingers before backing out of the driveway. The sight of his nose bent in the middle and his face streaked with red provided me with a small glimmer of satisfaction.

Dax looked over at me. Whatever he saw was enough to move him closer, his careful eyes taking in every detail.

"Are you okay? Did he hurt you?"

I could only blink and stare at the spot where Lucas had been moments ago as I attempted to make sense of what had just happened.

"Ivy." His body now stood in front of mine, but he was a blur in my vision. I couldn't move. The gentleness in his voice might unravel me. The sympathetic look on his face would no doubt make me cry. I had to look away. My hands covered my face as I held as still as I could and tried my best to hold back the tears. I was fine. Nothing had happened. Lucas was gone. I wasn't sure why my limbs felt so stiff.

"You need to breathe. Put your hands on your knees." With soft fingers, Dax held my arm, guiding me to bend over. He was careful not to get too close, like he knew I wouldn't want to be touched.

With deep breaths in and out, my nerves began to subside. Eventually, I straightened and met his gaze, which proved to be a mistake. Those eyes brought to memory a softness I'd only ever seen years ago in my garage. I tore my gaze away to keep myself from leaping into his arms.

"I'm okay," I said. "Just a little shaken up. Thanks for your help."

"I told you three knocks when you're in trouble is stupid," Dax said lightly, his hand still holding my arm. "You sure you're okay?"

Nodding, I reached for my doorknob, needing to be alone. "Yeah. I'm okay. Thanks."

"I'm going to call Beau and tell him to go look for that guy. Is he at the resort?"

I nodded. "Yeah. His name is Lucas Forester."

"Did anything else happen?"

I shook my head. "He got kind of handsy, but nothing I couldn't handle."

Dax stared at me for a long moment before looking to where Lucas's golf cart had been only moments ago. Finally, he swore and muttered something under his breath as he turned away, his phone pressed to his ear. He whipped back around. "Lock your door."

I would definitely be locking my door.

CHAPTER 14

Biology Class
Day 20

I looked over at the empty seat next to me before I flicked my gaze to Mr. Gray, standing by the whiteboard. Dax hadn't shown up for school today. Rumors of him getting into a fight and being suspended had been filtering through the hallways all morning, but I wasn't sure what to believe. Thankfully, there were no dead animals or scalpels in sight, so it wasn't like I needed him to be in class. It was actually nice having the desk all to myself. And you know what? It was even better not having Dax's annoying comments in my ear during the entire lecture. My gaze, once again, fell on the empty seat before I yanked my attention back to the front of the classroom.

I TOLD Dax I was fine. And I *was* fine. I closed the door, walked the three steps to the couch, and dropped my purse on the coffee table. Dax's voice on the porch was loud and humorless as he recounted the incident to Beau. He hung up soon after, and I heard him enter his apartment. His sounds were easily recognizable to me now. The thump of his shoes against the wall as he kicked them off by the door. The bang of the refrigerator closing. Cupboards were opened and shut repeatedly like he couldn't decide what he wanted to eat. The noises sounded sharper. Harsher. As though he was angry and had only the kitchen cupboards to witness his frustration. I heard the water run for a shower. I needed a shower. I wanted to wash off everything Lucas said, touched, or insinuated, but my gaze was trained on a scuff mark on the wall, so there I stayed.

Being a woman had left me vulnerable to unwanted attention my entire life. I'd had my body looked up and down by men I'd just met, ranging from simple curiosity to vile leering. Men had shouted crude things at me in parking lots. I'd been called sweetheart by male colleagues at the university. A guy at a party grabbed my butt once. He insisted he thought I was his girlfriend and had repeatedly apologized. I had laughed it off, even though it became clear the rest of the night that he didn't have a girlfriend with him at the party.

Lucas hadn't hurt me.

He had *terrified* me.

And I hated that he had made me feel that way. I hated that he thought he could *do* something like that to me. The second he had me pinned, everything I thought I knew about self-defense had vanished.

I wasn't hurt.

I was *livid*.

My fingers clenched at the same time they shook. I didn't want to give Lucas the satisfaction of my emotions, but there didn't seem to be enough air on the whole island to satisfy my needs.

My body itched to run a thousand miles, but I never left my couch. The breeze picked up outside, rattling my windows. I tensed at the sound. Another noise came from the window, and my heart lurched in my chest. I double-checked that the door was locked before sprinting to the back bedroom and making sure the window to the side of my bed was latched as well.

Once I heard Dax's water turn off, I trudged into the bathroom. In the shower, I did my best to scrub Lucas off my skin. I brushed my teeth, turned out the lights, and climbed into bed.

The silence sat heavy, emphasizing every creak, every rattle, and every ticking clock. The sounds must happen every night, but it felt different now. I forced another deep breath into my lungs and convinced my fingers to unclench their hold on my sheets, only to grab them again at the eerie hum of the wind outside my windows.

It was the second bang of the shutters against my window that did it. I reached for my phone in the dark.

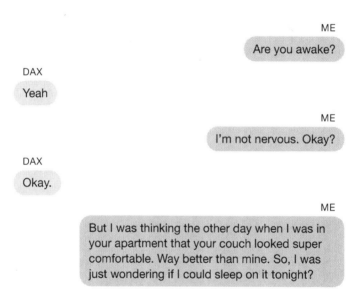

THERE WAS a pause in our exchange, and my heart died a little inside every second my text went unanswered. I sent the words out into the universe, immediately wishing I could gather them back up.

I was fine. I would be fine. Nothing had happened. I was nearly ready to tell him to forget it when my phone lit up.

DAX
I'll sleep on yours.

I DON'T KNOW why I felt like crying when Dax entered my apartment carrying a pillow and a blanket a minute later, but I did. So, of course, I didn't look at him. I busied myself with tucking a blanket around the cushions on the couch, since I didn't have extra sheets. I got him a glass of water. And an extra blanket. I made sure he knew where the bathroom was, even though it was literally his house. I told him I had chocolate milk and that I'd get him a glass.

My trembling hands had just grasped the jug from the fridge when I felt him behind me. His hand stopped me from grabbing the milk. He pulled me away, leaning forward to shut the fridge door before slowly gathering me into his arms. Like I was a fragile wounded bird, and he didn't quite know what to do with me. I didn't know what to do with me either, but my face pressed against his chest, and when his arms encircled my waist, my world finally grew quiet.

He smelled like soap and sun, and I breathed him in. Ever so slowly, his arms pulled me tighter while I nuzzled my face into his collarbone.

Dax pulled back, his dark eyes intense on mine. "I should have done a lot more than just punch him."

I smiled lightly at that, amazed at how my anguish over the last thirty minutes lessened at his words. Dr. Barb always spoke about the power of sharing a burden with someone. I had understood that in a therapy sense, but this felt different. Dax had done that just by showing up. I pressed my face back into his shirt once more. He had offered it, and I wasn't ready to give it up yet.

"I called Beau and told him where to find him. I doubt

anything will happen, but I feel better at least having him aware of everything that went down."

"Thanks," I said, touched that he would have thought to do that.

Dax held me for another minute, not speaking, until he bent over, picked me up at my knees, and carried me to my bed where he proceeded to tuck me in. My skin ignited everywhere his fingers lingered and grazed. He pulled my comforter up to my chin and raised his hand as if to brush my hair off my face before he seemed to think better of it and stepped back.

"Go to sleep, Ivy. Things will look better in the morning."

He was halfway through the kitchen when a smile crossed my face.

"You called me Ivy," I said proudly, turning to watch him kick off his shoes at the door and turn the light out before settling onto my couch.

"Don't let it go to your head."

"Too late," I called out.

"You were significantly less annoying tonight, so Ivy seemed fitting."

We were quiet for a few minutes, but I found I didn't want to go to sleep yet. Talking or hugging seemed to be the only way to calm my nerves. And Dax was all the way over there.

"What's our plan if Lucas comes back?"

"I can't believe you went out with a guy named Lucas."

"I've known a few Lucases, and they've all been nice," I insisted.

"Complete prep school wasters."

Despite myself, I laughed. "What's our plan?"

"I'm going to go to sleep. If he comes, you take him out this time. I'm tired."

I laid back against my pillow with a smile. The wind still hummed, and the windows still rattled, but the noise no longer bothered me. I did, however, find it ironic that, out of all the people on this island, Dax Miller was the only one I wanted on my couch tonight.

SEVERAL LOUD BANGS jolted me awake. I sat upright in my bed while I looked around in confusion. For as rocky as the night started, once Dax had settled onto my couch, sleep had come easily. Another loud thump at the door. I grabbed my phone off the nightstand. It was 1:00 am. Dax flung his blanket off the couch and strode toward the door. I wasn't about to leave Dax alone to face a drunk Lucas on the other side, so I scrambled over to where he was standing, his hand on the knob, ready to turn.

"Wait," I whisper-shouted, grabbing his hand to hold him off. "What are you doing?" I motioned toward the door. "Where's the peephole?"

"It doesn't have one."

"What?" I exploded in a soft-aggressive-whisper kind of way. "Why not?"

"I haven't put one in yet." His shrug was so casual. Dax's eyes drifted down at my bare legs clad in green shorts that hit me mid-thigh before glancing away. It was then that I realized underneath my cute, matching silky short-sleeved top, I wasn't wearing a bra. Nope. Last night, once I was settled under my covers and was certain Dax wouldn't see, I peeled off the inhumane contraption so I could sleep in comfort. I debated my next move. What if it wasn't Lucas, and someone was in trouble or hurt, and I had to race to the hospital?

"Shoot! Just a second." I scampered to the back bedroom, grabbed my bra off the floor, and dive-bombed into the bathroom in time for Dax to ignore me and open the door.

Inside the bathroom, my fingers fumbled with clasps and

buttons. When I finally burst out, Dax stood, leaning against the frame of the door, holding it open just enough to show half of his body.

"Do you know where she is?" my dad's voice broke through the quiet. It was one in the morning, and I was certain I was not in the mood for whatever he was here for.

Dax tossed a glance at me over his shoulder, controlled anger and defiance etched in the stiffness of his body.

He swung the door open wider, though still keeping a firm grip. But it was enough for my dad to see me walking out of the bathroom in my pajamas with my hair probably a fright.

But hey, at least I had a bra on.

My dad's eyes widened as he took in the pair of us. Dax stood with his bare chest and gray joggers slung low on his hips. I had noticed his bare chest at the door earlier, but I thought it was going to be the thing that would scare off Lucas, so I allowed it to stay naked. Not that he would have put a shirt on at my request. But…now it was going to be the thing that ticked off my dad.

Dad looked at Dax as though he were a piece of trash one might find on the sidewalk. "Your influence knows no bounds."

"This isn't what it looks like," I said.

Anger flooded my body at the way he looked at Dax, what he *assumed* about Dax, especially after the night we'd had. I didn't owe him an explanation. But he was still my dad, and I knew how this looked, and I wasn't about to go down on assumption alone.

"Dax lives on the other side of the duplex. He's here right now because Lucas ended up being a jerk, and Dax stopped him from hurting me. He's sleeping on my couch in case he comes back."

My dad attempted to step across the threshold, but Dax's arm remained firm, holding the door open but barring him access.

Clayton Brooks's Wikipedia bio states him being five foot eleven. He was five foot nine on a good day; Dax towered over him. My dad grew more stone-faced, but he stepped back.

With a scoff, he motioned toward me with his hand. "Well, I'm not sure what to believe. That's not the story Lucas told. You lied to me about where you were staying. Last week, if somebody would have called you a liar, I would have gone to my grave to deny it."

Dax snorted.

He scowled at Dax. "You got something to say?"

He leveled his gaze on my dad. "Yeah. She's your daughter. Some jackass just tried to take advantage of her, and you're taking his side to save face. She should mean a lot more to you than your precious campaign."

Daggers shot from my dad's eyes as he fought for control of his emotions. "Didn't you have an older brother once? Maybe you shouldn't be lecturing me about family matters."

Dax's hands curled on the door slightly. He took a second to recover before saying, "I'm not the one pretending to be something I'm not."

Steam poured from my dad's body as he took another step toward Dax. Bolting forward, I slipped underneath Dax's arm holding the door open and stepped between them.

"Time to go, Dad."

"You're coming with me."

"No, I'm not."

"So you can spend more time with him? You've already had one court sentencing. You don't need any more." He tried to grab my arm.

I reared back, fire, not blood, searing through my veins.

"How dare you come here and insinuate anything. You know nothing about him. Or me, for that matter."

"Time to go." Dax motioned the senator toward his golf cart.

My dad stared at him before shaking his head with disgust.

He was halfway to his golf cart when he called over his shoulder, "We're not done talking about this."

"We are," I said, taking another step forward as my dad retreated. I held myself back from clasping Dax's arm as he stood near the doorway, watching my dad leave.

Dax closed the door and locked it before turning around. For a long moment, he looked at me in slight disbelief.

"You've lived with that your whole life?"

Humiliation painted my cheeks. "It's election year. He's always wor—"

He lifted my chin in his hand, forcing me to meet his eyes, the touch of his fingers halting the words from my lips.

"Stop. He doesn't deserve your excuses. He doesn't deserve *you*. Got it?"

I blinked. Before I could overanalyze the sweetness in that statement, he pivoted and brought us back to lighter ground.

Dropping my chin and taking a step back, he said, "I've lived here three years without a single incident. You move in, and bam, constant trouble."

Another thought came to me as I threw my hands on my cheeks.

"My dad thinks we—"

"I know."

The tone of his voice had me looking up at him. "Why are you smiling?"

"I should've kissed you in front of him." Dax stepped around me and yanked the blanket off the floor before flopping down, re-situating the blanket over top of him. "If he ever talks to you like that again in front of me, you better buckle up."

I had just gotten off a date where a guy tried to steal a kiss—perhaps more than that. The thought of kissing Lucas triggered my upchuck reflex. Although his reasoning might have been flawed, the thought of kissing Dax gave my body a different reaction—if the tingles lacing my arms and the flood of saliva gathering in my mouth meant anything.

A delicious scenario suddenly burst into my thoughts. It began with teasing and flirting and ended with Dax pulling me closer, his hands gripping my—

"Hit the lights, would you?"

I bolted forward, remembering myself, and flipped the switch.

The cool sheets welcomed me as I settled into my bed for the third time that night. Stress had run its course, and I could feel the exhaustion settling in my limbs as I found the perfect position to rest my head on the pillow.

"Dax?"

"Yeah?"

"Thank you for all your help tonight."

A warm pause settled between us as I waited for his response.

"Ivy?"

"Yeah?"

"Anytime."

His voice and his presence in my space soothed and lulled, and I was almost gone when he pulled me back once more.

"Be sure to keep that bra on in case we get another visitor tonight."

I moaned and covered my face to the sound of his low chuckle.

CHAPTER 15

Biology Class
Day 23

"You got in a fight with Brock?" I said to Dax as he dropped into his seat next to me. Dax's fight with the class president and my prom date was the reason he had missed class last week. He had been suspended from school.

He laughed, sliding lower into his seat to rest the back of his head on his chair. His right eye was rimmed with black and green hues.

"Apparently, he only likes discussing the stock market to impress his girlfriends. I was hoping to grab some tips from him and he freaked out."

"You were making fun of him?" I asked.

He shrugged. "I just asked him a question. He kind of reminds me of you."

"Why?" I asked automatically, my tone prickly.

"It's that politician thing." He looked at me then, a deep knowing in his gaze that startled me. "You smile and say all the right things, but there's a lot boiling just below the surface. It's pretty entertaining to poke the really nice bear."

I moved my gaze over his black eye. "Looks like that nice bear poked you right back."

. . .

Two mornings later, I was on break at the cafe, stuffing my face with Marco's famous key-lime-pie pancakes with coconut syrup when my phone rang.

"Hi. Is this Caroline Brooks?" The woman on the line sounded bored. It was probably her polite secretary voice, but her tone and inflection sounded as though she was dreaming of a beach somewhere. She'd probably love Sunset Harbor.

"It's Ivy, actually, but yeah."

"Okay. This is Samantha from Kathleen Meyer's office at Vanderbilt. I'm calling about the class you were scheduled for later this summer and fall."

I snuck out of Marco's loud kitchen and slipped into the small office in the back of the cafe. This phone call could quite literally change my life, and I didn't think it was a great sign that Kathleen had assigned her secretary to call me. "Yeah?"

There was a slight pause before she deadpanned the sentence that would dash every plan I had made before coming to the island.

"Kathleen is sorry about the change in your summer schedule but ultimately feels you should serve your community service. Your eight-week course of Introduction to Statistics is scheduled to begin on Monday, August 5th. We are willing to waive the research you were supposed to do for this summer, but Kathleen needs you back in Nashville by Monday, July 22nd at the latest if you'd still like to keep your class and fellowship for the fall."

I clenched the phone in my hands. That was a week and a half earlier than I was expecting to leave.

"Why that early?" I asked.

"Because if, for some reason, you can't make it, we'll need the extra time to make other arrangements."

Any other time, it wouldn't be a big deal, but with my remaining hours at the cafe, every day counted. I had asked the cafe to schedule me out for a few weeks without pay. I couldn't cry off now. And I didn't want to. In a small way, it helped knowing Harold and Judy had one less thing to worry about while they were away for cancer treatments.

"Is that something you can do, Ms. Brooks? Or should we talk about giving the opportunity to another graduate?"

My mind raced to calculate.

T-minus ~~38~~ 29 days to exit
Dax hours remaining: 185

I'd be dead on my feet with no life, but I'd get my hours finished.

"I can do it. I'll be there."

There was another pause before Samantha reiterated, "You must report to Kathleen's office by 9 am on Monday, July 22nd, Ms. Brooks. Or else we'll be forced to re-evaluate our agreement."

"I'll make it work. Tell Kathleen to plan on me." While my words sounded bright and chipper, inside I was dying.

"Keep us posted if anything changes."

The line clicked off. I slumped into the desk chair in defeat. I imagined her writing a checkmark on the list next to her phone that said: *Call Caroline Brooks and destroy her immediate future.*

Check.

I just wouldn't sleep. Friends would have to come see me. Dax seemed to get along fine with a schedule like that.

This was my chance to stay connected to a university, researching and writing papers and rubbing shoulders with professors who might one day open a door for me. This job held the key to everything I had worked my butt off for the past ten years.

And it all stood to be flushed down the drain. If this postdoc fell through, I would be facing the biggest fear of every graduate student ever—being extremely overqualified and severely out of work.

LATER THAT AFTERNOON, I sat on the cold hard concrete floor of Dax's lobby. I had actually been looking forward to an evening of mindless Legos until I arrived and remembered that I still, in fact, hated it. I had organized one pile as best as I could, but I could never seem to find what I needed without scouring the ground for at least ten minutes. Beau and Phoenix had helped me find a couple of pieces on their way to see Dax—the Dax who saved me from Lucas and defended me to my dad.

We hadn't talked about the other night. The following morning, he left my apartment early to work at the shop, and I kept to myself. Sunday was the one day I gave myself time off, so I spent the day walking the beach and playing volleyball with Cat and Holland. But my heart lurched this morning when I found him sitting in his booth, waiting for coffee. He wasn't pushing me for much conversation beyond teasing, but there seemed to be a more gentle undertone between us now.

Watching Dax say those things to my dad on my behalf both humbled and humiliated me. I wasn't embarrassed by his words or his actions. It was the fact that it should have been me saying them. Conflict was something I'd been taught to ignore. Keeping my head down and smiling through the pain was the theme of life in the Brooks' household.

I found it difficult to talk back to my dad when, deep down, I still craved his approval.

And his love.

I knew what he was, but I also knew what he could be, and that knowledge waged a constant battle within me.

I picked up my Lego guidebook, squinting down at the small ball of Legos I had painstakingly crafted over the past few days and compared it to the picture in the book.

Then I looked again.

And again.

To my utter horror, the Lego piece in my hand looked different from the picture. Not a lot different, mind you, but the tiniest microscopic amount different. An amount that shouldn't have the power to ruin someone's already terrible day.

I flipped back the pages until I found where I went wrong. Fourteen pages back. Two days of work. TEN HOURS ruined. I threw the book down. It landed with a loud thump.

I didn't cry. Or scream. Instead, I slunk to the cold floor and lay there, allowing the numbness to overtake me.

Was I the camel? Because this straw was heavy.

The front door flung open. A man in grubby overalls thundered into the room, holding an invoice in his hand.

His stormy eyes landed on mine. "Is the owner here?"

I nodded, too far gone in my own misery to say anything. I just pointed toward the door that led into the garage.

Without another word, he strode past me, his footsteps heavy as he thundered his way toward Dax's space.

With my pity party essentially ruined, I picked up a Lego and held it in my hand. I imagined there would be eight-year-olds and parents everywhere who might understand this specific frustration—that I no longer felt.

Because...numb.

A voice, loud and booming, began shouting in the other room. Highly sensitive to sounds of anger, my body sat rigid while I strained to listen for what was being said. I debated for a moment before standing up, dropping my Lego in the pile, and making my way closer.

I stepped through the doorway. My attention first went to the man shouting while waving what looked like his invoice in the air while Dax listened, calmly leaning against a golf cart. Beau and Phoenix were seated on the chairs, watching the man yell at Dax. Beau smiled at me as I made my way toward them, pushing an empty barstool my way with his foot.

"We're out of chips. You don't happen to have any popcorn, do you?"

"You're the cop. Shouldn't you stop this?" I said.

His brow furrowed. "Stop what?"

"That guy yelling at Dax."

Laughter sprung into his eyes. "If this guy tries to throw a punch, I might jump in, but I just cleaned my uniform."

When I didn't laugh, Beau leaned in closer. "I doubt it will get that far. Dax can handle himself."

"You're way overcharging!" the man's voice boomed. "Just because you're on an island doesn't mean you can charge double the price of what I can get done on the mainland."

Dax shook his head and pointed at the invoice. "Listen, man, it costs almost double for me to get parts ferried onto this island, so I will definitely be charging more for that." He leaned closer and pointed at different parts of the bill. "That's the price of the part, including the extra shipping to get it here. This is my hourly rate to fix it. I don't have any secrets. It's all black and white. I told you the exact price on the phone when I called you."

"You never said a number this high. I would have stopped you."

"I read this exact invoice."

"Your hourly rate is extortion."

Dax laughed, running his hand through his hair as he noticed me sitting there for the first time. My skin came alive with awareness as his gaze landed on mine. "It's not."

"I'll be taking my business somewhere else next time."

"That would be great. But if you want your mower, you're going to have to sign right here and pay."

The man shook his head, grumbling under his breath. Dax looked at Phoenix and Beau and rolled his eyes, much to their delight.

The man pulled a checkbook out of his back pocket.

"Sorry, sir, there's no way I'm taking a check from you. Card or cash only." Dax folded his arms and waited unapologetically while the man's face turned a dark shade of red.

Biting his bitter tongue, the man reached into his pocket and pulled out his wallet, his pudgy fingers yanking out a stack of bills. "If you were any sort of business owner, you would at least give me a discount."

Again, Dax laughed, unfazed as he straightened up some tools on his workbench. "If I had my guess, you do this wherever you go, which is why you came to an island to get this fixed when you don't live here. You're probably not welcome anywhere else."

The man took another step toward Dax, to which Beau and Phoenix stood up from their chairs, the scrape of the metal against the concrete breaking into the tension of the room.

The man took a step back and threw down several one-hundred-dollar bills at Dax's feet before grabbing his push mower and storming out—at least, storming out as much as possible when pushing a mower that looked like a kid's toy to such a big man.

"You just lost my business!" he yelled as the door slammed shut behind him.

Phoenix let out a laugh. "You almost got beat up by a fifty-year-old man."

Dax's eyebrows raised. "You think he's that old?"

"At least."

Dax smiled, popping his knuckles. "I would have had to go easy on him, then."

I stood there entranced, watching his friends laugh together. Dax sauntered back over to a golf cart with a tool in his hand.

From what I could tell, he didn't hold any weight of the man's opinion of him on his back. But the tension from the conversation had filled my stomach with lead. That guy hated him. He would probably leave Dax a terrible review online somewhere, and here was Dax, just laughing about it with his friends.

How did he do that?

To stand up for himself without apology? To act without giving a thought to what others might think of him? Dax defended me and spoke the same way to my dad as he did this man. Even in high school, he never allowed anyone to treat him poorly. Teachers were disciplining him and at the same time asking for advice on motors.

I wanted that.

I didn't know how, but I wanted it.

Was there such a thing as a quarter-life crisis?

But how? How does one stop caring what people think? How do I stop caring that I'm disappointing my dad? How do I live a life on my terms?

I had no freaking idea.

"You still on the clock, Books?" Dax asked me a few minutes later, once the guys had left and I still hadn't moved from my spot on the barstool. My thoughts were jumbled in my head, and that was exactly how they came out to Dax.

"I messed up on the Legos, and I have to go back fourteen pages. So I'm just going to sit here for another minute if you don't mind."

Dax stopped what he was doing to look over at me. "Wait. What?"

"I messed up. And I hate Legos. My last two days have been for nothing."

He was silent for a long moment before he dropped his tool and walked over to me. "Show me."

Without a word, I followed him into the other room and sat down next to him as he flipped through the pages.

"I didn't realize I put this piece in the wrong way, fourteen pages ago. So now I have to rip this whole thing up and start over."

There was not a day horrible enough on this earth for me to cry over Legos in front of Dax Miller. So I sucked up my last breath and pinched my leg ultra hard to give my brain another hurt to process.

After a minute, Dax began breaking apart my Lego pieces. He flipped to the page I needed to redo and began fitting Legos into place with the ease and respect of someone who had clearly loved them his whole life.

"Chin up, Books. One hundred and eighty more hours, and you're home free."

"One hundred and eighty-four," I corrected miserably.

"Start organizing that pile over there. I'll work on fixing this mess," Dax said, nudging my foot with his leg. "The things you do to get me in here doing your work for you."

He seemed so absorbed in the booklet and Legos that he didn't seem to notice that I still sat where I was, my arms wrapped around bent legs, watching him.

"How do you speak your mind like that?" I asked, unable to help myself.

"Huh?"

"You almost got in a massive fight ten minutes ago, and now you're sitting here helping me with Legos like nothing happened."

"That wasn't a massive fight," he protested.

"It could have been. But you didn't even flinch. You just told him off."

"Yeah, because I didn't do anything wrong. I quoted him a fair price, and he was trying to bully his way out of paying."

"I know." And I did know, I realized. Dax was a lot of things, but deep down, there was something so honorable about him. I must have been a glutton for punishment asking this question, but I really wanted to know how a person could just turn emotions off like Dax seemed to do. "But how do you shrug off his opinion so fast? My mind goes blank when people are mad at me."

"Are you asking me for advice, Books?" He pointed at his inflated chest.

"Not if you're going to use that tone."

His lips lifted at the corners. "Alright. You want to know the secret?"

"Yeah."

"Stop making everything such a big deal. It doesn't have to be personal. You need to separate yourself. Lawnmower Joe from the mainland makes a career out of cheating people. That's not on me. And I have every right to stand up for myself when he tries it on me. So, just stop caring about people, and you'll be fine." He brushed his hands together like the matter was solved. I kicked him with my leg.

I remembered the way he held me after Lucas, the feel of his hands on my legs as he carried me to the bed. His words implied an aloofness, while his actions suggested otherwise. If anything, I think he cared too much about people. But I kept my thoughts to myself.

"It's hard to separate myself when the problem is my dad. It was easier in Tennessee, but here…" I trailed off.

"What's hard about it now?"

"He's right in front of my face. If I ignore his phone call he comes and finds me. He never called me in Tennessee."

"What's he making you feel bad for?" Dax asked, looking at me.

"Being here…ruining his campaign. Losing two of his sponsors." I gave a little laugh, like it was all funny, but there was a pang in my gut, reminding me how unfunny it actually was.

Dax set the Lego down and draped his arms over his knees, taking me in with dark eyes.

"He's making you feel bad because you're on the island?"

I shrugged. It could go either way—here on the island or here with Dax. My guess was it was more the latter, but admitting that to Dax seemed too forward.

Dax held up his fingers, ticking each off as he said, "It's not his island. It's your home. You have every right to be here. If he really thinks that, he's wrong. What's the next one?"

My lips pulled upward the tiniest bit. "I'm ruining his campaign."

"If he's that terrible of a politician that one accident is enough to sink him, that's on him. Your choices shouldn't be related to him in any way."

"But people do judge a politician's family," I insisted.

He shrugged. "He's not running for president, so I think he can calm down. Everybody in this town knows you, Books. It was an accident. Everybody has moved on. I was over it the second you stepped into my garage."

I looked to him in surprise. It took a long moment before I trusted myself to say something. "Was it my heartfelt apology?"

"Something like that." His voice sounded almost gentle even as he bit back a smile.

The mood shifted into something so soft I could hold in my hand.

"What was that last one?"

I thought back to what I had said. "He lost two big sponsors because of me—so he claims."

Dax rolled his eyes. "Okay. Now *you* tell me how he's wrong."

I blew out a breath. "He should have sided with me over the Lucas thing—or at least listened to me. But the problem became inconvenient for him, and he didn't want to deal with it. It's always easier to blame me instead of change his ways."

"Look at you go," Dax said, smiling proudly.

"What if I *am* in the wrong? I could do this with anything. I can't go through life pretending nothing is ever my fault."

"You won't. You'll make it right. That's why you showed up to my shop after the accident. You'll know here," he said, as he thumped at his chest. "Most people are more normal. If they make mistakes, they own it and then try to make it right. But there are always going to be people we have to protect ourselves against. Your dad is one of yours."

The simple way Dax spelled things out felt like something caged inside of me had been let free. For a brief second, all the twisted inner workings of my mind relaxed, allowing me to sit in a moment of justification and validation. Even though I knew my brain would re-complicate things soon enough, for now, the feeling of someone siding with me was liberating.

"It just takes some practice defying expectations, and then you'll be as cold and unfeeling as I am," Dax said lightly, rummaging through the pile of Legos once more.

"Was that your entire teenage life? Defying expectations?" I asked.

He held out his hands. "And look at me now."

I laughed as I began organizing the Legos into more piles. We didn't speak for a long moment while "Bad Moon Rising" by Creedence Clearwater Revival played in the background. The fact that I now knew the names of some of the songs on Dax's playlist astounded me at the same time my foot tapped to the beat.

Defying expectations.

My mind latched onto those two words, and they swirled inside me as the song blasted from the speakers. Dax had practiced for much of his life to block out opinions. I recalled the stiff way he spoke with his parents and the way he was always working. Certainly, a person could go too far with this idea. Still, my heart began to thrum with the itch to do…something. Anything. Scale a wall? Sure. Toilet paper a house? What time?

A restless energy began filtering through my veins, and I wasn't sure what to do with the feeling while I sat on the floor next to Dax handing him Lego pieces.

"So, when do you have to be back in Tennessee?" His voice was passively indifferent, but I thought I detected something else I couldn't place. Probably excitement.

"Just over four weeks now."

He looked over at me. "What?"

I filled him in on my phone call from earlier.

"If I can get all my hours finished in time, that's the plan."

"I think you forget that I've kindly provided you with a list of ways to reduce your hours." There was a reckless look on his face as he met my gaze.

While my racing heart skittered to a stop.

The list.

I had forgotten about the stupid list. The list he had made while knowing I would be too scared to do any of it.

And he had been right. I would have been too scared back then.

Honestly, I still was.

But now...the place deep inside, underneath my carefully crafted existence, felt empty. Hollow. Numb.

But underneath the numbness...the callus, new life began to grow.

I had one month to do one hundred and eighty-four hours of community service as well as do my part to help the cafe.

Even if I only did one thing off the list, it would save a lot of hours.

Then I remembered who I was. There was no way. Let's not forget that the list only had three things on it, and one of them was to spray paint a building. The other was driving an illegal car all around the island.

I was already on probation from one motor vehicle mishap.

There was no way I was doing any of it.

Dax only wrote the list because he was annoyed with me.

So, why was I still thinking about it?

Maybe I could secretly ask the owner of the clinic if I could borrow the ambulance for a bit? Dax wouldn't have to know.

"You're not going to do it, so wipe that look off your face."

I hadn't realized he'd been watching me. "Why? You worried I will?"

A smile brushed across his lips. "No." He paused and seemed to reconsider his statement before saying, "But if you did...what a way to start being brave and living life on your terms." He leaned closer. "Defying those expectations."

Now he was goading me. Usually, I would push him away or smack him in the arm for that, but this time, our eyes clung as my mind raced right alongside my heart.

I stood up and disappeared into the back room for a minute, feeling Dax's gaze on me as I left. Underneath the calendar of the beautiful and voluptuous 1960s women, Dax had tacked his paper onto the wall. I yanked the list down.

I'd spent my whole life living for others. Going to college for someone else. Getting my degree for someone else. Even getting a job at Vanderbilt for someone else. What would happen if I were to step a foot outside the mold? Or just, you know...dipped a toe?

I wanted so badly to feel different. To *be* different. I wanted one moment where my choices were mine. Even if it ended up being a mistake, I wanted to choose. I wanted to feel off-balance. And there was one person in this whole world who just might be game.

I strode back into the Lego room, the door hitting the wall with a force that made Dax jump.

"You've got to stop doing th—"

"I'm doing the list," I announced, sounding more assured than I felt. But I had made up my mind. Whatever was bubbling inside of me was now unleashed. A new life and energy pumped through my veins with a jarring certainty.

Dax's eyebrows raised in interest. "Do you remember the list? I'm pretty sure I didn't add a dance party on there."

"There's still time."

He snorted and looked back down at his Legos, as comfortable as I'd seen him in a while. "You're not doing it."

"I am. And first up, I'm getting a tattoo."

WELCOME TO SUNSET HARBOR

- Belacourt Resort
- Golf Course
- Noah's House
- Jane's House
- Nature Preserve
- Dax's Duplex
- Seaside Oasis Retirement Home
- Sunset Repairs
- Phoenix's Office
- City Offices
- Sunrise Cafe
- Scoops Ahoy Ice Cream
- Keene B&B
- Town Square
- Bakery
- Brigg's Apartment
- The Book Isle
- Cuts and Curls
- Tristan & Beau's House
- Capri's House
- Gemma's House
- Holland's House
- Beach Break Bar & Grill
- Public Beach

Gulf of Mexico

CHAPTER 16

Biology Class
Day 24

"Nice tattoo," I said, my eyes traveling all over the pink and slightly puffy skin. It was an old car, and honestly, it looked pretty cool—though I'd never admit that to him. "Did your mom take you to get it?"
Without skipping a beat, Dax said, "Nope. Your mom did."
I whacked his arm while he laughed.

I WAS SO ready for this tattoo.
So.
So.
Soooo.
Ready.
During these past four minutes, it was all I could think about. I kept envisioning a...something...on my arm, just where the sleeve would hit. And that...something...that *amazing* something would be the talk of the town. It was brilliant, really, killing two birds with one stone. I got to knock fifty hours off of my time, and if my dad happened to see me sporting a tattoo around town before I left, all the better.
Dax had been strangely quiet after my declaration. I had to

tell him three times before he showed any semblance of believing me, but when he did, he smiled. He even told me he'd take me tomorrow—if I still wanted to go. Then he handed me back my Legos, completely fixed, and walked off toward his garage.

He didn't believe me.

"Hey!"

He turned back around, his head tilted to one side.

"I want to go now."

Still, he watched me, calculating, and I shifted under his stare.

"I'll go by myself if I have to."

He didn't move. I guess I had to show my cards.

"Okay, I'm leaving, then. See you tomorrow, and be prepared to subtract fifty hours, buddy." My dramatic exit toward the door was halted when I realized my purse was still sitting behind the counter. I stalked back, grabbed it, and was halfway to the front door again before I remembered I needed to clock out. Dax's eyes trailed me with growing amusement while he held open the door for me to enter his garage.

"I'm doing it," I told him again.

"I can see that," came his reply as I stalked toward the calendar. I scratched in 8:00 pm for my time out and was surprised to find my hand shaking.

With excitement.

The lights in the shop went dark. I turned to see Dax waiting for me at the door. He had a bottle of Gatorade in his hands and something else. The warm yellow light from the lobby highlighted his silhouette in a way that had me catching my breath.

"You coming, Caroline?"

A relieved smile crossed my lips.

"Yeah."

THE ISLAND FERRY was located a few minutes south of Sunset Repairs. Dax didn't bother to take us in his golf cart, so we walked. The sun had almost met the horizon, and the creamsicle streaks of oranges and pinks lit up the sky. I couldn't take my eyes from the scene, breathing in the salty ocean air. There was nothing like sunsets on the island.

There was nothing like *being* on the island.

"Here," he said, handing me the drink and a granola bar. "Eat this. You don't want to get a tattoo on an empty stomach."

"Thanks," I said, accepting his offering. "Why not?"

"You don't want to pass out."

My steps slowed. "Why would I pass out?"

"From the needles? The pain? The smell? Take your pick."

I didn't answer him. Because it didn't matter. Each step toward the ferry brought me more clarity. I had never felt so good about a decision in my life. A tattoo was exactly what I needed right now. Something different, something…a little wild. At least for me. I couldn't wipe the smile from my face. My heart drummed in excitement. Nothing Dax could say would take that away.

He walked quietly beside me, my steps sure and strong as we made our way down the path. Every so often, my shoulder would brush against his, igniting trails of sparks down my arms.

"Do you want to talk about this rash decision?" Dax asked, slipping his hands into his pockets. His legs kept up with my determined stride easily, as though he were going for a light stroll in the park.

"Nothing to talk about. I've never been more sure of anything." I pointed to the road. "Is that a slug?!"

We bent down and examined a slimy, brown, oversized worm lounging on the dirt before continuing on our way.

"That reminds me of biology," I said.

He stopped short while I kept walking a few paces before my body knew to halt.

"What are you doing?"

A wicked gleam crossed his face. "Let's go grab him. I'll get a scalpel while we're out." He turned around, a man on a mission, striding toward the creature. "I'm adding him to the list."

He walked three steps before I grabbed his arm, laughing and pulling him back. He resisted only a minute before allowing himself to be guided again toward the ferry ticket counter. After a long moment, I realized my hand was still clutching his arm.

I removed it.

We'd been tracking the ferry's movements from the road, and now it was almost here. We jogged the rest of the way to the ticket counter. I reached into my purse, but Dax waved me away.

"This one's on me. I'm just happy to be here."

For that comment alone, I allowed him to pay for our twelve-minute passage to the mainland.

We boarded the ferry along with at least ten high school kids wearing hoodies and flip-flops with cameras strapped around their necks. It wasn't unusual to see people on the ferry at sunset, catching the golden hour. We even saw Judge Baylor in one of the seats on the top deck, but he only waved, his crinkly eyes taking us in.

We opted to stand on the deck. The sun drew close to the horizon, almost blinding us with its golden rays spread across the sky. I bounced up and down on my feet, unable to be still. Excitement and determination infiltrated every part of my being. I suspected that getting a tattoo would feel like stepping out of the salon after a bold new haircut. Something different than the way I'd always been. Something to shake me up. I had been one type of person my entire life. But I wasn't sure if I became that person because it's who I really was or if I became that person because I *had to*.

Becoming brave and defying the expectations of others was the first step for this recovering people-pleaser.

It was genius.

Unfortunately, the boat was the biggest buzz kill. The leisurely pull and tug through the water was in direct contrast to my bouncing feet and pumping heartbeat. I could have *swam* faster. I did a few quick right jabs into the air to keep my adrenaline pumping.

This ferry better hurry the freak up, or I might not even want a tattoo by the time we crawled into port.

I was aware of Dax observing me. I ignored his pointed looks and concentrated on the form of my uppercut.

"What are you going to get, Rocky?" Dax asked, leaning closer and resting his elbows on the ship. "A skull? Crossbones? My handsome face?"

I was working on my left hook now. "I haven't decided yet. Will they have a catalog to look through?"

That brought a smile to his face. "Yup. They'll have lots of options for you."

"Great," I said, going back to bouncing on my feet. "I'm so excited."

When he didn't say anything, I added. "Fifty hours down. That should put me at around one hundred and thirty?"

"I guess so."

"I'm so excited," I said. Had I already said that?

His eyebrows raised. "You trying to convince me or you?"

Okay, yeah, I had already said that. I smiled brightly. "Nobody. Just excited."

"You like needles?"

Did I *like* needles?

Of course not. But right now, I was an unstoppable bundle of adrenaline. I could handle the needles. Women pushed babies out of their bodies on a regular basis. I could handle a needle for five minutes.

"Wait. How long does it take? To get a tattoo?"

Dax shrugged. "Just a small one? I don't know. Probably an hour."

I sucked in a breath and paused in my bouncing. "That seems excessive."

He smiled, and my gaze fell to his arms, currently glistening in the glow of the setting sun. "How long did yours take?"

"Each of them probably took about four hours or so."

"How did you decide what to get?" I asked.

"Excuse me." We both turned to see a young girl with blue hair sticking out from under her beanie with an SLR camera slung across her neck. "Are you two a couple?"

I inched away from Dax. "No," I said. "We're just fr—acquaintances." Work associates? Jailbird and warden?

The girl's brow furrowed, taking us both in with some confusion. "Oh, sorry."

Dax continued to lean against the railing and smiled at the girl who seemed at a loss for words and not sure what to do.

"Did you need something?" he asked.

She drew in a breath. "My name is Whitney. I'm in a photography club, and I have an assignment due tomorrow. I need to take some pictures of a couple. I thought with the sunset it would be pretty, but...if you're not..." She trailed off as she motioned to a rapidly diminishing sky of color.

"We can do it," said Dax, standing up straight and startling me with his direct gaze. "We're trying new things today."

"Oh, thank you so much!" She turned and walked a few paces back to get in a better position.

"What?" I whispered to Dax, keeping light on my feet. "No."

He nodded toward the girl. "She needs help."

"But I'm..." I wasn't sure how to express my intense desire

to keep up with my constant movements and boxing stance. No, not desire. Need. I needed to be moving right now or else I might lose my nerve. But Dax was already making his way to where she was directing us. I couldn't say no, especially when it became clear that she needed him to wrap his arms around me. The things we women have to do sometimes.

"This is going to cost you," I whispered to Dax, my heart secretly thrilled as he pulled me to him so we were both facing the water, my back pressed against his stomach. I didn't know what to do with my hands, so I rested them on his forearms.

"I should charge *you* for this," Dax murmured, his lips somewhere close to my ear.

"Now both of you look off into the distance. Like you're thinking about how much you love each other," Whitney called out, a few yards away, a long zoom lens covering her face.

Dax's body tensed as though he were holding back a laugh. I elbowed him in the ribs.

"Um, can you stop moving your feet?" she asked me. "It might make the picture blurry." My heart sank as I forced my feet to stand still.

"Now, lean in close so your face is touching her cheek."

"Two hours," I whispered to Dax as I felt the stubble of his cheeks press against mine while the fire of adrenaline coursing through my body began to burn in a different direction. The slow and easy, white smoke and ember kind of direction—which was unfortunate when my body definitely needed the adrenaline of raging bonfire right now.

"Shh. Think about how much you love me," Dax murmured.

I opened my mouth to hurl a retort, something witty and sharp, but nothing came out. There were definitely things I could say that would shut him up or, at the very least, make him laugh, but then his arms tightened around my waist and my mind forgot all the words.

"Now, turn to face each other."

Dax turned me to face him, meeting my gaze unabashed with those dark lashes framing his eyes.

"Can you put your foreheads together?" Whitney asked, the camera hiding her face. "And um...pretend like you're laughing at something."

"No problem," Dax said, his fingers finding my belt loop and pulling me against his body. "She loves my jokes."

A smile came unbidden, though I tried to hold it back.

"You are looking at him so cute," Whitney said to me as Dax pressed his forehead against mine. "Stay just like that."

I stared up at Dax, amusement etched across his face.

"Shut up," I whispered.

"I didn't say anything."

"Now, put your hands on his cheeks," Whitney said.

I gave Whitney props for boldness as I placed my hands on his stubbled face.

"That's good. And then lean in close like you're almost going to kiss."

"Would you like her to kiss me? She'd be happy to." Dax blatantly ignored the stomp I gave his foot.

"No, that's okay. I don't want to make it too weird for you. I've got a few other poses to try, and we're almost to the dock," she said.

"Dry your eyes, Books," he whispered.

"You sure bring up kissing a lot," I said, giving him the side-eye.

Before he could respond, our dear, sweet photographer asked us to do the Titanic pose.

"Huh?" we both asked at the same time.

It got weirder from there, so I'll spare the details, except to say that it took disembarking from the ship and several long minutes later before I stopped feeling the imprint of Dax against my skin.

THE TATTOO PARLOR was down a few blocks and one questionable alleyway from the dock. For all the fire and guns I had when leaving Dax's shop, somewhere along the way, I had lost my steam. Thank you for that, Whitney. The closer we got to the parlor, the faster my mouth seemed to move.

"So have you ever TPed anybody?" I asked.

"Pretty sure nobody does that anymore."

"Nobody?"

"You were the last rabble-rouser of your kind, Books."

"It was really fun."

"I'm sure."

"There was this one time…" That was the part where my mouth started saying words, my hands flying every which way.

Very chipper.

It was exciting to do something fun. Out of my comfort zone. I was about to pick something meaningful to me that I would want printed on my body forever. This was great.

"And then I told my professor…"

There I was again. Off on another story my brain wasn't fully connected to, but my mind was a whirl of nerves and butterflies and pictures of skulls and snakes, and weirdly, Dax's face.

"And then he was, like, 'Whoa, you should really eat more cheese.'"

That's the statement my jabbering ended on as Dax led me to the small black painted building where I would be repeatedly stabbed in the name of art.

"You're not nervous, are you, Books?" Dax looked suspiciously like he was trying to hold back a laugh. But I couldn't waste my energy on him because as soon as he opened the door, the smell of cleaner and something else I couldn't pinpoint hit me in the face. Like a deer in headlights, I stood, gulping down air and momentarily stunned, until Dax's light hand at the base of my back guided me forward.

"Bravery starts now, Caroline," he whispered. "You ready?"

"If I do this, you have to start calling me Ivy."

A smile lit his face. "*If?*"

"When," I corrected.

He turned and nodded at the pretty brunette with a streak of purple in her hair and a colorful arrangement of tattoos on her neck and arms who was coming to greet us.

"Hey, Dax," she said, giving him a hug. "Long time, no see. Finally got off that island, huh?"

Dax smiled, leaning in for a quick embrace. "Hey, Jordan. I'm just here for a bit. You guys keeping busy?"

She shrugged. "It's steady, but not too crazy." I looked around the room with a critical eye. Several seats were occupied in a large room with a tattoo artist doing their work. Nobody seemed to be writhing in pain, but maybe they kept those customers in a private room. A soundproof room.

She looked at me curiously. "What brings you two in?"

Dax threw his arm around my shoulders. "This is my... acquaintance." I didn't miss the look he gave me at that word. "She's on a quest to find herself and is in dire need of a tattoo."

"A small tattoo," I supplied with a tight smile, clutching my hands together so as not to shake. "I've already found most of myself."

"Right," she said slowly, looking back and forth between us with a confused expression. "Do you have an appointment?"

"No," I said, trying hard to mask the hope in my voice.

Jordan looked at the clock and then down at her appointment book on the desk in front of her. "Well…"

"I texted Bernie. He said to come in, and he'd meet us here," Dax explained while I looked at him in surprise.

"He's back with a client, but he should be just about done."

"If you can hook us up with an empty room and a book of options, we'll wait for him there."

"I don't need a book. I want a butterfly." Goodness. Was my voice *always* that high-pitched? "A small one. Right here." I pointed at my upper arm.

She followed my movements. "For a small tattoo, usually you'd want it on a smaller spot on the body, like the back of the wrist or an ankle or something."

"Oh." I turned my hand to see the veins and thin skin on my wrist. "Does that hurt more or less than an arm?"

"A little more."

"We'll just stick to the arm, then. Maybe one day I'll come back for a full sleeve."

I was aware of Dax's chuckling as Jordan led us back into a private room. It looked similar to a doctor's office: two chairs against a wall, a large black reclined seat in the middle of the room, and small tables holding tools with wires coming out of them—the needles, I presumed.

Once we were seated and the door was closed, Dax was up again and striding toward the door.

"Bernie texted me to come find him. I'll be right back." The door clicked shut, leaving me in silence.

The smell of alcohol in this room made me lightheaded, but I couldn't stop gulping in the air. There were some other smells too. Maybe a little lemon cleaner? Burning flesh?

No. Not burning. Jabs and pokes–that was all the needles did, just little jabs and pokes. I could do that. I stood up and did ten jumping jacks. The cold, tiled floor pounded at my feet, pumping my blood and giving life back to my veins. I could do this. Tons of people had tattoos. If it really hurt that bad, they wouldn't go back to get more. This was probably a gateway tattoo for me. I'd love it so much I'd come back every week.

So, I settled in for some intense self-motivational speeches.

"You can do it," I whispered. Right hook.

"This is for Nashville." Left hook.

"I'm doing this." Right jab.

Maybe if I said it with more conviction each time, I'd be so pumped when Dax came back that all the worry would leave my face.

"I'm doing it." Right jab, left hook combo.

The only connection I had to butterflies was the fact that it was the tattoo the girl got in *A Walk to Remember*. Maybe I should have done a small book or something? Or a volleyball? A meaningful number sequence? Did I have anything in my life that warranted immortalizing it on my skin? A textbook? A stack of research papers? I didn't even have a movie I loved enough to use. TV was a luxury a stressed-out grad student could rarely afford.

Butterfly it was.

They were very pretty.

Right jab.

Didn't most of them have a two-week lifespan?

My hand covered my mouth.

They were probably crazy smart, though.

Left jab.

The door opened, and I had the sudden urge to throw up.

"Good news," Dax said, stepping into the room. "Bernie's tied up, but he said I could get you started."

"What?"

"Get you started." He said it like it was a no-brainer. Did this happen? Can people off the street get a person *started* on their tattoo?

My brow furrowed. "You can do that? Do you know how?"

"Yeah, I've done it before. I thought you might be less nervous."

I scoffed. "Who's nervous?"

He threw me a knowing look before nodding toward the door. "We could wait for Big Bernie if you'd like."

Big Bernie. I looked at Dax, taking in his eyes, soft with the exception of the slightest gleam. But I'd witnessed his capable hands do a lot of things with tools. A needle would probably be fine.

"No. I'll take you. I'd prefer punching you over Big Bernie if the pain gets too bad." I shook out my hands, trying to rid them of the shakes before sitting on the...operating chair? Was that what it was called?

"The tattoo is small, right?"

"Yeah."

"Does it hurt?"

"Not as bad as you're probably imagining. Lie still."

"I'm imagining a thousand knives stabbing my arm at the same time." I covered my eyes with my left hand. I didn't want to see any of the tools he'd be using.

"That's pretty close."

"What?" I unhid my face and turned to him.

He met my gaze with an almost sympathetic grin. "Not that bad, I promise."

"How did you pick your tattoos?" I asked, needing a distraction.

The rolling stool next to me squeaked as Dax sat down at my right side. The idea of him so close made me glad I hadn't picked a more risqué part of my body to ink.

"All of my tattoos mean something," he said. "Kind of like how butterflies are so special to you."

"Shut up," I whispered.

I went back to hiding, my body stiff as a board as the sound of movement from his chair inching closer to me elevated my heart rate.

Dax wiped something cold on my arm, the smell of alcohol suddenly filling my nostrils and making the room swirl.

"Take a breath," came his low voice.

I concentrated on breathing, slow and deep through my nose.

"You ready?" he asked.

I nodded, saying, "Do your worst," in all my dramatic glory, attempting to tamp down the dry heaves threatening to overtake my body. I then squeezed my eyes shut and braced myself for the pain.

"Fifty hours, fifty hours, fifty hours, fifty hours," I whispered under my breath.

The very picture of cool and calm.

Something cold and wet pressed against my arm again. Another alcohol swab? This place was very sanitary. Which was good. Great. The last thing I needed was some sort of infection. But my adrenaline was back, and I was ready to be stabbed. Time to get this over with already.

But Dax didn't swirl the alcohol swab. He kept it firmly pressed against my upper arm.

"Is this...to numb the spot or something?" I asked, my eyes still closed and my body tense. If it was, I wanted ice. A cold rag was not going to cut it.

No answer.

Finally, the pressure eased, and the cold left. I opened my eyes in time to watch Dax peel off the back of a temporary tattoo.

"I couldn't find any butterflies in the stack of press-ons they sell up front, but I thought this one fit you pretty well."

He leaned in closer and blew his cool breath across what looked like an open book with a vine of flowers coming out of the spine. In confusion, I blinked up at him.

"This is now worth twenty-five hours, Books." His lips held a ghost of a smile even as he tried to look serious. He held up a stack of identical tattoos. "I'm buying more so we can keep applying as needed. You have to wear it until you go back to Nashville, and it has to be visible every day for this to count."

For a moment, I lay stunned while my mind caught up to what had just happened. He had given me a fake tattoo. And it was beautiful–exactly the kind of thing I would have chosen if I had actually wanted a tattoo. How did Dax know?

One gentle finger brushed my chin, turning my face toward his as he spoke. "Lesson number one in bravery, Caroline. Never let anyone talk you into doing anything you don't want to do. Tattoos are something you need to think about for longer than a minute, and you should never make a decision like that when emotions are high." He leaned closer and waited until I looked him in the eye. "You don't need a tattoo to be brave or to stick it to your dad. And I'm not making you get one for our deal."

He was saying words. Sweet words, even. But all I could feel was the light touch of his hand on my face and the sudden relief coursing through my body. A breath expelled from my lungs while the tightness in my bones slowly melted away.

When I had collected myself enough to speak, I asked, "Does Big Bernie actually work here?"

"He's my tattoo guy."

"Did you plan this the whole time?"

"Yeah." He said the word so matter-of-factly I felt like an idiot to have been so duped. "People usually have appointments scheduled for weeks in advance to get into this place. I texted Bernie and told him I wanted to play this out, and he said he'd have a room ready."

I covered my face with my hands while embarrassed laughter bubbled out of me. And then I sat up, and slid from the chair, hesitating for only a moment before slipping my grateful arms around his shoulders. Maybe I'd get a real tattoo one day. But that day wasn't today, and for that, I was so grateful.

"Thank you."

His arms wrapped around my waist, gathering me close, the warm spice from his cologne tingling my senses and the strength of his body holding me upright.

"I was going to do it," I insisted, my face smashed into his chest. "I want that on record."

He patted my back, and I could almost feel the eye roll he was no doubt giving me.

"I know, Books. I know."

LATER THAT NIGHT, my song came knocking through the shared wall, loud and clear. Three distinct knocks with some before and after. I still couldn't place it.

DAX
Any guesses?

ME
SexyBack?

DAX
You're so bad at this.

Make sure you don't get your tattoo wet.

ME
I've got to be honest. I'm kind of liking this thing. I could be the world's most intimidating librarian.

DAX
I'm just glad I saved you from a butterfly.

ME
So all your tattoos mean something?

DAX
Yup.

ME
The car?

DAX
Yup

ME
You're a vat of information.

DAX
You're nosy.

My brother and I loved old cars.

ME
Loved?

DAX
I still love them. Night, Books.

CHAPTER 17

Biology Class
Day 26

"What do you call a DNA that's chilling?" I whispered.

Dax looked blankly at me, but I thought I detected the slightest flare of humor behind his eyes. Or it could just be annoyance. Either one worked great for me.

"Ivy. No talking," Mr. Gray called out, looking directly at me.

I slunk back in my seat, immediately chastened. Dax waited until Mr. Gray's attention had moved elsewhere and leaned toward me, catching the scent of my weakness in the air and pouncing.

"What's the answer?" he pressed.

"Shhh," I whispered, my eyes following Mr. Gray's movements.

Dax looked pointedly at our teacher. "You scared of getting in trouble, Books?"

"Nope." I swallowed.

"You started this," he said, not bothering to whisper. "Now I've got to know the answer."

"Shh." I whispered, my voice catching in my throat as Mr. Gray glanced at me again. When he had looked away once more, I hissed, "You don't really care."

"I care so much."

"It's cool genes, alright? Now shut up."

"Dax and Ivy," Mr. Gray called again. "Is there a problem?"

"No, sir," I stated, and with a raised chin I ignored Dax's teasing eyes for the rest of class.

T-minus 26 days to exit
Dax hours remaining: 153

CAT
You coming? Game starts in 20.

ME
I don't have time to go, so obviously I'm coming.

CAT
Perfect. I'll pick you up in ten. You at Dax's shop?

ME
Where else would I be on a perfect summer evening, other than indoors playing with Legos?

CAT
Ha, see you in a few.

I STOOD from my spot on the concrete floor, stretching my back as I did so. Even with the twenty-five hours from the fake tattoo, the math was not mathing. Dax's hours weren't going down as fast as they needed to be, but the evening looked too beautiful to waste.

The other night, I had been ready to accomplish the entire list. But since the other two items included theft, driving a car illegally, and damaging property, I was understandably stalled in my plan.

Dax sat on a metal barstool at one of the workbenches, filling out an invoice, when I walked in. A song I'd heard before but couldn't remember the name of played softly in the background. He glanced up, his dark eyes almost making me trip over my feet.

"I'm leaving early. Cat and some friends are playing volleyball at the beach."

Call me crazy, but a shot of disappointment seemed to flash across his face. It was gone so quick my only conclusion was that I imagined the whole thing. He turned back to his paperwork.

"You sure you have the hours to warrant a night off, Books?"

I scratched my time out on the calendar. "Don't care either way."

"That's the attitude."

He stood and sauntered over to where I stood, reaching up high on the shelf next to me to grab an oil can. His proximity and the smell of oil and cologne spiked my heart rate, and I took a step back.

"If you get bored, there are a bunch of Legos in the other room. They're really fun to play with."

He smirked but said nothing as he shuffled past me.

I walked all the way to the front door in the lobby before the song about loneliness hit the chorus. A small dose of guilt gnawed at my insides. Dax wasn't lonely. Right? Sure, he worked a lot, but his friends came to visit him all the time. He was too tough to be lonely. He didn't need anybody. He wouldn't even want to play volleyball. He would probably make fun of me for doing it tomorrow.

So why wasn't I moving?

Before I could overthink or change my mind, I turned around and strode back toward the garage, bursting into the doorway. Dax startled at my entrance as he stood on a fishing boat, the can of oil in his hands.

"Do you want to come?"

His eyebrows raised. "Play volleyball?"

"Yeah."

He raised his arms, basically giving me full permission to comb my eyes all over him. "Do I look like I play volleyball?"

My eyebrows raised as I eyed his muscles and tattoos peeking out of the bottom of his sleeve and asked, "Have you ever seen *Top Gun*?"

He smiled and took a seat on the boat. "Thanks, but I'm good."

"You chicken?"

Laughing, he said, "I guess so. Have fun, Books."

Suddenly, I wanted Dax to come play volleyball more than anything in the world. Other than when he came in for lunch sometimes at the cafe, I had never seen him anywhere else. He was at the shop until ten most nights. I did know he occasionally watched a game with Beau and Phoenix at one of their houses, because I'd heard them talking about it. And except for the night he took me to get a tattoo, I'd never seen him leave early before. From all appearances, Dax Miller should be lonely.

"Two hours." My eyes widened at what I blurted out. I counted my hours every night in my head like dollar bills. I couldn't just throw them away. And yet...

"Huh?" His voice was muffled.

"I'll give you two hours back if you come with me."

He set the oil can down and folded his arms across his chest. "I don't think you have two hours to bargain."

I didn't. If I had any sense in my brain, I'd be spray painting a building right now, but something about being with Dax made me forget all about the hours.

"I'm now sporting a tattoo, and I brought you a hamburger AND a drink the other day. Two hours."

"A fake tattoo. And you drank half of it."

"Not my problem."

I heard a huff of laughter before he stood to look at me, his hands resting on his hips. "Five."

I scoffed. "It will only take one hour to play the game."

"Four."

"Two, final offer. If you don't accept, I'll make your life miserable in this place."

He glanced up at his clock made from old boat propellers. "How so?"

"Say goodbye to all your tools neatly in place on your walls, that's for sure."

Still he didn't move, so I tried again.

"My songs all over your playlist."

A hint of a smile appeared just then. "You've already done that, and I've erased them all."

"I heard Bon Jovi earlier."

"Must have missed one." His soft voice caused a hitch in my breath. I forced myself to focus on my task of forcing Dax to have fun.

"Just come. Are you afraid you're going to have fun?"

He sighed, dusting his hands off on his pants. "Fine. Two hours, and if I do have fun, you're going to be in big trouble."

I held back my squeal and shot Cat a text, telling her I'd meet her there.

Surprisingly, Dax didn't make us wait to leave. He jumped down from the boat, and within minutes, the lights were off and the garage was closed. After a quick stop at the duplex to change clothes, we were headed south to the public beach.

It felt like we were skipping out on something, playing hooky even though we were leaving well past Dax's closing hours. I had hardly spent any time on the beach, and my body craved the sun—as did Dax's.

"Those legs are disturbingly white for an island boy," I said, eyeing him.

"I will turn this cart around, Books."

The vision of Dax wearing green-and-gray striped board shorts and flip-flops along with his white tank top gave him such a boyish charm it was hard to look away. It lightened something dark and became so appealing it had my face heating.

Families and sandcastles lined the beach when we pulled into the parking lot on the south side of the island. There were kids flying kites in the breeze, and the smell of cotton candy and hot dogs coming from somewhere made my mouth water. The breeze lifted my curls, and I immediately reached into the pocket of my shorts and pulled out the hair tie I always had there. My hair was almost tied in a top knot when I looked to Dax, startled to find him watching me before his eyes flicked away. He looked out toward the volleyball courts, a look of trepidation crossing his face.

I spotted Jane and Cat and Holland, along with several other friends, and began walking toward the court.

Dax fell behind me a few paces, looking slightly ill at ease as we grew closer.

"Come on," I said, lightly gripping his arm. "These are all your friends, too. They'll be excited you're here."

"Thanks, Mom."

I gave him a light push. "It's true."

"Because of my sparkling personality?"

"I mean, I don't like you, but that doesn't mean everyone else feels the same."

His reply was cut short when we were spotted by Beau and Phoenix, who immediately beelined toward us.

"Holy crap. Is that Dax Miller?" Beau's loud, friendly voice caused a smile to break out across my face while Dax's flushed with color.

"This is now worth five hours," Dax whispered.

I tried to tug my facial expression into something that wasn't a smile. All I wanted to do was grin at this moment, and I wasn't sure why.

Beau punched Dax lightly in the shoulder and looked at me, an awed expression on his face. "How'd you get him to leave the shop?"

"I threatened to key his golf cart," I said.

Beau nodded approvingly. "Threats and blackmail. I like it." Suddenly, his gaze locked on to my bare arm.

"Is that a tattoo?" His excitement quickly drew a crowd, and soon everyone was admiring my bookish beauty.

"Is that real?" Jane asked, glancing between me and Dax curiously.

"Ten bucks it's a fake," Cat stated, wearing one of our old volleyball team shirts tied in a knot a the waist.

"I don't know. She's been hanging out with Miller for a while now," Beau remarked. Suspicion laced his voice as he held Dax's gaze.

"You've got to pick better friends, Ivy," Phoenix stated, still looking as dapper as possible in jeans and a t-shirt—which must be his casual outfit. Everyone, including Dax, laughed.

Dax made a point to not be on my team. When we met across the net from each other, he leaned in closer.

"Five hours for whoever wins," he said.

I smiled. "Deal."

He wasn't the loudest or the fastest, or even someone who really looked like he knew what he was doing, but Dax Miller had the body of an athlete. Watching him try to hide how his face would light up after scoring a point or saving a ball was the icing on the cake for me.

We faced off at the net, where he hit it over and into a blind spot where my team, aka me, didn't get to it. Apparently, when one sits at a desk most of the day, one's vertical does not continue to gain height.

Dax raised his hands out like he scored points all the time. Newsflash: he didn't. "Weren't you on the volleyball team, Books?"

"That was a mercy point," I insisted, adjusting my sunglasses.

He laughed and waited for the next serve. It took a couple rounds, but I finally got my chance for revenge. Willing my legs to jump like they did ten years ago, I approached the ball Cat had set perfectly in my direction. Dax squared up opposite me, ready to block. My arms swung back, forward, and then connected with the ball at that perfect angle that felt amazing leaving my hand. The ball torpedoed down, humming past the hands Dax threw up in his attempt to block before burying itself in the sand behind him.

A beautiful kill.

I locked eyes with Dax and gave a little bow. Amusement lined his features, while he shook his head. On and on, we played like that. Even while the game and chatter played out around us, he was all I saw. I held a complete conversation with Holland, laughed at jokes I didn't actually hear, and gave the impression of a twenty-something-year-old woman hanging out with friends, but my mind was otherwise engaged. I knew when he felt out of place, because he'd cross his arms in front of his chest. I could tell when he forgot about feeling out of place, because he'd be laughing and high-fiving Beau and Phoenix. I knew, at any given moment, exactly where he was and who he was talking to.

I had no regrets on the hours spent to get us here.

Though he was careful to keep it hidden, I felt his eyes on me as well.

My team won, winning me back the hours I gave up to bring Dax here.

So, all in all, it was a wash.

Eventually, we ended up down by the water, standing in a cluster, some wading in to their ankles or knees. Beau and his older brother, Tristan, and a few of the other guys began regaling us with stories from the old days. Naturally, Dax's name came up in ways that got us all, including Dax, laughing. I wasn't sure why watching him joke and interact with our friends brought a burning sense of accomplishment to my chest, but it did.

There was something different about us that I couldn't put my finger on while we were there. But now, as we said goodnight and climbed into his golf cart, I realized what it was. There was an awareness between us that hadn't been there before. We went together. We left together. And all the time in between had been filled with covert glances, knowing smiles, and inside jokes. When it was time to go, Dax looked at me to see if I was ready. It felt intimate in the most casual of ways.

And something very much like...friends.

FOR THE RECORD, I wasn't lying in bed waiting for the goodnight knock. Since arriving home, I had given myself a pep talk, promising myself that I was going to stop getting distracted by Dax. I had a job to do, and I intended to do it. There was only pain in my future if I allowed myself to get attached to him. I didn't live here, and I didn't ever plan to.

I just happened to still be awake when he knocked. The end. When my phone lit up with a message a moment later, I only answered because there were definitely three distinct taps in that song, and he might be getting murdered. It was my neighborly duty.

DAX
Any guesses?

ME
Summer Girls by LFO?

DAX
I had to look that up. You're so embarrassing.

ME
Baby Got Back?

DAX
Nope. I think we're done for the night.

ME
White and Nerdy? By Weird Al?

DAX
You're definitely getting closer.

CHAPTER 18

Biology Class
Day 28

"Are you doing anything this weekend?" I asked Dax as the class sat waiting for the exciting documentary on genetics to load.
"That depends. Are you asking me out?"
I reared back. "No."
"Oh. Then I'm not doing anything."
I pushed his laughing body away from mine.

"IF I LICKED my finger and rubbed it against your tattoo, would it smudge?" Cat asked me as she and Jane sat in a corner booth the next day at the cafe. She watched me, her blonde ponytail swishing back and forth, as she waited for her opportunity to pounce.

I scoffed. "Of course not." I motioned toward her food. "Your pancakes are hot. You'd better stuff your face and stop asking questions."

She threw a sugar packet at me. "I gave blood with you once in high school, and there is no way you would willingly hand your arm over to a guy with a needle."

"Fess up," Jane said, leaning forward, the colors on her blue dress making her bright eyes pop. "We'll get it out of you eventually."

I blew out a sigh and glanced in every direction before leaning closer to my old friends.

"Okay, fine. It's fake."

"Obviously," Cat said, grabbing my arm and pulling me down into their booth. "The breakfast rush is over. You can sit for a minute, right?"

I glanced around and caught Jean's eye, motioning to the table and silently pleading with her to tell me I had to get back to work. But my horrible manager only smiled and gave me a thumbs up.

Resigned to my fate, I fortified myself with a bite of Cat's white-chocolate-macadamia-nut pancakes and told them about the tattoo, downplaying everything—for their sake and mine. Dax was a flirt and a tease. I had known that about him already, but nothing mattered when he was such a closed book, which was another thought I had while staring at my ceiling late into the night. I did think of him as a friend, but I really didn't know him any better now than I had back in high school. And that thought was actually quite depressing.

"Dax showed up to volleyball yesterday. He has NEVER played with us before. And the other night—apparently the night of the tattoo—his shop was closed up early. Lights off." Cat folded her arms triumphantly. "You like him. And by all accounts, he likes you right back. He likes the crap out of you."

"I'm sorry, are we back in high school?" I deflected, distracting them from my heated cheeks. "Do we have Spanish class after lunch? Do you need my notes?"

Jane laughed, but Cat brushed my comments aside, proving that my childhood friend knew me well. "What are you going to do about this?"

I pressed on a smile. "I'm only here for three more weeks.

I'm going to do my hours and go back to Tennessee. I can't stay. So I can't like him. The end."

"I don't think it works like that," Jane said softly, her brown hair curled at the edges.

Thankfully, we were spared an answer when a group of tourists walked into the cafe, and Jean was nowhere in sight.

The rest of the morning passed uneventfully. A few of the regulars commented on my tattoo. I had spent twenty minutes after my shower this morning scrubbing the remains off with coconut oil and pressing a new one on in its place. It would be a thousand times worse if people found out it was a stick on, but ultimately, I was surprised at how much my tattoo didn't affect anyone. Some made me lift my sleeve to show them the whole thing, some glanced away from it quickly, and some seemed curious only because it was something new about me. With the exception of Larry, who said I'd been hanging out with the mechanic for too long, nobody really seemed to care.

I felt the shift in the air the second Dax walked in. I knew it was him before I turned around to look. He sat in his usual booth along the front side of the restaurant and chatted easily with Jean as she walked by. By now, everyone at the cafe knew that Dax was *my* customer, no matter where he chose to sit. I usually made him wait a few minutes, but it seemed like each day those minutes got less and less. When I couldn't stand it any longer, I met him at his table with the coffee pot in my hands.

"It almost seems like you can't get enough of me," I said, filling his mug.

"The mediocre coffee here is spectacular."

A heated flush rose up the side of my neck. There was nothing special in the words, but his brown eyes were locked onto mine and his tone was warm and playful. Suddenly I felt as light as air.

"Ivy."

I turned when an intrusive voice came from behind me.

My dad stood a few steps from the door, looking like he'd come straight from a meeting. He wore gray trousers and a tie, with a white shirt rolled up at his forearms. He didn't give Dax a glance, only focused his steely gaze on me.

"I need to talk to you."

"I'm working."

He motioned around the nearly empty cafe. "Jean won't mind. I think you can spare a few minutes for your dad."

I hesitated, my teeth skimming my bottom lip. I'd been avoiding his phone calls since he showed up at my house after the Lucas incident. But he couldn't stay here. The last thing this cafe needed was Dax poking the bear. And by the look on Dax's face, he was itching to do it.

"I'll be outside." With a scathing glance at Dax, he turned and strode out the door.

I looked back to Dax, struggling to find words to fill the silence. Then I remembered I was a waitress.

"What would you like?"

"You don't have to go out there."

"I have to talk to him."

"Why?"

"Because he's…relentless. He'll be back in five minutes. It's easier to just go and get it over with."

I began making my way toward the door to do exactly that when my clothes caught on something. Glancing down, Dax's fingers gripped my apron.

"Hey," he said, pulling me toward him, his voice a low rumble.

"What?" I asked, a little breathless.

"You're okay to be here."

"What?"

He motioned toward the window. "You don't have to be

perfect to exist on this island. No matter what he says. You can mess up and still be here."

"It's not that simple. My dad—"

"It *is* that simple. Your dad will get over it."

I huffed out a laugh. "You don't know him. He doesn't *get over* things."

"That's not your problem then."

Drawing in a breath, I broke eye contact with him for a moment to gain my bearings. "I did screw up, though. And I think it really did mess with his campaign."

He shook his head. "It doesn't matter."

I gaped at him. "How?"

"Because your dad isn't part of this equation, Dr. Brooks. I am. And you could crash into my building ten more times and you'd still be okay."

Time stood still at that moment. The chatter and the clank of silverware went on all around me, dulled to a white noise. It was just him and me and the feel of his hand holding my apron. I pursed my lips and glanced away from the sweet intensity of his gaze. A girl could forget about a lot of things with a gaze like that. My eyes stung and I fought to regain control.

"Did you call me doctor?"

Though I could tell it pained him in this moment, he bit back a smile. "That's what you got out of all that?"

"I'll remember it forever."

"Not the real kind of doctor."

I went on like I hadn't heard him. "And ten more times? That's a lot of community service."

He was shaking his head at me while I spouted nonsense. Almost like he knew exactly what I was trying to do. But we needed a distraction. Dax Miller wasn't supposed to be sweet. I had planned on him giving me a hard time. I had planned on him being sarcastic. A closed book? Certainly. And he was all of those things. But charming? Sweet? A tamed rebel with a soft side?

I had to tread carefully or else I would be done for.

"So go talk to him if you need to. But don't take his crap. And don't let him make you feel guilty for taking up space in this world."

I tore my eyes from his and glanced to where my dad stood impatiently watching from the window. He tapped his watch.

I turned back to Dax. "I've got to go."

He still clung to my apron. He glanced toward my dad and then back to me.

"If you need to do something to stick it to your dad...I'm available."

A thrill rose gently up my spine at the ideas that grew from his suggestion. "Available? How?"

He shrugged. "I mean, if the idea of us being together is the worst thing for him..." he trailed off before looking at me. "Use your imagination." A reckless grin carved slowly across his face.

The smile, the wild look in his eyes, the untamed hair...High School Dax was back. I sucked in a breath, glancing around the cafe. We were past the lunch rush with only a few lingering tourists remaining. Nobody I knew.

Not that it mattered.

I wasn't doing...anything his eyes were strongly suggesting we do.

My hands found my hips. "I'm trying to keep the peace, not make things worse."

He shook his head. "Until you show your dad he can't control you, he'll never leave you alone."

The truth of his statement hit me with a sudden force, though I tried my best to deny it.

Folding my arms, I said, "So you're offering yourself up for this experiment. How noble."

He leaned back in his booth, temptation and vice oozing

from his lips. "Use me however you want. You and your mind are in complete control."

If I were being honest, my mind did wander for a split fraction of a moment. It was tiny. Microscopic. I took great comfort in the fact that nobody could have blamed me. He was leaning back in his seat in a white t-shirt with his arms resting on the table. Wild dark hair, curled slightly at the edges, fell in disordered array atop his head. His tattoos played peekaboo with me and suddenly I was somewhere else being pressed against a wall, bracketed by those arms.

He leaned forward, an amused smile touching his lips. "From the look on your face, your mind is kind of dirty."

I pushed against his shoulder, blushing hotly, effectively snapping out of wherever I had been.

"I think I'll be fine," I stated, stepping back from him as he let go of my apron.

"Suit yourself. The offer still stands."

I left him to his mediocre coffee while I slipped out the door to find my dad.

The sweltering Florida heat felt like walking into an oven. I wiped a bead of sweat off my brow as I picked my way toward where the senator was standing. When he saw me coming, he led me past another building on the more quiet side of the town square and slipped into an alleyway. I stopped a few feet away and squared my shoulders.

"Hi," I said.

He ran a hand through his hair but didn't make me wait long. "Ivy, I wanted to talk about the other night. Since you won't answer my phone calls, this was my only option. I was concerned when I went to find you and you weren't where you told me you'd be. When I discovered you were actually living next to—" He broke off, a tense chuckle seething out of his mouth. "As your father, who has warned you repeatedly against him, I was understandably upset. And you can't blame me."

My jaw clenched. "His name is Dax."

He smiled tightly. "I thought you'd be interested to know that the Foresters will not be donating money toward my campaign."

"If you were any kind of a father, you wouldn't want their money." I pinched my lips together, knowing I should walk away, but I forced myself to hold his gaze.

The senator went on like I had never spoken. "That makes two large donors who have pulled out since you arrived back on the island."

Don't let him make you feel guilty for taking up space in this world. You can mess up and still be here.

I wondered if Dax had learned that lesson himself.

My dad suddenly looked at something over my shoulder and smiled his big politician smile. "Hey, Bill! How are you?!"

I glanced back at the older man waving at my dad before moving onward. It was smart of him to come visit me in such a public place, where he was just a doting father visiting his daughter at work.

Well played, really.

"And do you know what the hardest part of it all is?" he went on. "I don't know what to believe. Lucas burst into our meeting with a cracked nose and blood dripping down his face, claiming that he was saying goodnight at your door, and all of a sudden, your overprotective boyfriend with the tattoos started going crazy and beating on him. He said he barely got away."

I shook my head, feeling sick at the lies. Feeling sick that he believed it. "He was pushing me too far, and Dax stepped in. End of story."

"You want to know the worst part? I stood up for you." He laughed bitterly. "I told them there was no way. She doesn't have a boyfriend, and she's staying at a friend's house. My daughter can be a lot of things, but she's not a liar. They looked at me like I had fallen for the oldest trick in the book—telling dear old dad you were staying at a friend's house and instead running straight to the boy I'd made pretty clear you were to stay away from." He swept his gaze down my arm, lingering on my tattoo. "And now it seems that boy is leaving his mark everywhere."

"I lied because I couldn't tell you the truth."

"I told you to stay away from him."

"I'm staying at his duplex to get away from you. So, it's really your fault if you think about it." I motioned toward the street where the man had just disappeared. "Maybe if you were the kind of person you act like in public, I'd have been happy to stay with you. But you're not. And you can't control me anymore." I started backing away. He stepped toward me, but I threw up my hands to ward him off. "I'm going back to work."

He might have had plenty left to say, but I didn't have to listen.

I turned the corner, out of the alleyway, striding toward the restaurant when the cafe door flew open and Dax stepped out into the sunlight. He was a few paces away from the door, before he noticed me.

My determined stride noticeably waned until my feet stopped all together. For a long moment, we stood there, staring.

Use me however you want.

My heart began pounding erratically. It felt like the beginning of a race, where all the runners were poised, ready for the gunshot. One of us had to move. I thought of my dad—siding with Lucas without even questioning me. Without even asking if I was okay. Blaming me for all his problems. My blood nearly boiled over. Yes. I wanted to make him mad. I wanted to scratch and claw and scream. As a child, I never had a voice, but right now, my veins were blazing hot.

I knew Dax wasn't going to make the first move. Even as he watched with a curious anticipation, he would let me lead where

I was comfortable, and for that, I was grateful. But I was tired of comfort. I didn't want to be careful anymore. I didn't want to be told what to do or what not to do. I wanted to feel alive. So I began closing the distance toward the one person who had a particular knack for making me feel everything.

He watched me coming, even braced himself for impact because I wasn't slowing. I didn't know if my dad would see this, I wasn't sure if I wanted him to, but Dax had given me an excuse and I was taking it.

Somewhere in my march toward him, I lost a bit of my nerve and instead of the brash, dominant kiss I'd envisioned, my hands stopped at his chest, and my lips stalled halfway to his mouth. With a trace of amusement lining his features, he slowly wrapped his arms around my waist, drawing me against him, moving us away from the windows of the cafe.

I raised myself up on my tiptoes, determined to finish what I started. Our lips were so close. The idea of it had seemed easier a moment ago, but now—

"Chicken," Dax goaded, his eyes sparkling.

My gaze narrowed, shooting him a warning look before I closed the distance.

Our lips came together gently at first—a series of sweet hellos in soft succession. Dax's hands stayed lightly at my waist, while mine remained tucked at his chest, sandwiched between the press of our bodies. A cry for more echoed inside me almost immediately, even while caution tinged the air. The heat from his chest seeped through my shirt and one of his hands glided up my arm before resting against my cheek. I shivered, wanting more, but I was determined to ground myself in some sort of reality. This moment didn't mean anything. It *couldn't* mean anything. And I needed him to know that.

I pulled back, blinking hard, my voice unsteady. "Just to be clear, this is about proving something to my dad. I'm leaving in a few weeks. And I don't like you."

A low breathy chuckle escaped his lips. The unfortunate kind that had me craving a life of beaches and babies and a warm Floridian sun.

"I don't like you either," he murmured, his left hand grazing my cheek to tuck a curl behind my ear. He glanced past my shoulder, his teeth sliding across his lower lip. "But we'd better put aside our differences, because your dad's about to get in his golf cart and he's looking this way."

"This was a bad idea," I whispered, unable to resist Dax pulling me closer.

"You started it," he said, a breath away.

"I did not—"

He was kissing me again. The soft, almost curious kiss we'd shared only moments ago was nowhere to be found. Dax's lips glided across mine in a way that curled my toes and had me arching toward him. His kiss was hot and smooth and controlled, the way he seemed to handle everything. I resisted my part as long as I could, but a girl could only hold back for so long before she breaks. And by the time Dax's hands skated up my sides, his thumbs brushing my rib cage, I had broken.

I broke so hard.

My lips parted against his, letting him in. And that was all it took.

He drew both of his arms tightly around my body, his lips never leaving mine. Then, hauling me against himself before lifting me off the ground, he turned us, setting me down gently before pressing me against the wall of the cafe. His hands took turns in my hair and on my neck before landing on my cheek. His lips melted into mine, stirring up emotions that definitely didn't make this *seem* like a bad idea. My hands roamed greedily up his arms, skimming past the tattoos on his shoulder before finding their place buried in the soft hair at the nape of his neck. As if on fire, his lips moved from my mouth to travel across my jawline and back again, not missing an inch.

In the back of my mind, I tried to remember where we were. Outside the cafe, in full view of the public. In full view of *my dad*. If he was even still around. Despite my insistence that this had all been for his benefit, I suddenly hoped he wasn't here. I hoped the entire town had decided to stay home on this otherwise unremarkable Friday afternoon. I didn't want to share this moment. I wanted it all to myself.

His lips were still on mine, but already I was mourning the loss of his kiss. The kind of kiss that would devastate me for a lifetime.

There had been so much talk leading up to this moment–the teasing, the goading, dancing around the heart of it all. But talk was just that. Talk. In this moment, our lips had painted us both liars. Big talkers. Hiding what we wanted most.

At least…hiding what I wanted most.

CHAPTER 19

Biology Class
Day 31

"I stepped in chicken poop in the hallway on my way here. I'm guessing I have you to thank for that," I said to Dax as I dropped into my seat next to him.

Dax's brow furrowed while he pretended to think. "It does seem like there's been a crazy amount of chickens around here lately."

"Where do you even get chickens?" The high school was on the mainland, but it wasn't like we were being overrun by farms this close to the ocean.

He pointed to himself. "Why do you assume it was me?"

I leveled him with a look that only made him laugh and turn away.

The chickens had arrived in the hallways just moments before the bell rang for lunch. Nobody saw them show up or knew how it happened; suddenly they were just there—six chickens and one angry rooster. The commotion raised afterward between teacher, student, and bird was one for the books. Watching the teachers tripping over themselves in the mad, chaotic fray as they scrambled to catch all of them would probably go down as one of my greatest memories of high school.

Not that I would ever tell Dax that.

T-minus 19 days to exit
Dax hours remaining: 124

THE SIGN above the door to Sunset Repairs said 'Closed', though I didn't pay it any mind. The doorknob turned easily enough, and I stepped inside. He was here. I knew he was. And I wasn't sure why it annoyed me so much. Actually, I knew exactly why.

The Fourth of July on Sunset Harbor was the stuff of American dreams. The entire day was full of activities from a pancake breakfast on the square, the parade, swimming and games on the beach, food trucks, and finally ending the night with dancing and fireworks. Holidays didn't get any better than this, and Dax wanted to skip out to work on some lawnmowers? If he wouldn't hire somebody to help him in his shop, I was going to do it for him.

I had spent the morning trying not to search for Dax while constantly scanning the crowds. At the town pancake breakfast, to give myself something to do, I had attempted to help Jane, who was in charge of the entire event, but she had swatted me away to eat and enjoy myself. Our island's own golf star, Walker Collins, served me pancakes along with Gemma, a pretty brunette I went to junior high with. Given her overall gorgeousness and the fact that I'd seen her with Beau at the cafe together recently, my suspicion meter was officially pinging.

To my surprise, Dax *had* eventually shown up at the pancake breakfast. Cat, Holland, and I had just sat down with our food, and within minutes, Dax and Phoenix slid into the seats next to us with plates full of pancakes dripping with syrup.

Though I tried to keep my composure, Dax's leg pressed against mine under the table and I struggled to think of words.

"So you'll leave your shop for pancakes?" I asked him quietly while the rest of the group began talking smack about the epic volleyball game scheduled later.

Dax took a drink of coffee steaming out of a red Solo cup. "I've actually been leaving my shop a lot more these days. And my pile of work keeps growing."

"Maybe you should hire some help."

"I have a girl working at my place, but she's a big distraction, and she's not that great with boats or tools."

I have a girl.

Nope. Nope. Nope.

I tamped down the butterflies begging for release and instead turned back to my triple stack of carbs and syrup.

That was the last time I had seen him all day.

All day.

Our kiss from a few days earlier had become a huge elephant in the room we didn't talk about. Even with all the jokes leading up to it, any attempt to make light of it after fell flat.

The sun had set, lighting the sky with a delicious golden hue. Fireworks would be starting soon. Dax had missed the parade, the beach games, swimming, food trucks, volleyball, and dinner. He had an island full of good friends hanging out on a major holiday, and he chose to hide himself away. Here I was, thinking he had made some good social progress the past week. I wasn't sure what he was so afraid of with his friends. There seemed to be a never-ending stream of people coming in and out, itching to talk with him.

Like me.

No, I was different, I told myself as I burst into his garage, ready to drag him to the beach. I wasn't doing it because I *liked* him.

I was doing it because...because he needed to appreciate what he had on this island.

There was no light on overhead, though I could have sworn I heard music. The familiar smell of grass clippings and motor oil greeted my nose as I used the flashlight on my phone to pick my way through the room littered with small motors. I kept the shop lights off because wherever Dax was, I wanted to find him first.

Again—and I can't emphasize this enough—not in a creepy kind of way.

In a *I will force him to have fun and remember what it's like to not be working all the time* kind of way.

I squinted out the back door window into the darkness, but other than the yellow glow of a light from the marina that illuminated the boats sitting in the water, I saw nothing. No indication that Dax was out there. The music seemed a little louder from where I was standing. I opened the three other doors leading to the storage closet, mechanical room, and the bathroom (again, not a stalker), and they were both pitch black inside.

I was about to head to the duplex to check for him there when the clank of a tool hitting the concrete sounded through the air and stopped me in my tracks.

He was here.

There was only one room I hadn't checked. I never thought to check because it was always locked. Once, when I had asked him about the mysterious third garage door with an entrance that required a code, he had only shrugged and told me it was storage.

Storage, my butt.

I stopped at the door, usually closed with a keypad on the outside, but today, someone had been careless, and the latch hadn't closed completely. My hands gripped the doorknob but stalled before opening. Unless he had randomly decided the Fourth of July was a great time to organize the storage room, Dax clearly didn't want anybody to know about whatever was in this room. What if he got mad? What if he pushed me away? What if this was where he buried his dead bodies? I really couldn't see Dax getting angry, but he kept so many doors closed, metaphorically and physically speaking, that I wasn't sure what would happen if I opened one and invited myself in.

Since the court sentencing, much of our relationship on the outside hadn't changed—with the exception of the kiss that will forever haunt my dreams. He still teased me. He still made me sweep his shop and clean his bathroom and answer his phones. But the fridge was always stocked with Coke, and my favorite bag of chips was always on the counter. Most nights, I would go home knowing I'd made it to a certain page in the Lego guidebook, but the next day, I'd be ten pages ahead, though Dax continued to deny it. And most importantly, he kept my Bon Jovi song on his playlist.

I swallowed. Of course, this could also be a secret weight room, and he's in there shirtless, pumping iron.

With sweat dripping down his neck and—

STOP it, Brooks.

Without further ado, I pushed open the door and stepped inside, the intro of the song "Spirit in the Sky" by Norman Greenbaum greeting me as I did so. When my eyes adjusted to the light, I dropped my purse on the ground with a thud. At the sound of the clatter, Dax, who was indeed standing shirtless with his back to me and holding a jug of oil, turned in surprise.

Surprise mixed with…horror? Shock? Trepidation?

With good reason because behind Dax, sprawled out in his secret garage with a secret code, on an island where it's illegal to drive or have in your possession anything but a golf cart, sat a shiny, burnt-orange 1969 Chevy Chevelle.

CHAPTER 20

Biology Class
Day 34

"Why'd you get a car tattoo?" I asked Dax, my eyes shamelessly roaming over his arms. Over the weekend, he had added an image of a sun and palm tree behind the car.

"Why not?"

"We live on an island with no cars. Shouldn't you have a boat on your arm or something?"

He shook his head. "No imagination, Books. This way, I bring the car to the island."

I GAPED AT THE SCENE, unable to take my gaze off of Da— his car.

He folded his arms across his chest, his eyes glinting steel.

"Five hours if you help me with this car, Books. Ten if you can shut up about it."

I couldn't help my smile any more than he could help the look of warning clouding his face. Taking a few steps into the room, I ran my fingers across the smooth orange paint.

"Ten hours? I don't know. For that price, it might be pretty hard to keep things quiet. You know, with all the gossip at the cafe." I turned to face him. "It's just hard to not say things sometimes, in the heat of the moment…"

"Fifteen hours."

I went on like I hadn't heard him, wandering to the front of the car, which was raised up on a lift. With my hand on the open hood, I peered down at all the pipes, like I had some idea what I was looking at.

"Off the island, fine. I mean, you're a car guy." I motion to his tattoo. "You're not hiding that. I'm sure people assume you own a car and that it's parked nicely in the garage—the garage on the mainland, that is."

I spared him a glance and was delighted at the smile softening his lips. For a moment, I was struck again by how utterly dangerous and alluring he could be. With his dark hair long and messy up top, and his jeans slung low across his hips, and the whole…no shirt thing.

Clearing my throat, I went on, "I mean, this is a 1969 Chevy Chevelle. I don't know how I could keep that a secret for only fifteen hours."

I thought I would impress him with my car knowledge, but instead his gaze narrowed, and he began walking toward me. I refused to back down from my stance of annoying him, even though my heart lurched at his growing proximity.

"That's interesting, Books. I don't remember you being much of a car girl. Unless you looked up my tattoo?"

A warm flush crawled up my neck. He took another step closer, and the fireworks this town had prepped for the party tonight had nothing on the sparks erupting inside of me.

"Doing some light internet stalking?" he asked.

I scoffed, taking a step back, my hand sweeping toward the car. "This is a classic. Everyone knows it."

"They don't. Unless they're a car guy." He folded his arms across his chest and gave me a knowing look.

"Or a car girl," I corrected.

"Or a car girl," he conceded. "Which you are not."

Okay, fine. Hand me a pair of binoculars and call me a peeping tom. So I looked it up on the internet. Big deal.

"Twenty-five hours or I'll tell the whole town what I know." The words came out bold, but the smile would not retract from my face. After a really crappy beginning to my summer, it felt good to finally have something on Dax. He had been fooling this town for so long, and look at the rule breaker now.

"Fifteen hours and I won't tell everyone you're now an accomplice."

I gasped while he laughed, husky and deep, his words bringing up memories of another night. And here we were again, ten years later, all grown up and—

FOCUS, IVY.

"Twenty hours. Or I'll tell Beau I'm a hostage, and you locked me inside against my will."

"Against your will?" His words mocked me at the same time the dark pools in his eyes spiked my heart rate. "He'll never believe that."

I blinked, glancing at his lips before yanking them away. Taking a step away from him, I fought to bring us back to where I had the advantage.

"Twenty hours. I won't tell anyone. And I'll help you for a while."

He looked amused at this statement. "What are you going to help me with?"

I looked around. I didn't have any ideas, but I knew I didn't want to go yet. The lure of the beach now felt lackluster compared to the spark flaring in his eyes.

"I can hand you tools," I began, ticking things off with my fingers. "I can get your playlist up to date. I can keep you hydrated."

Leaning back against the counter with his ankles crossed, he broke in. "Keep me hydrated? Can you explain what you mean by that?"

But he was also a master at getting reactions. He used to thrive on that, so if I was going to stick around, I needed to get a grip. He teased me to get under my skin, not for any other reason.

"I can grab you a Coke."

"The Coke that I brought here?"

"Yeah. And I'll grab it for you."

"What if I get thirsty for something else?"

My eyes flew to where he stood watching me with a playful expression.

"Stop," I warned.

He laughed softly before walking to the door. "I meant a lemonade or a Dr. Pepper. What did you think I meant?"

He left the room, and I waited with bated breath. Dax didn't lock me inside with an evil laugh, threatening to call Beau and have me framed, so I guess I should be grateful. But he was going to tell me no and kick me out. I knew it. He liked being alone. He didn't seem to need anybody, and I couldn't figure out why that thought bothered me. To my surprise, he returned to the secret garage, this time carrying two cans of Coke and a bag of Sun Chips. He shut the door, tossed the chips on the counter, and handed me one of the cans.

"I was supposed to get that," I said, popping the top, ridiculously excited he came back.

"I still haven't decided if what you can offer me is worth twenty hours or not, but I'm interested in playing this out. I've got some work to do underneath the car, and I could use an extra pair of hands."

My first thought went to Jane and Cat and our golf cart fantasies we had about Dax while eating lunch at the cafe. I took a sip of Coke to give my mouth something to do instead of smiling.

Dax grabbed something behind the door. He turned and held out the blue fabric of what looked like a pair of coveralls.

"Put these on."

I set my drink on the workbench and flung out the worn material several times. I wasn't sure how long it had been sitting in this shop, but I was going to do my best to rid the garment of any critters that might have crawled inside and made a home.

"Whose is this?" I asked, stepping one leg inside.

Dax rummaged through a few tools on the workbench. "Mine."

My motion of getting dressed skittered to a stop as his words sunk in, giving meaning and an intimacy to a crumpled pair of work coveralls.

"Do you ever wear them?"

Dax set a handful of tools on the counter. "Sometimes."

I zipped up the coveralls over my jean shorts and tank top. "Twenty hours," I told him again.

He looked me up and down, smiling at whatever he saw, and to my disappointment, he pulled a black shirt over his abs before grabbing a small box of tools he'd been adding to while I had changed. He nodded toward two rollers he had set out side by side and motioned me toward one. "We'll see."

The challenging look he gave me made me forget myself and crawl awkwardly onto the roller—or at least, give it my best attempt. The roller was extremely unforgiving for a newbie and kept sliding whenever I tried to heave my lower half on. Twice I landed on my butt while it slid out from underneath me. Dax bit back a laugh as he moved his foot to hold the roller steady without saying a word.

"I can do it by myself, it's just hard to maneuver in these clothes," I said, adjusting my position on the hard plastic.

"I have no doubt."

He slid onto his roller with the ease of a ninja warrior and scooted it next to mine. "Pop quiz. What's this thing you're lying on called?"

I scoffed. "That's too easy. Give me another one."

A smile broke out across his face, giving him such a boyish charm that I had to suck in a breath to quell the butterflies taking flight in my stomach. "I'd love to hear your answer."

"It's a…roller…scooter. At least, that's what my friends and I always call it."

He laughed, placing the small box of tools gently onto my stomach. "Down to nineteen hours now, Books."

He rolled under the car before I could stop him. I carefully followed suit, moving backward at a snail's pace until I reached his side.

"Hey! My answers don't change the hours. We agreed on twenty."

"No, we didn't. And your answers very much reflect your hours. You offered to help me, and I need somebody who knows what they're doing." He stopped rolling and looked at me. "Unless, of course…you don't."

Though it was dark underneath the car, it was light enough to see the humor lacing his eyes.

"Of course I do."

"Great. Now move your *roller scooter* over here. I've got a driveline for the car here, and I need you to help me hold it steady while I bolt it in."

"Hold the driveline," I repeated. "Obviously that's what we're going to do." I inched my way closer to him, aware of his low breath of laughter, but soon, all thoughts fled as he grabbed one side of the long pipe from the ground behind us, and raised it up.

"Hold it steady for me," he mumbled. I did as he asked while staring shamelessly at the man lying next to me. I had been cursing the appearance of his shirt only moments ago, but now it stretched taut across his body, giving peeks of skin and tattoos as he leaned and reached and deftly moved his hands, aligning the driveline just right.

"Pop quiz, Books. If I were to ask you for a socket wrench, what would you give me?"

I carefully turned the container of tools my way and peered inside. It was dark under the car, and though I could feel him watching me, seeing the tools was difficult. Good thing a socket wrench was one of the few tools I actually knew. I locked my fingers around the heavy metal wrench and passed it over to him.

"Twenty hours," I said proudly.

I felt his smile more than I saw it but to my confusion, he handed it back to me.

"What about a 9/16ths socket wrench?"

I peered back into the box of tools and debated. There were several sizes inside. I took a guess and handed it over.

When he took the wrench without a fuss, I declared my victory. "Twenty-one hours."

The veins in his arms bulged as he tightened the bolt. I swallowed, trying to think of something to push my thoughts in another direction. I wasn't going to be manipulated by manly arms and hands that could bolt drivelines.

"Phillips screwdriver."

Again, I breathed a sigh as I fished it out awkwardly and handed it to him with a confidence I was beginning to feel. "Twenty-two hours. You act like fixing cars is hard."

I was rewarded with a grin, but the punk didn't do anything with the screwdriver but place it on his stomach.

"Vise grip." He held out his hand expectantly.

"You can't just make up names."

He laughed. "I'm not."

After a long moment of rummaging, I confidently handed him a random tool I didn't know, praying I was right.

"And we're back. Twenty-one hours." He leaned over and

placed the tool back in the box on my stomach. "Let's see…I'm going to need a punch next."

"I thought you needed a *vise grip*." I held up my fingers in quotations.

"Just wanted to mess with you. Now I need a punch."

"I can do that."

Before I could try a fumbled attempt at boxing, his left arm shot out, pinning my hand to my side.

"You're a violent little thing. Does your dad know this about you?"

Our faces were so close. For a long moment, we stared at each other until I sucked in a breath and turned my face away. "There's no such thing as a punch."

"Twenty hours." He leaned into my space, tilting the toolbox on my stomach to see better while giving my nose a shot of his cologne. I didn't know what it was called, but I had to force my eyes not to roll to the back of my head in pleasure. He found what he was searching for and held up a small, smooth tool. "This is a punch." He dropped it back into the box. He didn't even need it.

"You're such a punk."

"Punk? What year is it?"

"According to your playlist? 1970."

He busied himself adding and tightening more bolts above our heads.

"Okay, if this is how we're playing it, let's see if you can answer a few of *my* work questions." I became distracted in attempting to think of something while the muscles on Dax's forearms strained to twist a bolt.

"Tick-tock," Dax mumbled before he moved his roller closer to me. His leg pressed against mine before he maneuvered himself out from under the car, only to roll back under again, this time on my other side. Before I could think or blink, his hand was on my thigh, rolling me closer to his side in a way that left me a mess of flutters, tingles, and a pounding heartbeat.

"Now I'm going to do the same thing with this end," he explained, as if he hadn't just grabbed my leg and destroyed me. He aligned the other side of the five-foot pipe just right and asked me for the 9/16ths socket wrench once more.

I handed it to him, to which he said proudly, "Look at how much you're learning."

"Alright, smart guy, 9/16ths is what point of an inch?"

"Huh?"

I smiled. "What is 9/16ths in decimal form?"

"Why would anybody know that?"

"You can't figure it out?"

"Can you?"

".5625." I smiled at him. "Twenty-one hours."

He blinked at me before a smile tugged at his lips. "I'll give that to you. That was pretty hot."

His words rumbled low in my ear, and my cheeks burned at his compliment. I had to look away.

"Okay," he said, "hand me the punch and a hammer while I pound this into place."

This was why he invited me here. He did actually need an extra pair of hands. Glad to know my coveralls weren't going to waste.

His coveralls.

I pushed that thought aside while I very capably reached into the box, pulled out the tools, and held them out to him.

"Twenty-two hours," I said proudly.

"I'll even let you take one for that. I'm so proud."

We settled into a routine. I now knew every tool he needed, so he couldn't trick me. Instead, Dax quizzed me on car knowledge. Questions like, what is a driveline? What does the transmission actually do? And I quizzed him on mathematics, ranging from easy to theories. Between his questions and mine, we each got very few right, but we worked seamlessly for the next twenty minutes. Much to the sinking in my stomach, I didn't delight in the questions as much as the accidental touches. My skin burned where his leg pressed against mine. My heart pounded like I'd run a marathon, but my feet hadn't touched the ground.

Finally, we settled on a score of eighteen and a half hours, thanks to a two-part math question Dax actually knew one answer to.

The popping sound of fireworks nearby greeted us as we crawled out from under the car. Dax slid out easily. I enjoyed a more *scoot-awkwardly-and-bang-my-head-on-the-bottom-of-the-car* kind of approach.

"Easy there, Caroline," he said, grabbing my roller and helping me slide out without further injury.

"Hey! It's Ivy. Or even Books, okay? Not Caroline."

"Why? That's your name, isn't it?"

"Yes, but it was my dad's mom, and she wasn't a very nice person."

"You kept smacking me underneath the car. Maybe your name is trying to tell you something."

At my best leveling gaze, he only laughed and began putting his tools away while I peeled off the coveralls.

"What do you have the car for anyway? You don't plan on leaving the island, right?"

"I plan on driving this thing all up and down the coast one day. It'll stay in the garage on the mainland when I'm finished. But I bought it all in parts, and I had to have somewhere to put it together."

"You ferried it over in parts?"

The amount of knowledge Dax had about cars astounded me. To have the skills to put together his own car was something not many could boast. And he wasn't even boasting about it. It seemed so matter-of-fact to him.

"Not ferried. I drove my own boat so I could sneak the parts inside."

"The little old ladies next door didn't catch you?"

"Thankfully, I guess they're not looking too hard at what I'm carrying."

The booming pop of another round of fireworks went off. I hadn't meant to be gone this long. I had forgotten my original purpose in finding Dax, with the excitement of the car and being with him. I had intended to drag him to the beach and force him to be around his friends and have fun.

"We should go watch the fireworks."

He looked my way and almost started to say something before he hesitated.

"What?" I asked.

"I was going to offer to let you drive my golf cart to the beach to watch them, but then I remembered who I was talking to."

I ignored his teasing. "Come with me."

"Nah."

"Why?"

"By the time we get down there, the fireworks will be done."

"They usually go for a half an hour. They just started." He was wavering, I could tell, so I added one more log to the fire.

"I'll give you an hour."

He looked at me, arms folded, clearly in a debate with himself.

"Two hours, then. Final offer."

An exasperated look crossed his face. "Keep your hours, you annoying pest of a girl."

He yanked open the door and motioned me to follow him. "Let's go."

I squealed in excitement, bolting out of the room before Dax could change his mind and lock me inside. Once outside, Dax strode to a cupboard above the workbench and reached for a key inside before putting it in his pocket. At the back door, he plucked two thin, black hoodies off a coat rack.

"Let's go," he called.

"Where'd you park your golf cart?"

"That's not what we're driving."

Confused, intrigued, and more than a little attracted to Dax Miller, I didn't even ask questions as I followed him out the door.

CHAPTER 21

*Biology Class
Day 35*

"I have a question for you," I began, leaning closer to Dax while Mr. Gray wrote something on the white board.

"I'm all ears," Dax said.

I stumbled a bit at his interest but pressed on. "Why did the DNA strand go to therapy?"

"What will you give me if I know it?"

"I'll try not to curse at you in my head as much."

Dax looked over at me, his mouth open in mockery. "Cursing? I'm shocked at you, Books."

"Do you know it?"

"Because it had separation issues."

My eyes narrowed. "How did you know that?"

He tapped at his forehead.

"Did you read the chapters?"

He looked at me. "Do I look like I would read the chapters?"

Dax glanced back toward Mr. Gray, but I thought I detected the faintest spot of color on his cheek.

. . .

Dax handed me one of the hoodies as we picked our way down the cracked sidewalk leading to the marina behind his shop.

Without thinking, I pulled it up to my nose and sniffed. The smell of cinnamon and sweet cologne settled over me.

I wasn't sure how I was going to handle being drowned in the scent that left me suddenly craving an obnoxious mechanic, but it looked like I'd have to do my best.

We put on the sweatshirts at the same time we reached the entrance, our heads turning toward a voice in the darkness.

"Are you stepping out on me, Dax Miller?!" It was a shaky voice, almost hard to hear over the sound of the fireworks popping off at random. Two older women sat on a balcony at the retirement center, across the grass from Sunset Repairs. This must be the famous Virginia, who by all accounts had developed a healthy crush on Dax.

"Isn't it your bedtime, Virginia?" Dax called back.

"I'm waiting for you to come tuck me in."

A delighted smile crossed my face as Dax covered his forehead briefly with his hand and let out an embarrassed chuckle.

"Go ahead and tuck her in," I whispered. "I'll wait."

His brows raised. "Is that how you want to play? Fine by me."

"What?" I asked.

Before he could answer or clue me in, Virginia called out again. "Who *is* that girl?" Her voice crackled as she threw a hand over her brows like she was trying to block the sun even though it was pitch black outside.

To my surprise, Dax threw his arm around my shoulders, tugging me against his side. "Sorry, Virginia! This one's been chasing after me all summer, but you're still my number one!"

I stood stunned in both shock and pleasure as his arm settled over me. I knew I should fight it, or at least pretend to fight it, for my own dignity. But like a glutton for punishment, I leaned into him more, wrapping both arms around his waist. He fit perfectly against me.

"What's her name? She doesn't look like she knows how to take care of a man!"

"Her name is Caroline Brooks. And I've been teaching her how to take care of a man. Sorry you had to find out this way."

"Brooks?! The girl who crashed into your shop?"

"And my heart," Dax lied cheerfully, ignoring my jabs to his stomach.

"You can have him, Virginia!" I called out. "I'm just using him for his boat!"

She cackled a loud laugh before waving us on our way. "Don't come back without a kiss that would make me blush!"

"Will do!" Dax said, happily pulling me along as we strolled along the dock, the wood rocking gently below our feet.

Dax held my hand and motioned me into a white boat with a green stripe around the perimeter. It looked exactly like the kind of boat I would imagine Dax Miller to have–built for speed, but also the kind of boat where he could sit quietly and take in the world around him. His hand gently let mine go as he moved to sit at the steering wheel. I sat on the white plastic bench seat lining the back of the boat. He fired up the engine, and soon we were backing out of the marina.

Bright fireworks of red, white, and blue burst in the sky above as Dax turned us around and drove quietly out of the marina and away from the glowing lights of Sunset Harbor.

I rubbed at my shoulders as we picked up speed, wishing I had been wearing pants. My goosebumps doubled as Dax slowed the boat to a stop and cut the engine.

"This is as far as we go."

"Why?"

"Because the ocean is freaking scary at night."

I laughed. "That's so true. Nobody talks about that."

Looking around, I gathered my bearings. He hadn't taken us

too far from the marina, but the view of the fireworks and the lighthouse on the southern end of the island would be spectacular.

Dax stood up, dug underneath a seat, and pulled out a blanket. "I've only got one blanket." His gaze held a question.

My entire body warmed at the possibilities his unspoken question evoked. Even as I wondered why I was doing this to myself when I was leaving so soon, I patted the spot next to me. He settled in, both of us sliding down in our seats as far as we could go without falling off. Our legs sprawled out in front of us, and our heads leaned against the backrest, finding the perfect vantage point for fireworks.

He flung the blanket out over the top of both our bodies. The pop of the fireworks, the gentle motion of the water, and his arm pressed against mine lulled me into a contemplative haze.

I hadn't been back for many July Fourths since I'd left the island. My parents had always played a big part in the town breakfast, serving pancakes and bacon with friendly smiles. They drove around in a golf cart with a sign hanging from the roof that said 'Senator Brooks' on it, waving enthusiastically at the crowds. Clayton Brooks ate up the Fourth of July, which was why my best memories from the holiday were with my friends.

"Do you do this every year?" I asked, suddenly curious about his family and why he wasn't with them.

Dax paused before he answered, "My family used to. I haven't done this for about fifteen years or so."

"Really? What do you do instead?"

"Work."

I looked at him, surprised by how close our heads were. "What does your family do?"

"Not sure."

"Why'd you stop?"

He adjusted his position under the blanket, nudging me with his arm. "You're kind of nosy, you know that?"

"Just give me something. I thought we were frien—"

The sentence got lost on my tongue. My unspoken word hung in the air between us. A word that seemed to say so much and so little at the same time.

He turned his head toward me. "Say it, chicken," he whispered.

A firework blasted overhead as his words led a trail of fire down my spine. His leg pressed softly against mine. I swallowed, waiting for him to move it back over, but he didn't. I was sitting somewhere in the dark ocean with a guy who I realized I trusted completely to keep me safe. Were we friends? I wasn't sure if my heart would be racing as much right now if we weren't at least...friends.

"Friends, Dax Miller. Can *you* say it?"

Another flurry of colorful fireworks showed his grin, though he looked at the sky again. "We've always been friends, Caroline."

I let the name go because there was something about the soft, almost sultry way it sounded from his lips. It didn't feel like my grandmother's name. It also felt much different than his other favorite—Books.

"Even after the things I said to you after that night in my garage?"

"Even after that."

"I'm sorry about that, by the way." I could only whisper, remembering the words I'd said to him. What I had insinuated about him.

"You're alright." His voice was soft, a feather grazing my skin, easing years of regret.

My heart began pounding against my chest. It must be the fireworks above us that had me so enamored. It surely wasn't the way he tugged at his hat before bringing his arm down again, this time the backs of our fingers skimming against each other ever so slightly.

"You were right. So much of my life to that point had been about keeping my dad happy—or at least attempting to. I don't think it ever really worked."

He waited a beat, rubbing a hand over his face. "I wasn't right. You're not anything like your dad."

I played with the edge of the blanket. "I was, though. Maybe I still am. But I never realized it until you called me out on it."

I kept my gaze fixed firmly on the fireworks, but I could feel him watching me.

"You were actually the reason I went to therapy."

"What?" he asked with some alarm.

I laughed. "I didn't go because of you, but because of what you observed about me. I couldn't get it out of my head. But it was the best thing I did. I had always known my dad had two sides to him, but it was hard separating myself from what I've always known. I hadn't realized how much of my entire personality had been altered in an attempt to make him happy. And honestly, even now, all my choices…" I trailed off. "It's hard to see where I start and my dad ends."

"Do you like school? Teaching?" Dax asked.

"I guess I'll find out." The last ten years flashed through my head until I pushed it away. I didn't want to think about my dad right now or my hours that weren't dwindling fast enough but at the same time…too fast.

I sucked in a breath. "Why don't you come out here anymore?"

He shifted in his seat. I didn't expect him to answer, so I was surprised when he did.

"My family used to come out here when I was a kid, every Fourth of July. Me and Trent would go fishing, and we'd paddle board and eat my mom's fried chicken and potato salad and watch the fireworks."

"Why'd you stop?" I could feel the mood shifting as I asked the question.

"Do you remember my older brother? Mason?" Dax's words were soft, a breath of air I would have missed if I hadn't been paying attention.

I thought for a moment. I didn't remember an older brother. I only knew his younger brother, Trent, from the student council in high school. But a hazy memory of Dax flickered through my mind just then. We must have been five or six playing at the playground together. I had been hurt, and he had helped me. I had never thought about that boy being Dax. He had been a kid wearing a Spiderman shirt like every other little boy at the playground. That was long before he became the Dax Miller I knew in high school.

"Not really. How much older is he?"

"Five years. He took off when I was thirteen. My family hasn't seen him since."

There was a moment of quiet while I absorbed that information. My mouth opened and closed a few times before it settled on, "Why?"

Another long pause. His words had cost him something, the way he kept running his hand over his mouth, like he wished he could take them all back.

"He was fighting a lot with my parents, about his future, stuff like that. That's what I remember, anyway. One day, he just packed up and left."

"You don't know why?"

He shook his head. "He left a note for my parents so we wouldn't think he was kidnapped or something. Said he was going to join the Peace Corps and to not contact him. He wanted to live his own life and didn't need us to do it for him. One day, we were building our Lego car together, and he was asking me about girls, and the next thing I know, his room was packed up and he was gone."

I sat stunned, my mind trying to make sense of a person's thought process in doing that to a family. To a brother.

"Do people know?" Though my dad had referenced it the night Dax punched Lucas, I hadn't heard a word before that. For a small island, that should have been big town gossip.

"A few close friends of the family know, but my parents have been pretty quiet about it. Mason took off right after he graduated, so I think most people assumed he was at college or just living his life somewhere. And…I guess he is."

The booms and pops of color lighting the sky became background noise, a distraction. I was desperate to keep him talking. He didn't seem to do much of that. Joking and teasing, sure—but speaking long sentences with meaning? Not so much.

"Were you close?"

There was a moment of silence.

"I idolized him."

Three little words, each filled with so much pain.

"What about now?"

I felt his shoulders move in a shrug as he breathed out a huff. "I'm indifferent."

"Did you ever talk to anybody?"

He paused, a furrow in his brow. "Like who?"

"A school counselor maybe? That's a big deal. That's a lot for a kid to try and process alone. Or what about your parents? Did you talk to them about it?"

"Oh, jeez," he said, his hand over his face. "Don't make me regret this even more."

I made a silent face into the night. My brain had a sudden overload of questions that needed answers. I had fired them off so quickly. Too quickly. But the gaps and holes in what I knew of Dax Miller were beginning to fill, and I was greedy for the knowledge. I attempted to ease him back in.

"Well, I am a doctor," I said, turning so he could see my grin. "You can talk to me."

He shook his head. "A doctor who sweeps my floors."

I poked at his side.

His low, easy chuckle made me think I could curl into him right now and not blink an eye, but I didn't.

"Did your parents talk to you about it?" Other than my brief interaction with Dax's parents at the shop, I didn't know them.

To my surprise, Dax spoke again. "It's hard because I was thirteen when it happened. I didn't understand everything at the time. All I knew was that my brother was gone, and according to his note, it was my parents' fault. They pushed him too hard, wanted him to go be a lawyer or a doctor or invest in real estate because that's what we do on this island. Looking at it now, I imagine they tried to talk to me, but I was so mad and..." he trailed off, biting his knuckle.

"Hurting," I said softly.

After a moment, he nodded slightly and whispered back, "Hurting."

"What happened after that?" I kept talking soft and slow, absorbing every little bit he was willing to give me.

Dax sighed, moving his hands to his face, rubbing up and down like he was washing it.

"What are you doing to me, woman?" he mumbled without any heat.

He didn't answer, so I pressed him again. "What happened?"

"Well...I started raising some hell."

A laugh gurgled out of me, and he shot me a smile. Heat flamed throughout my entire body.

"That's quite the understatement."

"Probably. All I knew was that my whole world had been turned on its head. Whatever bubble I was living in had popped. Suddenly, people I loved could just leave and never come back. And not because they were taken too soon–because they wanted to go. So I did everything I could to stop me from feeling like that again. I changed friends, got an attitude, and convinced myself I no longer cared."

"Did it work?"

"Suited me just fine for a few years." He grinned.

His attention turned to the fireworks. His pause gave weight to the moment—giving me a fresh perspective on the Dax I had known in biology—sauntering in and out of school, a devil-may-care attitude nipping at his heels. Impossible to read. Impossible to discipline.

"It was almost liberating once I realized that nothing really mattered. Nobody could touch me. Detention? Suspension? Juvy? Great. I didn't care. It all seemed so stupid. Why did any of it matter if people could just leave?"

I thought about thirteen-year-old Dax, who had his world completely rocked in the worst way. By the time he got into high school, he had been labeled a rebel. A troublemaker. A menace to society. When really, he was just a little boy with a broken heart and nowhere to go with his feelings.

A slight breeze picked up, and an unintentional shiver racked my body all of a sudden.

Dax sat up, running a hand through his hair. "Are you cold? We can get going."

"No, I'm fine." No way was I cutting this conversation early.

Dax eyed me. "I know what you're doing, Books."

"You can't blame me," I said, grabbing his forearm and tugging him back to our uncomfortable slouch on the seat. "These are the most words I've ever heard you speak."

He groaned but didn't put up the fuss I thought he might. Instead, he sat up again, leaned forward, and grabbed a five-gallon bucket he had sitting behind a seat. He set it out in front of us so we could have a leg rest before leaning back once again, pulling our blanket around us more securely.

"Wait. Why do you have a bucket?"

"To bail us out."

"Do you need to bail yourself out often?"

"Not *too* often."

"That's comforting," I said, as another shiver ran through

me. The middle of the ocean in the dark was indeed chilly, even in Florida.

"Alright, this is survival, Books. Don't get any ideas." In a move so smooth and natural, Dax slid his arm around my neck and pulled me against his side. His body exuded warmth, and I snuggled closer on instinct.

"So, you lived a life of mayhem all through high school. How long did that last?" I raised my head off his chest. "Or is it still going on?"

His lips curved in a smile before it disappeared. "It started slowing down my senior year of high school. It pretty much stopped after graduation. Most of my buddies left for college or enlisted somewhere, and I started working at the shop with Keith full time. I was on my own, doing what I wanted to do, and I didn't really have a reason to fight the system anymore."

"How did your parents handle those years?"

He sighed. "They didn't notice for a long time. They were still trying to do everything in their power to find Mason, but he just disappeared. He must have been planning it for weeks. Maybe months. When they did notice me, they didn't do much of anything."

My brow furrowed as my fingers played with a snag on the blanket. "Why?"

"At the time, I thought it was because they didn't care." He laughed, a little bitterly. "I was doing everything I could think of to get their attention, and it seemed like they couldn't have cared less. But now, I think they were too scared to push me too far."

"Why?"

His arm tightened around my shoulders. "I find you...annoying."

"Glad to see I haven't lost my touch," I said, tucking a wayward curl behind my ear.

"I found out that a kid has some leverage when their older

brother walks out on the family. They didn't want me to do the same thing, so they were willing to overlook a lot of stuff."

There was silence for a beat. Dax cleared his throat. "Anyway, that's the tragic past. I'm over it."

"Do people *get over* something like that?"

He drew in a ragged breath. "I don't know. Maybe not. But it hurts less now, and I *have* moved past it."

"Do you think he'll come back?"

It was the hesitation, the slight pause before he spoke, that had me listening intently. "Probably not. If he was going to, he would have done it already."

"But you still wonder sometimes?"

He didn't say anything. He didn't have to. It wasn't really a question.

"And the Lego car–that's the one you built with him?"

"Yeah."

And I had destroyed it. Guilt washed over me even as so many pieces of Dax began falling into place. How he had a mountain of friends who came to see him. Who adored him. How he kept them at arm's length.

"Is it like…a beacon for him? Having it in the shop window like that?"

Dax huffed out a laugh. "That seems like the cheesy ending of a movie. No. At least, I never thought of it like that. The car is huge and my mom wanted it out of her house. I told Keith about it, and he loved cars as much as I did, so we moved it to the shop. It became a thing with the whole town."

"How is your relationship with your parents now?"

Dax rubbed at his cheek. "It's getting better. In high school, I got a job at the shop, and Keith became an unsuspecting parent to me. I would have lived at the shop if he had let me. I started working, just doing some grunt work—cleaning bathrooms and sweeping."

"Interesting," I interjected.

"If you keep working hard, you could get a promotion too, Books."

I laughed softly.

"Anyway, I made it a point to never listen to anybody. But I listened to him. He was one of those guys who, if he told you he was disappointed in you, it would gut you for days. At least, he was that for me. I had him for all those years and didn't need much from my parents. So...after he died, I've been slowly trying to be better. To show up for things. I haven't been great at that yet, but..."

"It's easier to let people need you. It's probably a lot harder to allow yourself to need them," I said softly.

The breeze on the water picked up as we lay in contemplative silence underneath the stars. Dax pointed out one constellation, the boat rocking gently, before he dropped his fingers into my hair, softly playing with the curls. It felt like heaven.

"Do I need to pay you for this session, Doc? I think you might be in the wrong profession."

I smiled and buried my face in his chest.

"I love the straightforwardness of math. No games. Very few gimmicks. You just solve the problem and be on your way. People are much harder."

"And you like teaching at a college level?"

My stomach clenched. "I haven't actually done much of it."

His fingers moved in a soft line back and forth along my shoulder. "Why not?"

"You don't want to hear all of this."

His hand dropped to my side, gently tickling me while I squirmed and attempted to scramble away. I made it halfway up before he caught my arm and pulled me back down.

"After what you've put me through tonight, I want to know everything."

"Better be careful," I told him, becoming quite comfortable

using him as a human body pillow. "It's starting to sound like you might care."

"If anyone finds out, I know who to blame."

"Can you imagine the number of people that might come in and out of your shop if they thought you actually wanted them there?!"

"Quit stalling, Books. You like teaching?"

I thought about it for a moment. "I think so."

"You went through a lot of school for an 'I think so.'"

"There are a lot of hoops to jump through before you can teach. I've done some teaching at the high school level and that was great, but I was always aiming higher. A bachelor's never seemed like enough for me. Then my dad started telling people I was going to be a professor, and I ended up loving the sound of that. So I thought, why not just get my doctorate?"

"It astounds me how different we are," Dax said.

I laughed softly.

"Why do you have a fancy degree but haven't been teaching?"

I sighed. "Because the world of academia seduces you with the idea of this noble calling, and so you bust your butt for years, ignoring everything else, until it spits you out into a world where actual opportunities are so rare that somebody has to die or retire before a position opens up. I've spent two years doing a postdoc, which is basically a way to work at a university and bide my time, hoping something comes up or that a professor decides they adore me and will go to bat to get me hired somewhere. But there are too many postgrad students clamoring for jobs. I'm nobody special. If I can't do it, then someone will be there in ten seconds to take over."

"So when you go back to Tennessee, you'll be teaching?" Confusion etched around his voice.

"Only for a month. It's a fast-track summer course, but it's going to be my first chance at teaching, and I want it. I need people to see me teach."

"What are you doing when you're not teaching?"

"I'm on my computer, researching and writing. That's another way I could potentially get my name out there. Publish a few things in some journals."

"Wait. Do you hang out with people in Nashville?"

"Not much."

"So you've been giving me all this crap about working so much, and you're probably worse than me at being social?"

"I'm not worse!"

"I hang out a few times a month with Beau and Phoenix. The rest of the time, the entire island visits me on a regular basis."

"You don't understand. I *have* to do research and write papers to even have a chance at competing in the academia arena. *You* could hire someone and give yourself more of a life."

"What about your life? When does all the research and writing papers end?"

The words stalled on my tongue. I couldn't pretend to ignore how so many of my professors and colleagues hardly saw their families—or even the sun most days—working early hours and evenings, chasing something they might never actually catch.

But I've also known success stories. I've seen great professors doing great work and balancing it all, which lent to more upheaval in my mind.

"Seems like a lot to put on yourself so your dad can have something to brag about at parties."

"It's not just that," I insisted, his arrow narrowly missing his target. Because it *wasn't* just that. It *couldn't* be just that.

Was it?

But even now, the satisfaction of hearing my dad tell someone about my plan to become a professor and the proud inflection in his voice came back to me with startling alarm.

"Now, I'm overqualified for teaching anything else, so..."

"What does that matter?"

"Huh?"

"If teaching is what you love, why can't you teach at a high school? Or at a community college?"

I paused. "It's embarrassing, for one. I have a doctorate. I can't teach high school math."

"So, your noble calling has limitations on whose lives you can change?"

I sighed. "Listen, I probably said too much. There are lots of people who get jobs. Lots who love the research. Sometimes it's hard to see the forest through the trees. Every student of academia feels like this at some point. I just need to put my head down and do this next job, and maybe something will open up."

"When do you go back to Nashville?"

His fingers stopped playing with my hair, as if remembering the very real barrier between us. He shifted, edging slightly away from me.

I had just over two weeks left on the island. And once I procured secret permission from the clinic to use their ambulance (still working up the courage to ask about that one), I'd be done. After I...tagged a building. That, combined with my long hours at the cafe every morning, and I'd be finishing up my hours within two weeks. Easy peasy.

And then I'd leave.

Dax still wouldn't have his Lego car, and that was no longer sitting right with me, but maybe I could come back for a few weekends and help.

"Two weeks if I get the courage to steal an ambulance and spray paint a building."

After a long moment, Dax sat up, carefully extracting his arm from my shoulders. "Guess I'd better get the professor home, then."

He started the boat with rigid shoulders—an uneasy vibe humming between us. I still sat in the seat we'd both occupied a moment ago, hating the distance. Resenting the fact that my body was chilly on this Florida ocean and he was no longer there to warm it.

"Can I drive?" I asked, working hard to keep a normal tone to my voice.

Dax seemed relieved at the question breaking into the weirdness and sent a slow smile my way. "Not on your life."

"I'll give you back one hour."

"You might be the worst mathematician I've ever met." He rolled his eyes and motioned me over. "This is a freebie, Books. Don't get used to it."

He stood, and our bodies did a dance, moving around each other, his hand at my waist guiding me to the seat in front of the wheel. Suddenly, the boat hit a dip in the ocean, and I lurched forward, my foot tripping on the long rope that laid in a heap in the aisle. His hands were around me in seconds, our bodies now meshed together in a tangle as I gripped his shoulders for balance. He didn't pull away. His gaze dropped to my lips, and though he inched closer, he didn't partake.

"Chicken," I whispered, knowing this idea was bad but too far gone to care anymore.

Something snapped in his eyes, brandishing a fire that sizzled and burned. I held my breath as he grew closer, but his lips bypassed my mouth, settling somewhere near my ear. The heat from his breath spread like wildfire down my body. "You want to talk about opening my heart up? Fine. The kiss outside your cafe the other night was the hottest kiss I've ever had. I've been dropping tools in my garage ever since because my hands don't work right because I can't get it out of my head. I can't get *you* out of my head. But you're leaving. And I don't kiss girls who are leaving. No matter how much I might want to."

With that, he propelled me gently to the seat where, in a daze, I proceeded to drive us back to the dock. I didn't remember arriving. We were just there. His hands gripped my arms as I stepped off the boat, pulling me forward as I tried to find my stride. But my legs faltered, and my heart lurched. Dax had completely disarmed me, thrown me off balance yet again.

I needed Tennessee. I needed the space between me and my dad. This job was everything I had worked toward for the past ten years. So much of my blood, sweat, and tears had gone into finishing this degree—into becoming someone worth talking about.

But what did that even mean? Was it awards and accolades? Getting published in journals and magazines? Earning the title of professor and teaching future generations? Certainly, those were all good things. But if, at the end of the day, I went home to an empty house and my published works sat untouched on dusty shelves, was it truly important?

After falling into bed that night, my ears perked up at the sound that I was waiting for. I had heard it so often by now I could almost detect a rhythm that was familiar, but it was over too quickly. He definitely had to knock using both hands for the beat. I'd have to remember to record it next time.

DAX
Any guesses yet?

ME
I need a hint.

DAX
If you haven't gotten it by now, I can't help you.

My parents' BBQ is tomorrow. You coming?

ME
Do you want me to come?

DAX
Yeah

Rebel Summer

> **ME**
> What about what you said on the boat?

DAX
> We're friends, Books. Unless you're worried about not being able to keep your hands to yourself?

> **ME**
> Won't be a problem.

AND IT WOULDN'T BE.

DAX
> I'll pick you up after your shift at the cafe.

> **ME**
> Sounds good, buddy.

DAX
> Dork

CHAPTER 22

Biology Class
Day 48

My stomach tightened as Dax dropped into his seat next to mine. So much had happened between us in the twenty-four hours since we last sat here, and every moment pinched at my nerves. I kept my gaze locked onto Mr. Gray, my back stiff and my neck straight. Every part of my being except for my eyes focused intently on the guy sitting next to me. The way he slouched in his seat, just enough to look bored but not enough to fool me into thinking he wasn't paying attention. After a while, Mr. Gray started a documentary about ecosystems.

Dax nudged my leg with his.

I turned and met an expression brimming with mischief.

"We could use a lookout tonight. You up for it?"

"Nope," I whispered, turning my attention back to Mr. Gray. Hating the coldness in my voice, while at the same time hiding behind it.

There had been many emotions coursing through me last night, but the shame of my dad looking at me as if I were on a brazen path of self destruction seemed to overpower everything else. I had made it my business to never give him cause to worry about me, but all it took was one moment of being in the wrong place at the wrong time for none of that to have mattered. The worst part was, my dad hadn't even seemed surprised. Angry, yes. Disappointed, absolutely. He acted like he had always known that this would happen–that I would do something to screw up his campaign. I had already screwed up his life by just being born, so I suppose it made sense that he was just biding his time until I repeated the offense. And yet, I hadn't even messed up. Unless you count getting into the cart with Dax. Now my dad assumed I was about to trade in all of my plans for Dax Miller.

"That boy is trouble."

"You've got plans after graduation. You'd better not do anything to screw that up."

"He'll be in the exact same spot in ten years. Causing trouble in or in jail somewhere. Mark my words."

I could hardly stand the guy, but my dad refused to be convinced.

MARK AND TRUDY MILLER lived in a nice neighborhood on the south end of the island. The house was white with blue shutters and had a picket fence and a porch swing. It looked like the absolute opposite of the kind of home I expected Dax to hail from. I kept waiting for a sweet old grandmother wearing a pink cardigan to slip out the front screen to sip her iced tea on the porch.

"I expected more bars on the windows." I leaned forward to take in the cozy home. "Are you sure this is your house?"

He leaned across me and pointed. "See that window on the second floor?"

"Yeah."

"I used to sneak out of there at night. The tree next to it provided the perfect ladder."

"So your house was just a cover for your clandestine activities. That makes much more sense."

"Exactly. Pretty sure my twin bed and Spiderman sheets haven't changed since I left."

I paused while taking in that delicious tidbit. "Does that mean you slept in Spiderman sheets when you were in high school?"

He blinked. A hint of smile played across his lips before he stepped out of the cart. "Not one word, Books."

"So, the whole time we were in biology together, you were going home to snuggle up in your superhero sheets?" I asked out loud, walking toward the door, absolutely adoring the visual that gave me. "That's gonna cost you a few hours—at least. And that's being generous."

His low chuckle met my ears as his arm slung across my shoulders on the walk up. "That tattoo has done a number on you."

I breathed out a laugh, hoping he was done touching me, while at the same time praying he wasn't. We were standing on the front walkway leading to his parents' house. We shouldn't have been touching. As if he suddenly remembered our conversation the night before, he released me.

I had almost sent Dax a message tonight, canceling on him before he picked me up. But I couldn't send the message. I couldn't say no. I didn't *want* to say no. But I also couldn't see how this wouldn't go down in flames.

"Hey, you two!"

Trudy stood in the doorway, waving us closer. She wore white slacks, a pink floral top, and dangly gold necklaces. I could see bits of her son in her rich, coffee-colored eyes.

"Hey, honey," she said, pulling him into a hug. Dax stiffened for a moment before he slowly wrapped his arms around her.

"Ivy, I'm so glad you could come." She gathered me into a soft embrace, the friendliness of her manners making me miss my own mother.

"Thanks for having me," I told her. "Happy birthday."

"Thank you," she said, patting Dax's cheeks. "My two boys are here. What more could I want?"

She ushered us both inside an expansive home that smelled of warm bread and cinnamon. Trudy chatted with Dax as she led us farther into the house—Dax's childhood home. Along the way, we passed picture frames filled with images of smiling faces of three little boys building forts and younger versions of Trudy and her husband in front of the Disney World sign. A child version of Dax outside in a yard, with dark hair and a dirty tank top, bursting with gnarly teeth and a grin that wasn't unlike the one he'd given me earlier on the drive over. He had his arm extended as far up as it would go, wrapped around a taller, light-haired boy wearing a smile that was nearly identical.

What more could she want?

I was willing to guess.

She led us past the kitchen decorated in whites and natural woods to the deck out back. Mark Miller stood tall at the barbecue grill, looking like a golfer in his khaki shorts and a tucked-in pastel polo shirt. He couldn't have dressed more differently from Dax if he tried. Dax's younger brother, Trent, stood at the grill with Mark, the pair laughing over something as we stepped out onto the deck. Compared to his lean and tall family, Trent was shorter with the build of a football player. He wore cargo shorts and a tank top and upon seeing his brother, an excited grin.

He whooped before running over and grabbing Dax by the waist to lift him up in a brotherly version of romance. Despite himself, Dax laughed and, after a moment, hugged him back.

Trudy beamed at her sons, a glossy sheen in her eyes. But I couldn't seem to ease my mind, knowing what I knew about Mason. Was she thinking of him now? Missing him at this moment? Or had enough time passed that she didn't mourn his absence at every occasion anymore? Was there a callus now where there used to be an open wound?

Trent and Dax were now standing on the grass, catching up. Trent regaled Dax with a tale that involved animated hand gestures. Dax saw me watching and motioned me closer with a flick of his head.

"Oh, sorry! I forgot you brought a girl over." Trent took me in, blocking the sun from his eyes. "Wait. Ivy?"

Soon, I was the one wrapped in one of Trent's hugs, though it was much less romantic, thank goodness.

"How are you? I thought you were the one who ran into his shop?"

I smiled awkwardly. "Guilty."

Dax's dad came over and gave me a side hug. "Hey, glad to have you."

Trent still looked puzzled. "You're hanging out together? After all that?"

"They became friends." Trudy beamed at me while I stood in the middle of this ping pong match, not quite sure what to say.

"They already knew each other," Trent insisted.

"They graduated together but didn't really know each other," Trudy said to Trent.

"They were partners in biology," Trent explained with a laugh. "They knew each other, trust me."

Dax seemed to shrink slightly.

Trudy leaned forward to tap Dax's chest. "What? You didn't tell us that."

Trent laughed. "She's the reason he passed the class."

My body stilled. What?

"No," Trudy said. "He graduated because Keith told him he had to if he wanted to keep his job."

Trent snorted. His loud frankness in comparison to his brother was shocking if not, at this very moment, wildly interesting.

"He was always going to have a job with Keith. The guy loved him. We all knew that. Teachers, threats, suspension, bribes... None of that worked on Dax. But...put a pretty girl who can hold her own against him as his lab partner, and it was all over."

I froze. Dax froze. The rest of the family began talking, moving, their voices muffled in my head. Our eyes locked together, mine in curiosity, his in…defeat? Or something else? My brows raised at him in question as I waited for his response. It was the crinkle of his nose and nearly imperceptible shrug of his shoulders that caused the grin splitting across my face.

Eventually, the burgers were done, and we all sat chatting at the table, munching on chips and potato salad while I watched this sweet family re-group again after Trent's long absence. Trent was gregarious. Happy and interested in everything going on around him. It was no wonder the fun-loving kid I remembered from student council had gone on to become this person. And his parents were similar. If it wasn't for the crinkle in Mark's eyes when he laughed and the mischievous grin he shot his wife on occasion when he teased her, I might have insisted Dax was adopted.

LATER THAT AFTERNOON, the heat had become unbearable enough that we moved our chat and key lime pie into the cozy living room. Dax sat beside me on the couch, our legs next to each other. Yesterday had ended on a note of boundaries, but today, I found myself confused again. The pull of Nashville was always on my mind, but nothing like the force of nature it had been when I first arrived.

Mark slapped his hand on his knee and looked at Dax, "Well, do you mind if we take a look at my golf cart real quick, son?"

"Sure."

The men stood, and Mark and Trent made their way toward

the garage, but Dax turned to me before leaving. "We'll just be a few minutes. You alright?"

"Yeah." I smiled. "Do you need me to show you how to…crack open that…carburetor real quick?"

His mouth curled upward. "I'll call you when I need you."

He and his dad left for the garage, and it was only when I turned back to his mom, who was watching me carefully, that I realized I still had a sloppy grin on my face. I dialed it down to what was hopefully a more friendly vibe for the mother of a guy I was…friends with.

"Your house is beautiful," I told her, suddenly desperate to fill the silence.

She smiled. "Thank you. Was it the kind of home you expected Dax to grow up in?"

I laughed, somewhat awkwardly, at her piercing truth bomb. "I definitely expected more black paint."

She smiled good-naturedly but didn't say anything else. Her gaze was heavy on me, and I fidgeted under her scrutiny while scouring my mind for something else I could chat about with this woman. I wasn't sure why I wanted her to like me so much, but I did. It turned out, I didn't have to say anything.

"Whatever it is you're doing with Dax, please keep doing it."

My eyes lifted to meet hers. "What?"

"It's been wonderful watching him today. With you. He's like a whole different boy."

I opened my mouth to say something, but nothing came. Thankfully, she was just beginning.

Trudy's eyes were glossy. "We have another son. Mason. Has Dax told you anything?"

"A little." My voice came out soft, matching her tempo.

She nodded, gathering her thoughts. "After Mason left, it was like I had lost two sons. Dax became so angry. He blamed us for pushing Mason away. And maybe we did. I don't know. If I could go back, I would." She paused to wipe under her eyes, then took in another ragged breath. "But then Dax started changing, stopped caring about things. He stopped playing with his little brother. He stopped trying in school. He was getting into all sorts of trouble. When he laughed, it was only to make fun of something. He moved into Mason's old room, and I was terrified he was going to leave one day too. We just *lost* him."

I wiped at the lone tear slipping down my face as she continued.

"He's been doing great the past few years. He's a good worker. His business has been thriving, but he still keeps such a tight wall around himself. Mason leaving devastated all of us in such different ways." She met my gaze. "But today, with you, he was so much like the old Dax that I kept double-checking that it was really him. His eyes are shining again, and as a mom…" Her face morphed into a pained expression as she tried to gain control of her emotions. "As a mom, that was the best birthday gift I could have ever received."

"I don't think I have much to do with that. He—"

She shook her head. "It's you. I probably could have guilted him into coming to the barbecue today because it was for my birthday, and Trent's here, but he would have left the first chance he could. But he stayed, and he visited, and he laughed, and he had a smile on his face while watching you for most of it."

When I could only gape at her, she smiled.

"I mean no pressure on you about any of this. I don't want to pry into your relationship, but I couldn't let the day go by without telling you thank you."

I wasn't sure I could speak with the way my heart was touched by her words. I hadn't done anything but show up with her son because I now craved being with him.

"Dax is a good person," I said. Inwardly, I blanched. It sounded like I was placating her. My paltry words weren't enough for all the good things I was discovering about her son.

"I mean, he's actually helped me a lot with some things, and..." I floundered, there was too much I wanted to say and not enough words to do it. His mom stared at me, a smile growing on her face, and took pity.

"He is a good man. I'm so glad you see that in him."

The rest of the afternoon passed with more chatting, and we even played Trudy's favorite card game while we ate cake and ice cream. Dax seemed to relax more the longer we stayed, teasing his brother and even giving his mom a kiss on her cheek when we left. At first, I'd been shocked at the family and house Dax had grown up in, but now it felt exactly right.

We didn't say much on the golf cart ride back to the duplex. My mind was too busy churning with everything I'd learned about Dax and his family. So much so that when we arrived at our driveway, and he turned off the key, I couldn't help but speak.

"Your mom told me you moved into Mason's room after he left."

He had been about to exit when he paused before turning a slightly horrified gaze back at me. "What all did you and my mom talk about?"

"I now know that you and your brothers used to have a thing about streaking in your backyard."

He smiled, but there was an overtly casual way about him, and he didn't move a muscle. "Only when we lost at cards."

"Why'd you move into his room?"

His first instinct was to brush me off. I knew it was. I could see it in his eyes. So, it surprised me when he leaned back against his seat, his fingers playing with the steering wheel.

"Because I thought he was going to come back."

"Why did you think that?"

"Because I was thirteen. All I knew was my brother was gone, and I didn't know why. I used to go looking through his room for clues, thinking I could track him down. But then I found this old Swiss Army knife I'd given to him for his birthday, and he had loved it—at least, he told me he did. So, I kept thinking he would come back to grab it. He used to love the TV show *Survivor* and had always talked about doing something like that, so for a while, I thought he was trying to make it on the island by himself, which meant he was probably missing his knife. So, I slept in his room for a few months, waiting for him to come back for it. Once I discovered how handy the tree next to the window was, it became my room permanently."

He huffed out a laugh, giving the impression that it was no longer important. That he no longer cared.

But he couldn't fool me anymore.

I hadn't fully grasped the enormity of emotions a person needed to work through when someone abandoned their family, but I was starting to understand the tip of the iceberg. I'd taken psychology classes in college that had helped me understand more about death. The grieving process was brutal and heart-wrenching, and the enormity of emotions a person faces for the rest of their life never goes away.

Abandonment was another sort of tragedy on a similar scale.

I imagined the grieving process was similar. Someone you loved was no longer there. Life's universal sorrow. But there was a merciful finality with death that was absent here. The devastation brought to this family held no ending. No coffin. No closure. Which meant there was still hope to be shattered every day that failed to bring their son home.

Or brother.

Hope was the real tragedy here.

Later that night, the knocking came softer this time, but by now, I knew the tune, though I still hadn't figured out the song.

DAX
Thanks for coming tonight.

> **ME**
> I had fun. Thanks for inviting me.
> Do it one more time.

> **DAX**
> That's against the rules, Books.

> **ME**
> You break the rules all the time.

HE STARTED AGAIN, louder and with more distinct knocking. I sat up on my bed and finished out the tune with him, a smile on my face.

> **ME**
> It's confusing with all the knocking. Is this song from my generation of music or yours?

> **DAX**
> Mine.

> **ME**
> Any hints?

> **DAX**
> I just gave you one.

> **ME**
> Any more?

> **DAX**
> Sweet dreams, Books

CHAPTER 23

Biology Class
Day 48

"Did you get in trouble?" Dax asked, his brow lightly furrowed.

I gaped at him. "Yeah. Why did you think I was trying to get you to leave?"

"He obviously knew you didn't steal the golf cart."

"You wouldn't know that by talking to him."

"What did he say?"

I wasn't about to tell him that my daddy said I couldn't hang around him anymore. This wasn't a drama on Lifetime. Other than being forced to sit next to him for a class, we never ran in the same circles. And we never would. My dad was right. Dax would never leave the island.

"It's fine. Just...I'm not getting messed up with you. Okay? The second I graduate, I'm out of here."

"Messed up with me? What do you mean by that?"

I swallowed, ignoring the slight edge in his voice.

"Nothing."

"Oh. So your dad doesn't want you hanging out with me? Is that right?" This looked like it amused him in some way, which made my blood burn. He had caused the entire incident and he thought it was funny.

"No. He doesn't." I folded my arms.

"Why?"

My foot twitched under the table. It wasn't in my nature to be direct, but Dax wasn't going to stop until I told him the truth. The words of my dad from the previous night spat easily from my lips.

"Because I'm graduating valedictorian. I'm headed to Vanderbilt. I'm leaving this island. I'm not going to be working the same job I worked at in high school for the rest of my life. Take your pick."

For the tiniest moment, he looked as though he'd been shot, betrayed in some irreparable way, and I knew it would be that image that would haunt me for the rest of my days. But then I blinked and his self assured smile was back in place and I wondered if I imagined the whole thing.

T-minus 15 days to exit
Dax hours remaining: 100

THE NEXT WEEK whirled by in a mixture of delusion and a whole lot of fun. My shifts at the cafe were nearly over. The blue tarps were taken down, and the windows on Dax's shop finally got replaced. And Dax and I found a thousand things to do outside of his shop that had nothing to do with Legos.

All for hours, of course.

But with bargains like these, who could possibly blame me?

For a mere ten hours, Dax had to sit with me at the farmers market for the cafe. For only five hours more, I convinced him to contribute a few of his tools and random things he'd made in the shop. The propeller clock was purchased by the honorable Judge Baylor. Several knives made out of old lawnmower blades and sheathed in material from an old boat sail were claimed by several teenage boys in town. It was as delicious as I imagined, sitting next to Dax and watching his face flush with embarrassment from the praise.

And the twenty hours Dax offered me to TP my dad's house was worth every second. The summer was slipping from my fingers, the Lego car was at least a month away from completion, and worst of all was the growing attachment I felt for Dax Miller.

Really. Who would have seen this coming?

"How many hours do you have left?" Dax asked as we sat on the floor, side by side, with the Lego guidebook between us. The song "We Built This City" played loudly through the speakers–louder than usual, but Dax said the song deserved respect, and apparently that meant volume. He had taken to helping me more lately, since we'd been spending so much time away from his shop the past couple of weeks. The nights spent doing Legos with him became the best part of my day. It turned out that Legos weren't the worst when someone was doing them with you.

"Last count, I had ninety-eight."

His brow furrowed. "Since when?"

"Since I did a bunch of your invoices the other night."

He stretched and took a drink of his Coke. "I think I'm getting robbed."

I didn't want to talk about the hours. About how there was no way, save stealing an ambulance and tagging a building, that I would be able to get it done in time before I left in exactly one week.

And I had to leave. Right? It would be so dumb to walk away from a career I'd spent ten years building.

So, I sat there, ignoring everything but the feel of his arm against mine while we listened to a new mix of seventies and eighties rock. When an N'SYNC song I'd secretly added a while back came on, I began bopping to the beat, carefully hiding his phone on the other side of me. Dax began patting the space on both sides of him, and when he couldn't find what he was looking for, he tackled me as I squealed in protest. He then proceeded to roll me gently to the side. My shirt had ridden up a few inches in our scuffle and I held my breath as his fingers grazed my bare stomach as he located the phone.

It was at that moment, with me lying on the ground and half of Dax's body leaning over me, that the door to the shop opened, and Sunset Harbor's local senator stepped inside.

Impeccable timing, per usual.

I scooted out from under Dax and stood as my dad strode toward us. I expected rudeness and snarling, so I braced myself for it. What I got instead was much worse.

"Hello." His voice was pleasant, and I was immediately on guard. He ignored Dax completely, choosing instead to ask if there was somewhere we could go to talk.

"Right here is fine," I said.

That pulled him briefly out of his facade, a slight crack in his armor, but he quickly righted himself and said, "Good news. I spoke to the judge. I told him about your job and that they needed you back sooner than we thought."

"How did you know about that?" I broke in.

"I called your department."

Of course he did.

"Anyway, the judge said he'd give you permission to transfer whatever community service hours you have left here to a business in Nashville."

I gaped at him. "What about the Lego car?"

My dad rolled his annoyed eyes toward Dax. "I'll personally pay to have it built."

"No thanks," Dax said, his arms folded as he looked at my dad.

"I still owe Dax a lot of hours. That's not fair to exchange that for something else."

"Well, I told the judge you've been spending plenty of time with him, so I was pretty certain you'd maxed out your hours."

"You had no right."

"You're doing it, Ivy. Pack your bags because your plane leaves on Monday." He took a step toward me, teeth bared. "I didn't pay for the last 8 years of college so you could throw it all away for the town mechanic."

"Dad—" I began, my body filling with rage.

"No," my dad said. "You have a career and a life that is nowhere near this island. You are not going to waste it here." He stepped back toward the door, saying firmly once more, "Three days. Then you're on a plane to become the professor I paid for you to be."

The door slammed shut and my week of delusion came to an abrupt end. I had a job waiting for me. People depending on me. And a dad who hated me. He had dropped his bomb and fled the scene so quickly I didn't have time to yell all the things now circling in my head. How dare he. How *dare* he. The fact that he was still so much a presence in my life, dictating and controlling, always for *his* own good, made my fingers itch to fling and smash with rage.

"Your dad seems to think I like you way more than I actually do," Dax said, watching me carefully.

I couldn't even find it in me to smile.

"I gotta do some work in the garage." He lingered, even as he spoke of leaving. His hand played with the towel hanging from his belt. "Listen, you've officially served all your hours for me." He smiled with a sweetness that broke me. "I'll tell the judge you're good to go."

Then he walked into his garage, closing the door between us.

I stood staring at the mess of Legos I'd created. A numbness began to spread over my body, officially killing any sense of loyalty or respect I'd tried to have for the senator in my life. What had it all been for? So I could spend years of my life in therapy and still be stuck in the same endless mind games? Being twenty-eight years old and still never measuring up to his impossible standards? To the standards he holds for everyone but himself.

I didn't want to feel anything anymore. I wanted to act

without thought—without feeling. And suddenly, I knew exactly what I wanted to do. What I needed to do.

I strode toward the door separating his garage from the lobby and flung it open, Dax and I both jumping as it smashed against the wall.

"You've got to stop doing th—"

"Is your car drivable?" My voice came out strong and sure. Because I *was* sure—about this, anyway. I might not be exactly sure about my immediate future, but I was going to earn my hours from Dax.

However I had to do it.

A slow smile, sweet and reminiscent of something a bit more reckless, crossed his face.

"I thought you'd never ask."

CHAPTER 24

Biology Class
Day 48

He leaned closer, his eyebrows raised. "It sounds like the Senator's got your life all planned out for you."

The bite stung, but I refused to examine why. "No, it's what I want."

His brows lifted. "Okay. Let me ask you this. You know what really happened last night. Why does anything else matter? The police didn't catch us. You know that you didn't steal it. Why are you mad?"

"Because my dad thinks I did. Or at least thinks that I helped you."

"Well..technically," he began to say until I kicked at his foot underneath the table. He rolled his eyes as laughter spat from his mouth.

"You know what happened," he said again. "So why does it matter what your dad thinks?"

"Because he's my dad," I said.

"And the fact that he doesn't believe you isn't a problem for you?"

"He doesn't care who did it. It's the fact that I was involved at all that makes him mad. It can mess with his public image. It can mess with our public image." I told myself to stop talking, but the words came anyway.

Understanding settled on Dax's face. "That explains it. I thought the whole fake persona was just the politician stuff, but looks like it runs in the family."

We chose two a.m. for our drive time.

Caffeine, Sun Chips, and Dax's teasing made the wait until the middle of the night bearable. We didn't talk about the reasons why I was doing this, those would come later. I was certain of it. This was a last hurrah. The perfect ending to my summer with Dax Miller.

After I'd made my declaration, we hung out in the garage together. I definitely put in a few more hours, but this time, I was helping Dax in his shop, filling out invoices while he worked on a fishing boat he'd pulled inside on a trailer from the marina.

"It's time," Dax said, as he turned off the lights before hitting the button to open the third garage door. One yellow bulb hanging from the ceiling was our only source of light.

He paused, his hand on the door of the orange car he'd hand-built in this garage. "You having second thoughts, Books?"

"No."

And I wasn't, strangely enough. I wasn't a daredevil by any stretch of the imagination, but nothing was going to stop me right now. After a life of rules and regulations, I was determined to do this. I held my hand out in front of me. There were no shakes, no tremors. No guilt. This could potentially be the biggest mistake of my life, maybe my career, but I knew with absolute certainty that it wouldn't turn into a regret.

He held open the driver's side door, motioning me closer. "You ready?"

"Obviously, I was born ready."

He huffed out a laugh, his dark eyes flashing with intrigue, taking in my short overalls and t-shirt with small red hearts all over it.

"Okay, Trouble. Let's go over the rules."

"Rules?" I walked toward him, trying hard not to internalize the fact that he looked like James Dean, in his jeans and white shirt with a really cool car behind him. "I've influenced you more than I thought."

"Number one. If you harm one hair on this car's head, so help me..." he said.

I folded my arms and gave him a look.

"Number two. I drive first."

"You think because you spent two years of your life building this car, you get to drive it first?" I said.

"No. I just don't trust you backing out of this garage."

I glared at him, but since I had smashed into his building earlier this summer, I let it slide.

"Number three. We're not doing the whole route. It's too risky with your history of driving on this island, so we're going to just go up to the resort's entrance road, and then back down to the north end of the town square, then back to the shop. About one mile total. It should take three minutes."

"You sure that's worth it for one hundred hours?" I asked him.

He studied me for a moment too long before saying, "Yeah. Everybody on this island has their windows open, so we can't draw attention. We'll drive slow so it sounds like it's a golf cart going twenty-five miles per hour past their house. Got it?"

"Your rules make you sound like a little old lady," I said.

He shot me an annoyed look. Before he could change his mind, I ran around to the other side of the car and slid onto the bucket seat of the dark interior. The smell of leather oil and the snug proximity of the seats inside the car drew me in like a moth to a flame. Dax slid in beside me and shut the door, enclosing us. Almost reverently, he put the keys in the ignition.

"Moment of truth," he said.

He turned the key. The engine growled to life with a low purr, producing a smile on Dax's face, and some sort of manly moan of pleasure spewed out of him.

"Should I leave you two alone for a minute?" I asked, running my hand along the dash, taking in all the details.

Dax grinned, leaning his head back against the headrest with a sigh. "I did it."

I watched him with a smile. "Dax?"

"Yeah?"

"It's pretty freaking cool," I said, pride for him practically billowing out of me, which I, of course, had to tamp down with some teasing. "Just remember who handed you the wrench to put in that driveline."

He blinked before rolling his head toward me, as if he were coming out of a daze. "We're about to take the car of my dreams, that I built, on a test drive, Caroline. That's a pretty bold move to be talking dirty to me right now."

My hands lifted to cover my heated cheeks while the hum of his low laughter scattered goosebumps around my skin.

Dax put his arm around the back of my seat, his fingers brushing past the hair at my shoulders as he looked behind him and ever…so…slowly…backed out.

I let out a dramatic gasp, my hands flying to the dash.

Dax swore, slamming on the brakes while his hands flew off the wheel. "What?!"

Laughter in the form of nervous, high-pitched giggles erupted from me. Leaning forward, I hid my howling face behind my hands while he swore again. If this was living on the lam, sign me up, because so far I was having a great time.

He growled lowly before he backed out of the garage, closed the door, and crept toward Main Street. Just before we entered the street, he stopped, looking down the road illuminated by a row of yellow lamp posts.

"Last chance to back out, Ivy."

The use of my name on his lips jarred me slightly, grounding me for a moment when I had been somewhere lost in the clouds.

Were we actually doing this?

As Dax's eyes waited patiently on mine, my mind raced to find the turning point that had brought me to this moment. The crash had been the tip of the iceberg to a summer I had no idea I needed. The list. The tattoo. Dax. Learning to separate myself from who I was and who I'm becoming. The baring of souls while sparks flew above us.

And between us.

Life was messy. Jobs were messy. People were even messier. But for the first time since I'd left the island ten years ago, I had an attachment to my life that I'd never felt before. One filled with connection and friendships and people I loved. Other than a job, I had nothing in Tennessee to go back to. Before now, my existence had been more about marking things off of a checklist —hoping what I accomplished measured up to an unknown standard. My decisions had always been controlled and concise —black and white. But tonight, I was dipping my toe into the gray.

Maybe tonight would end up just being a funny story to tell. Or maybe there would be consequences. But my heart was ready to leap from my chest, the smile on my face refused to fade, and I knew there was nowhere else on earth I'd rather be than driving Dax's car around the island. Come what may...I was here for all of it.

I mean...obviously I *hoped* nothing would happen in three minutes.

"Wait," I said, my fingers fumbling with the radio dial on the dash. "We need theme music."

Since it was Dax's maiden voyage with his car, I set the dial to the oldies station—the kind I imagined grandparents everywhere listened to in their cars. And when "Centerfield" by John Fogerty began playing, it just felt right.

"Now I'm in," I said.

He still looked unsure. "You don't have to do this. I'm giving you the hours either way. The car started, and that completely rocked my world. That's enough for me."

"I want to do it."

"Are you sure—"

"GO!" I yelled.

He waited a beat, still looking at me, before his excitement to be driving his car refused to be contained any longer. His grin grew even wider as he turned onto the main road heading toward the resort and got his baby up to the agreed-upon twenty-five miles per hour.

It was a bit…anticlimactic, to be honest. I mean, the car was amazing, but we were crawling.

"How bad is it killing you to go this slow?" I asked. The beat to the song on the radio was going faster than we were.

He rubbed his hand along the wheel trimmed in red. "In my mind, we're flying down an empty freeway right now."

"How do you plan to get the car off the island?"

"I'm sure Beau will help me, but I'd probably have to let him drive it on the mainland for a while after."

We approached the entrance road to the resort where Dax turned the car around and threw it in park.

"It purrs like a dream," he said, as he unbuckled his seatbelt. "Alright, you're up, Books."

I went to open the door, and nothing happened. I jiggled the handle and pushed my shoulder against it, but nothing budged. Dax leaned across the seat and tried it himself. After several attempts with his body half leaning against me, Dax reached his hand below, feeling around the door frame.

"Is this… Did you bring your purse?"

"Yeah."

"The strap is stuck in the door."

It must be noted that, by this time, parked so long in one place, Dax's car began to feel like a sitting duck. Though I was still happy to be doing this with Dax, my heart rate was picking up...just a smidge.

"Why'd you bring your purse?" Dax gave it one more tug to no avail before sitting up.

"It has my license."

We waited a beat, the words hanging in the air for about five whole seconds while we both registered my incredibly dumb thought process. Dax broke first, a snicker bursting free, before I followed suit.

There was a smile in his voice when he said, "Alright, I can't open it. Just come out my side."

It took some finagling in the bucket seats, but I maneuvered my way to Dax's side of the car. Then I stepped out and allowed Dax to get in before me.

It was about the time when Dax was attempting to maneuver his six-foot frame across the seats of a confined muscle car that I began to glance around the darkened streets. My self-awareness heightened the longer we sat here. And then Dax's leg went haywire, accidentally pressing the horn for what seemed like ten years, blaring a distress signal to the entire island.

We both froze. My hands covered my mouth.

"Did that sound like a golf cart horn to you?" Dax asked, his voice frantic.

One lone chortle escaped my mouth before I clamped it shut. And then another came, and it was hopeless. Soon, I was leaning on my knees, sucking in air as tears began falling down my face.

Dax poked his head out of the car. "Hey, Crazy Girl. Rein it in. We've gotta move."

Right. Yes. I swiped at a few tears before I climbed inside and closed the door.

"Okay, we're going to head back to the shop."

"Wait. You said we could drive down to the square."

"Well," he checked out the window behind him. "That was

before I blasted the horn for the entire island to hear. We can't go anywhere near the square, we—"

"We're doing it, Grandma!"

The dark look Dax shot me filled my rebellious little cup to the brim.

I began laughing and pressed on the gas, growing bold enough to punch the speedometer up to a whopping thirty miles per hour.

I was just past the bend in the road next to Dax's shop, heading toward the town square, when he leaned forward, peering out the window.

"Hold up," he said.

"What?"

"There's lights coming our way. In front of us."

I squinted to see where he was pointing. Sure enough, just past the streetlights of the town square, a lone golf cart was idling up the road, headed toward the east side of the square, directly in our path.

"What do we do?" I asked, my heart picking up speed while I watched the lights slowly growing closer. "If we go back to the shop, he'll see us pull into your garage."

Dax looked all around. "Okay, punch it, and we'll go around the square on the other side and wait for him to pass."

I brought the car up to a breakneck speed of forty miles per hour, the nerves in the air heightening the exhilaration I felt. "Maybe from a distance he'll think we're another golf cart."

"The car is twice as wide. They'll know," Dax said. "Turn off the lights. There's enough light from the street for us to see."

I immediately began pressing buttons and flipping switches around the car while my heart began to thrum chaotically inside my chest. The blinkers and windshield wipers began blinking and flapping in disordered mayhem, which resulted in me pushing levers and buttons at random. Dax leaned forward and caged my hands against the wheel while he turned off the lights.

Without the headlights, the streetlights became more visible, lighting corners of the town square and casting a golden hue as far as the light could reach.

"Turn here. We'll go around the square this way," Dax whispered.

"Why are you whispering?" I teased as we passed the cafe. "That guy can't hear you."

He looked at me, his mouth slightly aghast. "I need you to answer me seriously. Are you on something right now?"

I swatted his arm, but didn't answer. I was too busy checking my rearview mirror while racing down the street, making a dash for the corner to hide out before we were spotted. We were playing the ultimate game of hide and seek, and it was completely exhilarating.

"Not bad," Dax said, flipping around to watch out the back windshield. "I could have used you back in high school."

I put the car in park, with the back bumper barely visible, as we both watched out the back window for signs of the golf cart. Eventually, it appeared and kept ambling up the road toward the resort while Dax and I released a sigh of relief.

When we no longer saw the brake lights from the cart, we turned back around in our seats. My fingers drummed the steering wheel.

"Where to next? Should we cruise the whole island?"

"Let's get you back to the garage, Hot Rod."

Somewhat reluctantly, I put the car into drive and was about to move again when Dax cried out.

"Hold up, another cart's coming. From the resort."

"What are these people doing? It's two in the morning!"

"Hold on, let's see where he's headed. If he's going south, he won't see us."

I waited, my body tensing slightly, though not as much as I would have expected. Dax even made the thought of probation violation insignificant.

"He's coming this way! We gotta move."

"What?! Why?"

"Go! Go!"

It was killing Dax to not be in the driver's seat. I knew that, but we also didn't have time to switch. I threw the car into drive and circled the south end of the square, passing the Book Isle and pausing at the stop sign near the Cut and Curls Salon, where I pulled out far enough into the road to look both ways. My stomach dropped with a thud.

"There's another cart!" I gasped, pointing at another set of headlights making their way from the southern tip of the island.

Dax swore. "We're going to get boxed in." He whipped around, looking up and down the tiny island for a place to hide a car.

"Flip around, and we'll try hiding at the baseball field. We've got to get off the road."

"Won't they see us?" I asked, taking a hard right and following the road as best as I could without our headlights until we came to the empty field at the south end of the island.

"Hopefully with our lights off we'll stay hidden," Dax said.

"I just...drive on the grass?" My foot slipped off the gas as I hesitated, pointing in front of me.

Dax was busy looking out the window for any sign of the oncoming carts. "Yeah! It's fine! Go!"

His frantic gesturing caused me to gun the gas pedal even as I squinted at a dark spot on the grass in front of me. "What is th—"

"Watch out for the ditch—"

The car lurched forward and stuttered as I suddenly remembered the small ditch-like dip full of grass that surrounded the field, creating a barrier between the field and parking. A low groan shuddered through Dax's body as the packed dirt and weeds scraped hard underneath the car.

"I'm sorry!" I shouted, my panic and the forward jolt of the car making me step on the gas even harder. We flew from the dip, possibly catching air, while Dax buried his face behind his hands in horror until I rolled the car to a stop. Glancing out the window, I gathered that we were somewhere out in left field.

I felt that hard.

Without a word, Dax put a hand on my arm and pointed directly in front of us as one of the golf carts pulled up to the side of the bookstore. Whoever it was, if they were looking into the distance, they would have a perfect view of Dax's car.

The moon wasn't too full, and we were in the middle of a field, so I was sure we'd be fine.

But still, we leaned forward, watching out the window, awaiting any sign of movement from the cart.

"It's probably Briggs," Dax said, his voice low. "He lives above the bookstore."

We waited for him to get out of the cart, straining to see movement. But the cart remained dark. Had he gotten out already? Though I still wasn't as panicked as I probably should have been at this moment, even I was feeling ready to get back to the safety of Dax's garage.

"Maybe he's looking at his phone or something," I said.

We were silent as we both stared out the window, daring something to move inside or outside of the golf cart.

"He's probably inside," Dax said after a long moment. "We don't have a good view of the back door into the shop, so he could have slipped inside without us seeing. But let's wait it out for a minute, just in case."

I sat back in my seat, my tense shoulders relaxing slightly. I sucked in a full breath through my nose and willed my heart to calm. The quiet hum of the car seemed a direct contrast to our plight only moments ago. We weren't out of the woods yet, but for a moment, we needed to be still. The cart that had been coming down from the resort ambled past the field without braking or slowing, causing us to breathe easier.

"Are you nervous?" I asked Dax.

"Not for me."

"Why not?"

He met my gaze. "What are they going to do to me?"

"Probation? Fines? Jail? How bad on the island's sin scale is driving a car?"

He shrugged. "It's illegal, so they could do a lot of things."

"But you're not worried?"

He laughed. "The judge has been breathing down my neck to get his lawnmower back. He's not sending me away. It's you I'm worried about."

We faced forward once more to watch out the window. In the quiet, my ears tuned in to more things. The light tap of Dax's fingers on the arm rest, the plastic sound the seats made when we adjusted our positions, and the radio…which had been background noise most of our time in the car.

Our attention stayed locked on the cart next to the book shop while a song with a familiar tune began to play. It needed no introduction, really. Even I knew this song. Everyone in America knew this song. My shoulders swayed to the beat. I made it through the entire first verse, singing along in my head, but as the lyrics began working their way to the chorus, my hand gripped the steering wheel in anticipation of everyone's favorite moment of the song. My fingers gave the three distinct taps at just the right part when I stopped.

My body froze.

It was a facepalm kind of moment. I wanted to laugh and cry and start the song over. I wanted to memorize every word. Of course it was this song. It perfectly captured my entire summer with him. But mostly, I sat in awe and wonder at the song Dax had dubbed mine when it was really a song Neil Diamond had written long ago about a girl he'd named "Sweet Caroline."

The song was nearly over before I gained the courage to look at Dax. He was leaning back in his seat, one arm resting near the window, holding his head with one hand, watching me, waiting for me to figure it out in his calm, patient way. Something flashed across his face just then. Something dangerous. Something alluring. Something that made my breath hitch and my stomach tighten with nerves.

"Sweet Caroline," I whispered, turning to face him, my head leaning on the back of the seat.

"It's your song."

Was his voice always this low? The deep rasp and the overtly casual tone had the same effect on me as someone skating their fingers down my spine. His face was illuminated only by the sliver of moonlight through the window.

"Do you want me to drive back?" he asked.

"Yeah."

The lyrics of "Sweet Caroline" raced through my head as I moved to unbuckle my seatbelt. The words washed over me. What in that song made him think of me? The title? A verse? Or was it...everything? I wanted it to be everything. But wanting and having were two very different things.

I had just stepped out of the car when he said, "My seatbelt is stuck. I can't get it at this angle."

Confused, I leaned down, my hand resting on the open door as I peered inside, trying to see what the problem was. He had a whisper of a smile curling his lips. That should have been my first clue. He wore a t-shirt today. Only the barest hint of tattoos peeked out from the bottom of his sleeve. I loved the ink on his skin, but seeing him without them in this moment softened him somehow, even as my heart bid caution.

"It's stuck?" I asked.

"Yeah."

The prickles on my skin flared as I crawled back inside, kneeling carefully on the driver's seat in an effort to lean forward and examine his seatbelt. The air in the car vibrated with energy. My body trembled with anticipation.

There were so many moments in life that a person could miss because of overthinking. Over-analyzing. My time up until this point had been full of weights and measures. Bars and graphs. Everything compartmentalized and in its place. I hadn't had a place in my life for Dax Miller. My time with him had been a constant state of calculating, analyzing and rejecting. No matter how hard I tried to spin it, X plus Y could never equal Z.

Therefore, I couldn't have it. Him.

But this...

This.

I leaned in close and pushed his seatbelt button. It released immediately. As did the thundering of my heart.

"Liar," I whispered.

He brushed back my hair from my face before cupping my cheeks under his palm. His thumb trailed across my lips and cheeks and every freckle, leaving me feeling exposed and tingly and flooded with a craving that threatened to consume me.

His lips found a corner of my mouth. My toes curled.

"Every word," he murmured.

"What?" I whispered, his proximity snatching the breath from my lungs. My hands moved to his shoulders to keep me upright.

He pulled back, his eyes half-lowered with heavy lids. "Every word of that song belongs to you."

The sentence hung in the air, his sweetness cracking the wall that had always been between us. I was done. He was done.

Our resistance had been breached.

It happened too quickly to think. Too fast to stop. Or had it been more like a crescendo, slowly building up pace and tempo over the summer? At this moment, there was nothing left to reject. Maybe I *could* have it all. I could refigure the sequence. I could—

His hands slipped to the back of my neck and pulled my mouth to his. The tug and slide of his lips tangling with mine sparked a fire low in my belly. There was no hesitation on my part. I met fire with fire.

Growing impatient with our position, Dax's hands found my hips, lifting and pulling me across the seat before settling me across his lap. I pressed in close. My hands, now free to wander, slid up his shoulders before slipping to the back of his head, losing themselves in the curls at the base of his neck. We were insatiable, giving in to the thing we'd both denied ourselves for so long.

He pulled back slightly, his lips wandering across my jawline before I pulled his mouth back on mine. His arms pressed and cradled me closer while my body relished in the feeling of being completely cocooned in his arms. Those arms that had protected and defended me all summer long.

There was something about being with Dax in this moment that calmed my nerves and eased my fears. And then I realized why I hadn't been nervous to be in this car with him. To be risking this moment with him. Because with him, I was safe to fall. I had *always* been safe to fall. Safe to be less than perfect. The feeling was both addicting and liberating. There was a power in feeling safe with someone–safe to make mistakes and to be completely yourself. Safe to trust someone that much.

We'd been trying all night to not get caught. Who knew that getting caught would be the best part?

As if the universe had heard my bold thought, flashes of blue and red lit up our cozy oasis. A tap on our window had us pulling apart, blinking in confusion, me still on Dax's lap and his hands around my waist.

"What in the—" Beau stood, gaping at us, as he began to yell. His words were muffled by the closed door between us, but we had no trouble interpreting his meaning.

He was ticked.

CHAPTER 25

Biology Class
Day 49

Mr. Gray began his lecture at two minutes past the hour. It wasn't unusual for Dax to be late. I slouched in my seat, my hand holding up my chin, and kept my gaze forward. Our conversation from yesterday ran through my mind on a constant shuffle.

The words I had said on repeat.

He never came.

BEAU FLIPPED on the light in a large room at the police station. A low hum sounded before the small island's version of a jail lit up in fluorescent lights. The room boasted two small holding cells tucked side by side against the wall. They were cage-like and gave the impression of sturdy chicken wire wrapped around all sides. Honestly, it looked like something anybody could order off the internet. Each cell had a twin-sized bed with a questionable blanket and pillow sitting skewed on top and a metal toilet right there in the open room.

The cell on the right looked like it had been used more as a storage room than to hold prisoners. Boxes, old books, and a couple of dusty printers that looked like they'd come directly from the 1990s lined the floor and bed. Directly across from the holding cells was a large desk with a tidy stack of papers, a computer, and a plaque that said *Officer Beau Palmer*.

"Are you serious?" Dax asked, after we had a chance to soak in our immediate future.

"I had four calls from the retirement center alone, telling me about a car sighting, and at least seven other calls from people around the community."

"How about we just —" Dax began.

"Nope!" Beau held up his hand in front of Dax's face. "You guys dragged me out of bed at three in the morning for something as dumb as this. I'll be doing paperwork all day tomorrow, and I'll probably still be taking calls all night."

It appeared that Beau was still grumpy.

As if on cue, Beau's phone began to ring. He picked it up, glanced at it, and groaned before silencing the ring.

"Sorry you got dragged into this, Ivy," Beau said. "But if I make him stay, I've got to make you stay too."

"It was my idea. I should be the one staying."

Seriously. Why wasn't I worried? This whole thing still felt like it was some grand adventure. I was still on PROBATION from the last time I screwed up. This was serious stuff. But also, I just had the best kiss of my life.

So…

That was probably where the wires were getting crossed.

"Alright, pick your cell," Beau said, striding forward to the first cell without all the boxes and shoving a key in the lock. "And yes, you are sleeping here tonight. I'm that annoyed."

The door opened with a squeak and a clank. He moved to the next and tried all seven keys on his chain before kicking the cage in frustration.

"Shouldn't you have a keypad or something?" Dax asked, his arms folded and amusement pouring out of him. "Can't every halfway decent criminal pick locks nowadays?"

Beau turned toward his friend. "Can you?"

Dax made a face. "I plead the fifth."

"Do you even know what the fifth is?"

"Yeah. It's the one where I don't have to say anything."

At this point, I was internally pleading with Dax to shut up, but we both saw the moment Beau snapped.

"That's it. You're sharing this cell. Dax, you'd better be a gentleman and let her have the bed." He motioned us to move forward.

"I told you I'd let you drive it for a week," Dax said, the humor not quite gone from his face.

"You didn't even tell me you had a car on the island. For two years?! I'm going to need it for at least a month before I even think about getting over this," Beau said.

We humbly stepped inside the cell as Beau quite dramatically locked us inside.

"If you need it, the toilet is conveniently located next to the bed. It's the middle of the night, so I don't have to get you any food." He strode to the mini refrigerator sitting next to his desk and pulled out two water bottles. He hesitated half a second before muttering a string of words under his breath and grabbing a half-eaten bag of Tootsie Rolls. He handed us both a water bottle and me the bag of candy before backing away.

"Don't share that with him," he told me, pointing at Dax. "And I'm not staying here, for your information. After what I just saw in that car, there's no way." He shot Dax a stern look. "And just so you know, there are cameras all over this room. Don't do anything I wouldn't do."

"Are you talking about that one camera right in the middle of your desk?" Dax asked, watching his friend in some amusement.

Beau stiffened, glancing quickly behind him. "There's more."

Dax laughed, giving the bed a kick with his foot. "What's the year on this bad boy?"

"It's definitely older than any of us." He turned off the light, which immediately kicked on a few yellow security lights, casting a golden hue about the room. "But you'll be on the floor, so it doesn't matter. Sweet dreams. Hopefully I'll remember you guys are here in the morning."

"The accommodations are lovely. Thank you," Dax called pleasantly.

There were more inaudible grumbles before the door slammed shut.

A moment of silence passed between us where Dax stood almost sheepishly running his hand through his hair as he looked around before his gaze fell to me.

"I've never brought a girl here before."

A laugh bubbled out of me as I looked around our home for the next few hours. The frumpy-looking bed held almost zero appeal. The toilet looked clean enough but was missing a few walls around it. But Dax was here with me. It was all a big adventure. A dream. We couldn't be in trouble if it felt this easy to be here.

Right?

I pulled out a Tootsie Roll from the bag Beau handed me. "Do you think he's more upset because we drove the car on the island or that you had a car and didn't tell him?"

"Definitely the second."

"Why didn't you tell him?" I asked, popping the candy in my mouth.

He shrugged. "That's a lot of information to put on a cop. Are you planning on sharing that bag, Books?"

I pretended to think. "I don't know... Beau specifically told me not to."

"Ten hours to the first person who can knock over the camera on his desk."

I laughed, looking at the small camera facing us. "Do you think he's watching us right now?"

"All I know is that I'm not peeing in here with that thing pointed this way."

I shot him a look that made him laugh. "You better not be peeing at any time in this cell."

He nodded toward the candy bag. "Ten hours?"

"Fine." I pulled a handful of candy out of the bag before handing it over to him. There was a narrow slit of a window in the center of the cage door. It was wide enough to deliver meals to people sitting inside and toss Tootsie Rolls toward the desk. My first attempt glanced off the corner of Beau's desk.

"Pathetic, Books," Dax said as he lined up his shot. I laughed when his attempt didn't even make it to the desk.

"Eh, I'm not too worried," I said, getting into the game. My enthusiasm began to wane, however, when after five minutes of trash talking and goading, the closest we'd come was wiggling the camera a bit.

"Are you regretting driving the car?" he asked, throwing another shot, his candy landing in a pile on Beau's desk.

I thought for a moment. "No. I keep waiting for regret to show up, but so far…I'm still on a high."

Dax shot me a look. "Maybe the high is from something else."

Heat bloomed on my cheeks as wide as I took in a shaky breath. I needed to get a grip. I was in jail with Dax Miller.

JAIL.

This was not a time to flirt. I needed casual Dax and Ivy back if I was going to survive the night here. Currently, I had enough energy zipping through my body to power a small building.

"You mean when I actually got to drive the cult classic 1969 Chevy Chevelle?"

"The second-best thrill of the night."

He leaned casually against the cell door, one hand in his pocket as he studied me. Every part of me wanted to walk up to him and bring us back to where we had left off in the car.

Judging from the smoldering fire in his gaze, I'd bet he'd be willing.

Instead, I clasped the wall of the holding cell to keep me from moving toward him.

But my brain had already taken flight, soaring high in the clouds. I relived the strength of his arms pulling me onto his lap. The softness of his fingers brushing the hair from my face. His warm body pressed against mine, and the—

"Are you leaving on Monday?"

His careful question pulled me from a car of tangled limbs and back to reality. His stormy eyes on mine.

"According to my dad." I threw another candy, and to my shock and amazement, it was a direct hit. The camera tipped backward. I raised my hands in triumph.

Dax smiled. "Ten hours."

Suddenly, I felt hollow inside. Like I'd spent all of my money riding a carnival ride that ended too quickly and left me feeling empty and slightly nauseous. The hours didn't mean anything anymore. This past week, I had gotten really good at fooling myself into thinking that reality didn't exist for me. That my summer on the island would never end. I walked farther into the cell, still not tempted by the frumpy bed and instead, sunk down the wall onto the cold ground at the foot of the bed.

"Do you want to go?" Dax sat against the opposite wall from me, his legs stretched out in front of him.

Did I want to go?

That was the question of the hour.

"I've worked my entire life to get a job like this. I finally get to teach a class. I don't think I have much choice."

"After the class, though? From what you told me on the boat, you'll be doing more research.

"But I will be teaching one day," I insisted. My voice was strong and clear, though in direct contrast to my cloudy thoughts. "Look, I know what I told you on the boat. It probably sounded bad. It's a great career, and it's paid for now, and I think I'll enjoy it. It's just hard to find jobs right out of graduation, so I...it's hard to..." I trailed off, not knowing what to say or how to end it. My brain was a mess of words and numbers. My heart hadn't even entered the chat.

His jaw clenched slightly as he looked away. "As long as it's *you* that wants it. That's great. But life is hard enough without trying to manage somebody else's expectations."

I didn't have to ask who he was referring to.

"Look, things with my dad go back a long way."

"Tell me."

I scoffed. "We're literally in jail right now. We don't need to get into all of this. We need to sleep."

Dax nodded toward the bed of questionable sheets. "You first."

When I visibly wavered, he pushed one more button. "I'm guessing that it was your daddy issues that got us here, so it seems fitting to talk about."

"We're here because I wanted to finish my hours. How nice of you to figure out a way for me to—"

"Ivy."

He was waiting for me to speak. I could feel my body slowly shutting down as the excitement from the night began fading.

I waited a moment before I spoke, doing my best to sort through twenty-eight years of complicated emotions into something I could tell Dax.

"It was hard growing up with my dad. You know how he is. Nothing I ever did was good enough for him, so I always knew I had to be something great for him to love me. Or do something great."

"How did you know that?"

"Know what?"

"That you had to earn his love?"

"What do you mean?"

He shrugged. "Even after everything with my parents, I never doubted they loved me. Why did you?"

A memory from long ago bubbled up to the surface. It wasn't a moment I'd forgotten. It was the opposite of that. I couldn't have forgotten it if I tried. And I had tried. It had been repressed, pushed down, and even denied on occasion. But never forgotten.

"I think I was nine. My parents were fighting in the kitchen, and I was hiding in my room under the covers. I remember hearing my mom walking down the hall, probably to go cry in her room, but my dad followed her. He probably forgot I was even home, or maybe he thought I was asleep, but I overheard him tell my mom that getting her pregnant with me was the biggest mistake of his life."

Dax didn't move, his body tense except for the smallest tick in his jaw.

"They had been about to break up, but then they found out they were pregnant with me, so they got married instead," I said, a humorless laugh billowing out of me. "I've unpacked a lot of that in therapy already, but it's easy to see how my entire childhood was spent proving my worth to a man who would never see it."

He moved his hand across his mouth as he watched me. I grew self-conscious at his sympathetic gaze, turning me into a water spout that refused to turn off.

"I was doing really well in Tennessee—or so I thought. But since coming to the island, I've realized I only thought that because I wasn't around him. Anyway, I know he doesn't have the capacity to feel love in that way. I know this. My mom knows this. Angela will figure it out eventually. So I can't figure out why it still hurts so much?"

"Because he's your dad," Dax stated softly.

I took a breath, fighting for control of my emotions, before adding, "It's kind of funny... After all my therapy, I can diagnose everything he says and does. I know all the narcissistic behaviors. I know he won't change. I can name all the emotions I'm feeling whenever I'm around him, but I can't seem to ever fully overcome them, and it sucks. So, when you ask me if I want to go to Tennessee? I have no idea. I'm so lost in not knowing if I want to go because it's really something I love, or if it's something I think I love because it's what he wants for me."

I sunk down on the floor, curling on my side, my head resting on my arm. I had run a marathon tonight, between the adrenaline, the kiss, getting caught, and now sitting in a cell. I wanted to sleep, but my brain whirled too much to settle just yet.

And then Dax spoke.

"It's interesting how people move in and out of our lives...how they kind of...shape us. There's a lot of potential havoc to be had just from being close to someone."

Though his voice was light I could feel the pain behind his words.

"Do you think you'd be different if Mason hadn't left?" I asked softly.

After a moment, he cleared his throat, bending one leg at the knee to rest his arm on it. "I wonder if I would have turned out more like Trent."

"A doctor? I don't know... I've seen your handiwork with a scalpel. I wasn't that impressed." I sent him a teasing smile, sensing that we needed a moment to regroup.

He shook his head, a reluctant smile forming on his lips. "After all my work in biology, it's ironic that you're the one with the doctor tag on your name."

I laughed. "So you think you might have been different if Mason was still here?"

"I don't know. I was on track to be like Trent before Mason left. I wasn't as hard core with the books, but I was a pretty good student. Never caused much trouble. But when he left, everything changed. Keith saved me in a lot of ways because he taught me how to be good at something. And I loved it. I love taking things apart and fixing them with my hands. The mechanics of how things are built just make sense to me. So maybe I would have been exactly the same either way."

"Or maybe you found what you loved because of Mason."

There was a pause in the air as we both contemplated the idea of that statement.

"So, if I ever see Mason again, I should be thanking him, huh?" His voice was soft, reminding me once again about hope.

"I think you became exactly who you were meant to be. And you should be proud of that."

"So, extremely good-looking and smart?" he teased.

"Yeah." I couldn't even say it sarcastically. I meant it too much.

"Thanks, Doc."

I laughed, my head feeling fuzzier by the minute. "I thought you said you weren't going to call me that unless I could operate on your leg."

"I've said a lot of things. I can't be held responsible for all of them."

"I wonder what I would have been like if my dad had been different," I said.

"You probably would have been a lot funner in biology."

A soft laugh escaped me. "If you were closer, I'd kick you for that."

"Get over here then."

I bit my lip as his words tempted and toyed with me. Notwithstanding the fact that he would be a much more comfortable place to lay my head than the cold floor, I had a strong suspicion I would have a hard time letting go of Dax if I were to crawl over there now. And there was too much unknown whirling in my mind for me to be another person wreaking havoc on his life when I left.

"You light up whenever you talk about teaching. It's in your blood. I watch you at the cafe. You like people, and people like you. With or without your dad, I think you're right where you're supposed to be." The words were said with such softness. Achingly so. As if he were preparing us both for something.

"Guess we're both better off than we thought."

That statement was going to be my last. I could feel myself slipping, until the tiniest little nugget of information from his brother came flying back into my conscience. It knocked and clanged noisily until I had to get it out. Now. Not tomorrow. There was something about talking in the dark that made a person brave. I'd be too chicken tomorrow.

"Dax?" I asked.

"Hmm?" His voice was heavy with sleep.

"Did I really help you graduate?"

The room fell silent except the sound of a ticking clock somewhere on the wall. He waited so long to speak I thought he had fallen asleep.

"I was about to quit. The counselor told me I had to take biology and an English class to graduate, and I didn't want to do either one of them. I told Keith I would get my GED later, and that would be good enough. He told me I had to try it out for three weeks to see how it went. I was on my final week, just messing around, until I could tell Keith it didn't work out. And then Mr. Gray switched my partner."

A flame dipped low in my belly, sending sparks zipping though my veins.

"And she must have been sweet and smart and a really good influence—" I began.

"She was the bossiest, most annoying girl I'd ever been around," he interrupted while I broke off, laughing.

"She made me work, didn't put up with my crap, and had a smile that lit me up for days. I couldn't have gotten her out of my head if I tried."

I covered my face with my hands. It was too much. More than I bargained for. More than I was ready for. But I snatched the words from the air and kept them anyway.

"Dax," I said, taking a deep breath. "You lit me up too."

It wasn't wasted on me that I used past tense when the way I was feeling currently made me yearn to use present, but my heart was still fragile. This awakening in me was still new, and there were still so many unknowns. So, I kept to myself the fact that Dax Miller had done a number on me this summer.

But I had a house and a job and a life in Tennessee.

"I'm going to regret telling you this," he began, "but I'm half delirious right now. I know you Googled the tattoo of my car, but have you ever looked closer?"

"Huh?"

"Maybe you should."

"Wait. What?"

I could hear the smile in his voice. "Goodnight, Caroline."

All of a sudden, the tune of "Sweet Caroline" was being knocked on the floor of the holding cell. With a grin on my face, I made a mental note to examine Dax's tattoos more thoroughly in the morning, and with my body half numb from lying on the concrete floor, I slipped off to sleep.

SOMETIME LATER, I felt myself being lifted up off the hard ground. I became slightly more aware when Dax placed me gently on the bed.

"Ew. I don't want to use the pillow," I mumbled, trying to move my head away.

"I've got something covering it. Relax."

Carefully, I let my head fall back, waiting for something to eat me. Instead, I was enveloped in a soft, uneven pillow that smelled exactly like Dax. His shirt. His hand brushed a hair out of my face, and I felt a soft kiss on my forehead before he moved away.

"Dax?"

"Yeah?"

"I thought you didn't kiss girls who are leaving."

"Are you leaving?" His voice was as soft as his caress.

"I don't know."

"Then there's your answer."

WELCOME TO SUNSET HARBOR

- Belacourt Resort
- Golf Course
- Noah's House
- Jane's House
- Nature Preserve
- Dax's Duplex
- Seaside Oasis Retirement Home
- Sunset Repairs
- Phoenix's Office
- City Offices
- Sunrise Cafe
- Scoops Ahoy Ice Cream
- Keene B&B
- Town Square
- Bakery
- Briggs's Apartment
- The Book Isle
- Cuts and Curls
- Tristan & Beau's House
- Capri's House
- Gemma's House
- Holland's House
- Beach Break Bar & Grill
- Public Beach

Gulf of Mexico

CHAPTER 26

Biology Class
Day 50

I sat up straight as Dax made his way across the room toward our table. My limbs felt strangely disassociated from the rest of my body. My hands tried to find their natural place toying with my hair, then resting on the desk, before finally coming together clenched tightly in my lap.

He settled in beside me, dropping his bag on the ground and plopping his phone onto the desk with a sigh. We were careful not to touch. Our shoulders kept a respectful twelve-inch distance between them.

"Dax, I'm sorry for what I said the other day. I was just...mad." I winced at the awkwardness of my speech. The apologetic words that had been burning in my head the past couple days were nowhere to be found when I finally had my chance.

Dax turned to me, his eyebrows raised appreciatively. "Wow. Did your dad's PR manager help you come up with that? That was pretty good, Books."

"Dax," I began.

"It's fine. We're good."

"Why do you look like we're not?"

"We are. It's not like we're friends. We only have a couple days left until graduation. And then...you're off to change the world, so...we're good. Just be sure to tell your fans who did all the heavy lifting in your high school biology class."

BEAU DIDN'T FORGET about us.

At promptly 8:30 am the next morning, the door to the jail flew open with a loud bang. Beau stepped inside, dressed in his full uniform, and flipped on the lights. Dax and I stretched and yawned. Him from his spot on the floor and me from the bed—which had been surprisingly comfortable as far as jail beds go. I hated to give up my Dax-scented shirt pillow, but I tossed it to him anyway.

Beau walked inside the room and plopped a humongous book on his desk. He then picked it up and plopped it down again before looking over at us.

"Oh, I'm sorry. Did I wake you both?"

"Not at all," Dax said, his dark eyes running over me in a way that made me jealous of whoever gets to wake up next to him for the rest of their life. I self-consciously tucked my wild and matted hair behind my ear.

"After I dropped you two off," Beau said, looking at Dax, "I moved the car back to your secret storage room, like you told me. I hate you, by the way, in case I forget to tell you today."

"I love you too, buddy," Dax said, coming to stand by the entrance of the cell, his hand leaning on the door. "How'd she run for you?"

"I don't want to talk about it." Beau pulled out his phone and held it out in front of him, pointing toward us. "But I am getting a fun little souvenir for myself. Say cheese."

He pocketed the phone before coming to stand before us. I slid out of the bed, straightening my shirt and short overalls. I had been surprised at how well I'd slept after breaking the law. Even in my sleep-drunk state, the kiss scene from the car played in my head and dreams all night.

Jail sleep might be the best sleep. Who would have known?

"So, here's the thing," Beau began. "Judge Baylor's beautiful wife, Nancy, was up taking the dog out last night and happened to see what looked like a car driving past her window. So, naturally, she woke up the judge. Guess who he called right away?"

Dax pointed at Beau.

Beau nodded. "That's right. Me. He called me at 2:30 in the morning to check it out. But guess what? I was already awake, taking calls." He looked at Dax. "Pretty bold move to drive a car when you work next door to a retirement home with people who never sleep at night—and a girlfriend still on probation."

See? This is the problem. Even now, as my stomach clenched and the bubble I'd been living in began to deflate, hearing Beau call me Dax's girlfriend brought me right back to sunshine and butterflies.

"Was that your golf cart watching us last night on the square?" Dax asked, a smile hovering on his lips.

"Yup."

"What does that mean for us?" I asked, trying to remind myself that I was in trouble.

"The judge wants to talk to you both in ten minutes."

A thud landed in my stomach at that. It looked like I hadn't completely gone off the rails. The thought of Judge Baylor looking at me in disappointment might be the thing that brings me back down to reality.

I looked down at my wrinkled clothes and touched my face, no doubt looking like a raccoon with mascara under my eyes. "In ten minutes?"

Beau sighed and strode to a cabinet located near his desk and rummaged around before he stood in front of us again and handed us each a flimsy, travel-sized toothbrush wrapped in plastic and a small tube of toothpaste to share.

"You guys have five minutes to brush your teeth, but that's

it. Your sink doesn't work, so you'll have to use the bathroom down the hall. Then we need to head to his office."

He unlocked our cells, stepped aside, and motioned us toward a hallway.

Dax grabbed Beau's arm, forcing his friend to look at him. "Listen, I'm sorry I didn't tell you about the car. I didn't want you to have to hold onto that knowledge as a cop. Besides, I didn't actually plan on driving it on the island. I just needed somewhere to work on it."

"Wait." Beau turned to me. "Was driving it really your idea?"

The look on my face must have said it all, because Beau only smiled and shook his head. "Maybe Dax wasn't reaching too high after all." He motioned down the hallway. "Bathroom is the first door on the left. You now have four minutes."

The hallway had its own pulse as we walked together toward the unisex bathroom. Or maybe it was my mind that was thumping. The carefree night of driving a car with Dax would stay with me for a long time, no matter what happened. The feeling of being numb to all reason except wanting to be a little crazy. Having a little adventure. It all gave me life. A buzz of excitement. But…crazy had consequences. And now, I was headed to see the judge.

Again.

Dax opened the bathroom door for me, watching me as I brushed past him, my arm sweeping against his.

The door closed automatically, the click of the lock making me jump. He handed me the toothpaste. My trembling fingers dropped it immediately on the counter. Until that moment, I hadn't been aware I was shaking. As I reached for it, Dax grabbed my hand and held it steady in his. We were so close. I could feel the heat from his chest vibrating out of his black t-shirt.

I could have stayed like that all day, but Beau's loud thumping on the bathroom door, giving us a three-minute warning, did the trick. I pulled my hand from his grasp and began brushing my teeth.

He did the same.

I wasn't going to look in the mirror. I didn't need his disheveled brown hair and mischievous smile confusing me further before I discovered my fate. Our fate. But my body refused to care what I thought, and my eyes darted upward. It was a wild pitch, but he caught them perfectly, holding me hostage. He scrunched his nose at me until it became too much of a chore to hold back my smile.

We spit our water out and wiped our mouths with a paper towel.

I faced him, gulping down a breath of courage. "I'm so sorry, Dax. It was my idea, and now you're going to get in trouble."

Dax had built a life here. He had a good job and was well-liked in the community. He had turned so much of his life around, and I hated the idea that he might be in trouble because of my wild night sowing oats.

Beau banged against the bathroom door. "One more minute. And for the love, you'd better just be brushing your teeth in there."

Dax ignored Beau, and with a finger on my chin, he lifted my face up to meet his. He wore a small smile on his face, as though he found all of this funny, which immediately had my thoughts racing. Maybe I had started him on a path that would make him spiral. He'd been doing so well. His mom was going to kill me. What had I done?

I put my hands on his chest, trying to shake sense into him. "Dax, this could be bad. We're going to see the judge. What if you get in trouble? What if I ruined your whole life?"

"Eh. I was just the accomplice." He breathed out a laugh while I glared at him. Laughing was for five minutes ago. I tried to move around him, but he blocked me.

"Hold on, Books," he whispered, his hands holding me in

front of him. He held my gaze for a long moment, his humor apparent, but something else too. Something sweeter that wrapped around my insides and squeezed.

"There's nobody else on this earth I'd rather share a jail cell with." Warm brown eyes scattered across my face as he leaned closer and whispered, "I'd do it all over again if it brought me right back here."

I shook my head at him, but the smile wouldn't be repressed. Ever so slowly, I turned him to the side, peeling up the sleeve on his t-shirt. His shoulder displayed an impressive sunset on the beach, a palm tree, and his car. I had always been the most fascinated by the car, but there was something else underneath that looked familiar. Something I should have put together long before now. My face burned in secret delight as I looked up at him, my fingers splayed over the ink.

"A DNA strand? You used to hate those jokes."

A soft smile touched his lips. "I was laughing on the inside."

All of my tattoos mean something.

"I didn't think I'd ever see you again," he said, turning to face me once more, his hands on my shoulders. "Not really. But that time with you changed me for the better."

"Alright, I'm coming in!" Beau yelled through the door.

Dax groaned before yanking open the door. "Can't two people brush their teeth in peace?"

Beau escorted us to the judge's door before leaving us alone to our fate. Dax's tattoo revelation was currently squeezing my heart into a thousand pieces, but I had to put that aside for another day.

The judge was in session.

There were no attorneys or court reporters. It was just Judge Baylor seated at his desk. He motioned for us to sit down while I searched his face for clues and found none. Dax's shoulder pressed into mine, his easy-going presence calming my jittery hands.

Judge Baylor looked at us both for a long moment, his hands clasped together on his desk. I sat up straighter in my chair, and I noticed Dax doing the same.

"Been out for a little joyride together, I hear?" His voice cracked as though he found humor in the escapade, but the comedy of it all wasn't quite as evident on his face.

I was determined not to hang my head low, so I looked him in the eye and said, "It was my fault, Your Honor."

"No, it wasn't," Dax protested.

Judge Baylor leaned back in his chair, watching us. "Are you both aware it is against the law to drive and have in your possession a car or truck on this island?"

"Yes, Your Honor," Dax said.

"And you still did it?"

"I wanted to, and I insisted," I said quickly. Dax lightly stepped on my foot.

"You've been doing quite a few things together around the island, if the gossip hit my ears correctly." He looked at Dax. "Whenever I drove past your shop after work headed home, your lights were always on—oftentimes, well into the evening. You worked yourself to the bone. But ever since Ms. Brooks's arrival, I've been seeing you in quite a few places—the cafe, the Fourth of July breakfast, the farmers' market." He motioned to the propeller clock on his wall. "I love my clock, by the way." Dax and I both gaped at him. Judge Baylor chuckled at our reaction before continuing, "I even heard from my granddaughter that the two of you were playing volleyball on the beach the other night."

Looking at Dax, he added, "I didn't know you were the volleyball type."

"Believe me, I'm not, Your Honor."

A twinkle shown in Judge Baylor's eyes. "There is a lightness about you now that wasn't there before, and I like it."

He leaned forward, straightening a handful of papers on his

desk. "However, you were also hiding an illegal car in your garage. How did you even get it here without being seen?"

Dax cleared his throat. "I brought it over in parts, Your Honor."

Judge Baylor stared at him, slightly dumbfounded. "In parts? You pieced together an entire car from parts?"

"Yes, sir."

The judge blinked before chuckling and shaking his head slightly. "Well, whatever this town pays you for your services, it's probably not enough. That's impressive, son."

Dax flushed slightly at these words while a feeling of pride on his behalf filled my entire body.

He pointed at Dax with his big paw. "However…illegal."

He shifted his judicious eyes back to mine. "And you, Ms. Brooks. This is the second time in less than two months you've been in to see me. Before that, you were a perfect student, graduated college with honors, and went and made yourself into a doctor of mathematics." He darted a glance to the fake tattoo peeking out from the bottom of my sleeve. "Since your time back on Sunset Harbor, you've been avoiding your service hours, if the empty window display in Mr. Miller's shop tells me anything, and you willingly drove an illegal car on this island. Your father seems to think your time here hasn't been a good influence on you."

It took some work to school my expression at the mention of my dad.

"But let me tell you what *I've* observed." This man, and his low Southern drawl, was beginning to give me whiplash. I wasn't sure what to think or where any of this was going.

Dax's leg bumped lightly into mine.

"You're causing public disturbances now, but you feel more like a real person than you ever did before. There is a stiffness in perfection that's difficult for people to relate to. There's a loudness about you now and a spark of life in your eyes that wasn't there before."

I sensed more was coming, so I sucked in a breath while my heart pumped wildly.

"However, you also recklessly drove an illegal car on my island in the middle of the night."

Reckless was debatable when our top speed was forty miles an hour, but there was no need to bring that up.

Judge Baylor sighed, his hand covering his mouth as he stared thoughtfully between the two of us.

"I still have one question, Ms. Brooks. I recall giving my permission to let you transfer the rest of your service hours to Nashville so your career wouldn't have to suffer for your accidental DUI. You are set to leave in two days. You're still on probation. My only question for you is, why?"

Dax sat up in his seat. "Your Honor, I told her she could bargain her hours down if she did it. I forced her hand."

Judge Baylor raised his eyebrows. "Is that true, Ms. Brooks? Did he *make* you do it?"

I glanced at Dax before looking back to the judge. "No."

Dax scoffed. "I gave her a list of bogus things to do to lessen her hours. It was my fault for putting the idea in her head."

He looked interested at this. "What was on the list?"

A hint of a smile crossed Dax's face. "Get a tattoo, tag a building, and drive a car on the island."

Judge Baylor's face grew serious as he looked back and forth from Dax to me. "Did either of you spray paint a building?"

"No," I said at the same time Dax said, "She is much too chicken for something like that."

His stare grew cold. "You had both better be too chicken for that."

"We are," I assured him, kicking Dax with my foot while he hid a smile behind his hand.

"I've never been one for convention," Judge Baylor began. "In my courtroom, I want to serve the people how I see fit more than be someone's executioner."

Executioner. What a word.

I willed my hands to not fidget.

"It seems to have been a summer of both good and bad."

Judge Baylor had a flair for the theatrics. We stood there, a captive audience, awaiting our fate.

"The good I see in both of you now far outweighs the bad. And that tells me that making noise about this or putting you in jail for a few nights"—he peered down hard at us both—"might not be the right decision. So, your punishment will be time already served along with a day of community service performed together. I'm thinking a beach cleanup would be just the thing." He glanced up at the clock on his wall. "And Mr. Miller, your car better be on the 9:30 am ferry off this island."

Turning to me, he said, "Ms. Brooks, since there was no harm done, and nobody got hurt, I will allow my initial decision to transfer your remaining hours to Nashville to stand. I don't want this to set you back on a life where I assume you'll do far more good than you did last night. This is all unofficially official, and if I see you back in my office anytime soon, I won't be this nice."

I blinked at his dismissal. His speech hovered in the air like a cloud before it rained over me.

Over my parade.

His punishment had been better than anything I could have dreamed up. He'd been kind and generous. He gave me the out I needed.

So why didn't it feel right?

My entire life, I'd been afraid of mistakes. I'd made choices based on what others deemed fit for me. I created an entire life out of an illusion. My dad's happiness wasn't on me anymore.

Nobody could make a man like him happy. It wasn't about me. And it never had been.

Did I want to teach?

Yes.

Did I want to teach in Nashville?

No.

The word created such a visceral reaction the moment I allowed myself to think it. Relief poured from my body as I dared to let go of every expectation I'd put on myself. Every expectation I'd allowed others to place on me.

This summer with Dax had been about more than a court sentence. It had given me space to slowly reconstruct new dreams for myself. Dreams that involved more people and less studies. More time spent teaching and less behind a computer. A dream of raising children on the same island I loved as a child. And spending time with a brown-eyed man with a teasing smile who had become such a part of my life that I couldn't let go if I wanted to.

And I didn't.

Suddenly, my direction was clear.

Dax had stood and was shaking Judge Baylor's hand.

"Your Honor." My voice was strong and clear, cutting into their low voices, like a woman who knew exactly what she was doing. I didn't have any clue what I was doing, actually, but I did know what I felt, and when a girl feels like that, she doesn't go to Tennessee.

He and Dax looked at me.

"Yes?" Judge Baylor said.

I drew in a breath as I fought to find the words. "I'm not sure the punishment fits the crime."

Dax gaped at me slightly as I realized how bold my statement was. Holy crap. The ways this could backfire on me were countless, but I wasn't stopping now.

"What do you mean?" the judge asked, a perplexed expression drawn on his eyebrows.

"Well, Your Honor, I've been pretty bad."

We could have heard a pin drop for how quiet the room became. A part of me wished I would have tagged a building so I could have had more things to add to my summer resume, in case he needed proof. An accidental DUI, violation of my probation, TPing my dad's house, and an illegal driving spree felt like it needed one more thing.

But alas, I kept going. "And I think I need to stay here and deal with my consequences."

Dax stood still, watching me with a knowing, bemused expression that melted me into a puddle.

Understanding lit the good judge's face. He glanced back and forth between Dax and me and chuckled.

"I applaud your sense of conscience, Ms. Brooks. I can't say I saw that coming, but…" He glanced at Dax. "Maybe I should have."

"I revoke the initial sentence. I hereby sentence you to jail time already served. You must complete your service hours remaining to Dax Miller. You and Mr. Miller will do two beach cleanup days. And I'd like you to organize a community effort to get the Lego car up and running. I miss it, and I know the tourists miss it as well. Anything else I can add to your sentence, Ms. Brooks?"

I couldn't hold back the smile if I tried. "No. Thank you, Your Honor. That's perfect."

He glanced at the clock. "Mr. Miller, you now have twenty-five minutes to get your car to the ferry. I suggest you run."

Dax looked at me, but before I could stand, the judge said, "I'd like to talk to you alone for a minute, Ms. Brooks." To Dax, he added, "She's staying. Under no circumstances will there be kissing in my office. This will be the perfect punishment for you. Go get your car off my island."

Dax bit back a smile and gave me a look that told me he would definitely be seeing me later. He opened the door.

"And Dax?" the judge began.

"Yes, sir?"

"If you're going to start having more of a life, why don't you hire somebody to work for you so I don't have to wait two weeks to get my lawnmower back."

A grin crossed Dax's face. "Will do, sir."

Judge Baylor glanced at his watch and looked back up at Dax. "Your time starts now."

With one last look at me, Dax bolted out of the judge's office.

Once he was gone, I turned expectantly to the judge, bracing myself for whatever he might tell me.

He leaned forward at his desk, a big smile on his face. "I didn't have anything to tell you. I just didn't want that young man getting distracted when he only has twenty five minutes to move his car."

I laughed, bringing my hand to my face, attempting to hide my flushed cheeks.

"Ms. Brooks."

"Yes?" I dropped my hands in my lap.

This time, the expressive look on his face was filled more with wisdom than teasing. "As a judge on this island, there are always people who don't approve of my decisions: neighbors, friends…politicians."

My eyes flitted up to his.

He kept going. "That's something we all have to learn to live with. But we still have to make decisions—we have to take charge of our own lives. Our freedom to choose is the most important thing we have in this country, even if it might hurt or anger somebody else. Part of life is knowing that there is going to be disappointment sometimes." He leaned forward, his chair squeaking. "But when it comes to matters of your life and your heart, it shouldn't be you that's disappointed."

I nodded, grateful for this man's kindness toward me. "Thank you."

"And off the record, Ms. Brooks—even teenage altercations included, you'd be hard-pressed to find a better man in the world than Dax Miller."

Smiling, I stood up to go. "I definitely know that."

CHAPTER 27

Biology Class
Day 52

It was our last day in class. The last five minutes, actually, if the slow tick of the clock could be trusted. The last biology class of my high school career. Dax drummed his fingers on the table, ignoring me to listen to a song through his earbuds.

To my surprise, he suddenly turned toward me, a determined aloofness in his eyes.

"I've got a question for you, Books."

I blinked at him. "What?"

"Why is DNA so good at solving crimes?"

His face was so carefully passive, you almost wouldn't know that we'd ever had any moment between us outside of this class.

My lips twitched ever so slightly. "Did somebody read the chapters again?"

"Quit stalling."

"I don't know."

His eyes shot up. "Did you *not* read the chapters?"

I hadn't. My brain had been too occupied with other things.

"Not yet."

He leaned toward me. "Because it has all the inside information."

The bell rang so I grabbed my backpack and stood up to go. "You're right. That is annoying."

"Exactly. Have a nice life, Books."

NEWS of our escapade had spread like wildfire, at least according to the dozens of text messages from this morning that I had yet to read on my phone. I left the judge's office with a surprising (given the lack of sleep) spring in my step. Beau was nowhere to be found, and I became almost positive Dax had taken him on the ferry with him. He had some apologizing to do, and I was willing to bet the two boys had pulled off on a lonely stretch of road to break the car in.

The island looked different now that I was staying.

The sunshine and ninety-degree weather at ten in the morning? Cheery.

The sweat dripping down my neck? Charming.

The fact that I could still listen to Dax knock on my wall a tune that was now imprinted on my heart? Divine.

Seeing my dad sitting on the front steps of my duplex in his expensive running shorts and t-shirt? Nerve-wracking.

And then, strangely exhilarating.

There had been so much truth I'd had to face the past few weeks that now I actually craved it. So much inside of me sat simmering below the surface, begging to be freed. There was a power in giving feelings a voice. And I had a lot to say.

He stood at my approach. His hair looked matted at the edges, like he'd been sweaty before it dried in the breeze.

"I tried calling you," my dad called out.

"I haven't checked my messages," I said, stopping a few feet away from him.

"I imagine it's difficult to check messages when you're in jail."

Shrugging, I said, "Beau didn't take our phones away. And it was just the holding cell. Not jail."

By the look on my dad's face, he didn't appreciate my spelling out the difference.

"I'm not even going to give voice to the stupidity of what I heard went down last night." His jaw clenched as his arms folded across his body. "I just want to know what the judge said."

"He told me I could finish out my community service hours in Tennessee if I wanted."

Relief poured over his face.

"I told him I was staying."

His eyes darted back up to mine. "What? Why would you—"

"Because I'm staying."

"No. You're not."

"I am." A cool calm spread through me along with a breath of laughter. My voice didn't waver. A weight I'd carried for so many years began to lighten as I realized that this man's opinions didn't mean much to me anymore.

"You're not going to waste ten years of schooling because you decided to sow some wild oats this summer."

"I'm not wasting them," I said. "I'll still be teaching, but I'll find somewhere nearby."

"What? A community college? No." He shook his head adamantly while I grew bored of the conversation. "Not my daughter."

"Am I your daughter? Your name comes up as *The Senator* on my phone."

His jaw ticked with anger. "I'm very aware that my career means nothing to you, but—"

"Probably because your career means *everything* to you."

"That's not true." He shook his head adamantly.

"I've never once voted for you," I said, a faucet unwilling to be shut off.

His next words stalled on his lips as a look of betrayal etched across his face.

"Even when you used to send me the absentee ballots at school. I always voted against you. So maybe instead of trying to give me life advice, you should think about why your daughter, one of the only people who truly knows you, wouldn't vote for you."

He reared back slightly at this. And it was enough for me. The honest truth of my statement suddenly felt so heavy. So sad. I had already put years of therapy into mourning the father I had grown up with. Looking at him now, I found myself mourning the father he could have been.

"We're not done yet," he stated as I brushed past him and took the stairs up to my door.

"Yes, we are." When I grasped the door handle, I turned back. "Listen, Dad. I'm staying. I'm going to figure out what I want to do next, and you're going to have to deal with that. I don't want to be angry. I don't want to fight anymore, but if that means I can't talk to you, then so be it. I'll smile at you at the cafe. I'll pour your coffee. I'll even wave to you on the street. But until you're willing to try for something different, that's where our boundaries will have to stay."

And then I walked inside, feeling strangely liberated.

THE REST of my morning passed without Dax.

After my dad left, I got my phone call to Vanderbilt out of the way. They had been unsurprisingly understanding about the whole thing, which confirmed my suspicion that they would have no trouble replacing me. There were still things I needed to decide. I had a house in Nashville I would need to sell or rent. Eventually, I'd have to go back to pack up my house.

Noon rolled around with still no sight of or even message from Dax, which was fine. I was absolutely certain he and Beau were out on a joyride right now. And good for them. Hopefully, the friends had made up and buried their hatchets.

I attempted a nap after lunch but quickly decided that pacing my floor, listening for any sound of Dax returning, was more fun. When the cafe called at two in the afternoon, extremely short-handed and asking me to work, I couldn't get out of my house fast enough.

Had it all been a mistake? Why wasn't he texting me?

Maybe he forgot his phone. Maybe he didn't get the car on the ferry in time, and Beau had to arrest him. Maybe—and this idea was rapidly taking flight in my head—I had scared him off.

It was just now occurring to me that neither Dax nor I had ever really talked about our feelings. We danced around things, sure. This morning, brushing our teeth, and our late-night conversations began to blur in my mind. Then I went and more or less proposed marriage to Dax Miller inside the judge's office. Maybe not marriage, but it had been pretty clear what I was sticking around for. *Who* I was staying for. That was a lot of pressure on a man who had gotten comfortable carving out a life of not needing anyone.

I picked up my pace to the restaurant, needing something to occupy my hands and hopefully quiet the noise in my head. It was all going to be fine. Why do brains do these things? They find that tiny seed of doubt and then plant it, sprout it, and let it fully bloom all within minutes.

Dax had been ready to kiss me in Judge Baylor's office—a good one too, by the looks of it.

So, shut up, brain.

But seriously...where was he?

"What's with you?" Cat asked a while later, sitting across from Jane in a booth at the cafe.

"Huh?" I asked, wiping up some water drops on her table.

"I asked you three times if anything happened between you and Dax while you were sharing a freaking jail cell, and three times you told me the daily special." She leaned forward with a laugh. "I don't want clam chowder."

"Oh, sorry." I checked behind my ear for my pencil and found it. "What do you want?"

Jane bit back a laugh as I looked at them both in question.

"You've already put in her order," Jane said, smiling. "We just want to see how things are going with Dax. Though, by the looks of you, I think we could guess."

I opened my mouth to say something when a jingle at the door to the cafe drew my attention. I'd been looking up at the sound all afternoon. And every time, I'd been disappointed.

This time, however, a man with dark, rumpled hair and wild and sweet brown eyes, wearing a delicious pair of jeans and a black t-shirt strode inside. He scanned the cafe until his gaze locked on mine—where it stayed, swallowing me up. My heart came to a stop as I watched him. Feeling shy, all of a sudden, I tucked a loose curl behind my ear, waiting for him to tell me I had misread a few signals.

I wasn't crazy. I hadn't imagined it all. But...what if?

And then...the tiniest tug of his lips started my heart up again. From across the room, he began making his way toward me.

I heard the girls sitting in the booth gasp and whisper, but all I could think about as he approached was the gleam in his eye that made my insides quake and my hands clench together.

He stopped in front of me, a pace away.

"You staying, Caroline?" His low voice caused goosebumps to scatter across my skin.

"Do you want me to?"

He reared back slightly at this, confusion etched in his brow. "What?"

I fingered the tie on my apron. "I just...want to make sure...

I was pretty bold in the judge's..." I trailed off helplessly, tangling my words. I didn't want to put any pressure on him, so if he didn't want me, I was going to give him an out.

Dax looked down at Cat and Jane, who weren't even pretending to hide the fact that they were watching this discussion with rapt attention. He held his hands out as if to have them explain something.

Cat shook her head, giving me a look. "I'm so sorry, Dax. She's into math and stuff. Some things she's pretty clueless about. But she's been messing up our orders all morning because she can't stop thinking about you."

His lips tugged upward at that and he turned back to me. "Can you go on break?"

I glanced around the busy cafe, not seeing Jean anywhere. "I don't kno—"

"We'll watch her tables," Jane said, grinning, her eyes dancing. "You go show her what's painfully obvious to the rest of us."

"Great." Dax grabbed my hand and whirled me around to follow him as he strode toward the kitchen in the back of the restaurant.

"Dax!" I pulled on his hand. "I can't just leave them to watch my tables!"

"Yes, you can," came his obstinate reply. "You just got out of jail. You're a wild woman now."

A chorus of delighted catcalls from the restaurant regulars followed us as we burst into the kitchen.

"She's going on break!" Dax called out as we flew past Jean and a laughing Marco, and out the back door.

By the time he released my hand and pushed me gently against the back wall of the cafe, I was blushing and laughing and completely head over heels for Dax Miller.

He stepped closer, one arm around my waist and one hand behind my neck, pulling me into him as he kissed away every doubt. He was very thorough about this business, to which I could only feel grateful.

"Where were you?"

He leaned in, nuzzling my neck as though this wait had been too long for him as well.

"I forgot my phone in the holding cell. And then I took Beau with me, and he wanted to exact his revenge by keeping me away from you as long as possible."

I laughed, throwing my arms around his neck to drag myself even closer to him. "I'm sure you were just miserable, driving that old bucket of rust up and down the highway."

His arms tightened around me. "It was the worst. And actually, Beau wasn't planning to torture me quite so long. The car got a flat tire down the highway. I didn't have a spare, so we had to get towed into a tire shop and wait forever to get it put on. Then the ferry was late. Then I couldn't find you. It was like the universe was trying to punish me for letting you take the car out last night."

I leaned up and kissed him, slow and sweet. "If this is being punished, you better lock me up."

"I'm sorry you got in trouble," he said, his eyes sweeping across my face as if he was memorizing every freckle.

"I'd do community service with you any day."

He grinned. "My kind of woman."

I took a breath. "Dax…I like you so much it scares me. I'm worried I won't be enough for you. I'm worried that my brain has gone to mush, and I can see myself forgetting all about teaching because I just want to sweep the floors in your shop so I can hang out with you. You've jumbled me up in all the best ways."

His smile slayed me just then. As did the way his hands slid up my sides to land on my shoulders and neck. As did the kisses he wielded at that spot just below my ear. And along my jawline. Until I captured his mouth with mine.

When he'd had his fill, he stepped back.

"Books, I was gone for you in high school and it took about ten seconds of you being back to realize not much had changed."

It was too much. The sweetness. *He* was too much. But he wasn't done.

He leaned in closer, "So gone that I would clean the shop bathroom every day before you got there."

A laugh sputtered out of me. "I knew it."

"And I'd leave my shop doors open to blow in dirt so the floors would be dirty enough to sweep every day. I ate at the cafe more times this summer than I have my entire life. I wanted you by me. But I knew you were leaving and so I kept trying to deny it and push you away, just like everybody else in my life."

I brushed at a strand of his hair on his forehead.

"Books, I'm not good with words. I hadn't realized how much I had shut people out of my life after Mason left. I made it my business not to need anyone again. And then you showed up and I suddenly needed every second with you."

"It was incredibly annoying," he said, as he kissed my nose and made me laugh.

"You're exactly who I want—who I've always wanted." He glanced down, running a hand through his hair. "I just never thought I could have you."

"I think you're pretty good with words," I said, smiling up at him.

"I'm better without words, though," he said, his nose brushing softly against mine.

"My kind of talk," I said. "And what about—"

His impatient lips interrupted mine, making me forget everything else.

CHAPTER 28

Day 1

I lay dazed and flat on the playground wood chips, gasping for a breath that was stalled somewhere in my lungs. Ten seconds earlier, I had been running up the equipment stairs toward the slide, ready to race down again, when an older boy with messy red hair and freckles had beat me to the slide and shoved me out of his way.

Except, out of his way on the crowded landing meant a five foot drop down the opening of the playground set. I fell backward, arms flailing and banging my head against the fireman pole until the ground met my back.

Once the breath came back to my lungs, tears leaked out of my eyes. It wasn't the pain as much as feeling hurt that someone would be mean enough to push me in the first place. I was careful not to cry out, but instead I sat up and wiped my eyes while searching for any sign of my parents–though even at five years old, I knew the Fourth of July breakfast going on across the park would have their attention.

A dark haired boy wearing a blue and red Spiderman shirt squatted before me. I blinked up at him, my eyes adjusting to the harsh sunlight behind his head.

"Are you okay?"

"Yeah," I said, sniffling and wiping my nose with the back of my hand.

"He pushed you," he said, pointing at the red-haired boy laughing raucously and chasing another boy around the perimeter of the playground.

The boy in front of me looked familiar.

"I'm Dax. I've seen you at my school before."

I shrugged. "I'm Ivy."

"Now he's chasing my older brother," Dax said, his eyes following the young offender.

He turned abruptly to me, holding up his hands, and showed me what looked like a Spiderman web-shooter contraption attached to his wrists.

"You want me to get him?"

I stood, brushing the dirt off of my hands and nodded solemnly, injustice burning a hole in my wounded heart.

He slipped one of the web shooters off of his wrist. "You want the other one?"

Grasping it lightly in my hand, I replied. "Yeah."

He helped me secure it onto my wrist while giving me a crash course in all things Spiderman and web shooters.

Then we were off.

THE LAUGHTER from men and boys filled the lobby at Sunset Repairs. I hadn't realized that pizza, a plethora of brown sodas, and a Lego monstrosity on steroids was the key to happiness. I never had siblings. I never understood the power of the Lego. How it brought grown men and young boys together, bonding them for life amid Star Wars relics and dinosaur replicas.

Dax had given me his permission, after paying him in an hour's worth of kisses, to open up the building of the Lego car to the community. And the response had been epic.

Angela loaned me an old projector collecting dust in my dad's basement, which made it possible to project the pages of the guidebook on the wall so everyone could be looking for the next pieces. Pretty soon, an impressive assembly line formed while I sat there with an almost spiritual satisfaction, watching the car get built. It was just one day, but these guys were as good as professionals. The size of the Lego car had already doubled from where I had it, and it had only been an hour.

Some friends from high school had even come to help out—Beau; Beau's brother, Tristan; Noah Belacourt, the island billionaire who owned the resort; Phoenix; Briggs; and even Walker Collins, the island golf star, stopped by for a slice of pizza and promptly began searching with the others for missing pieces. It felt like a high school reunion of sorts, and watching the easygoing camaraderie between everyone...it only made me happier that I'd chosen this life.

Dax closed up the shop early. He stood by the sparkling new windows, chatting with a teenage boy wearing baggy pants and a beanie, probably regarding the position of part-time help Dax had posted online. He had already hired one person full-time, but he was now in search of a teenager looking for an after-school position that he might have some influence over. The legacy of Keith McMannus would live on forever in the form of seventies music and inspiring goodness.

Dax looked relaxed and friendly today. His jeans looked fitted, and combined with the allure of his tattoos peeking out from underneath his sleeve, I couldn't tear my eyes away. We'd been caught having too many public displays of affection lately, so I busied myself with passing out drinks and brownies to anybody who wanted some. And if the entire island ran out of brownies, I'd swim to the mainland to get more if that meant everybody stayed here and worked on the car.

Pretty soon, the girls of the island filtered their way into the shop. It was fun to see Cat and Jane and a few other friends I hadn't seen in a while, but they proved much more distracting to the guys than all the pizza and brownies combined.

The best surprise of the night, however, was when Dax's parents and Trent, who was headed back to the mainland the next day, stopped by to lend a hand. Dax shot me a curious look before he greeted them, giving his parents a brief hug. But it was watching Dax and Trent laughing together while searching for Lego pieces for the car that held so many memories of Dax and another brother that had me blinking back tears. This family was on their way to rebuilding—this time with Dax—and it was beautiful.

And surprisingly, Angela stopped by.

Her brunette hair was pulled up in a high ponytail as she strode into the lobby.

"Hey." She said, smiling at all the testosterone kneeling together over a pile of Legos. "That's so cute."

I smiled and looked at where she was pointing. It really was cute. "Thank you for coming."

She smiled. "Your dad wished he could come, but he had campaign obligations on the mainland today."

I nodded, understanding her perfectly and appreciating her efforts. I doubted much would ever change with him, but setting boundaries had become easier for me. I wasn't sure what my dad's and my relationship would look like down the road, but I was hopeful for a somewhat peaceful existence.

The car was over three-quarters of the way built, and the way the crowd still stuck around, it was looking like it might get completely finished today. Nobody even complained about Dax's music, and when a specific song came on toward the end of the afternoon, the entire group began singing. Young and old alike seemed to know the words. I was laughing at the enthusiasm of Beau and Trent busting out the words, but it was the chorus that caused my eyes to find Dax's.

And when he motioned to me with the flick of his head to meet him in the garage, I didn't hesitate.

When he lifted me up to sit on his workbench, for easier access to my mouth, I had no complaints.

"So, is 'Sweet Caroline' an old favorite of yours?" I asked between kisses, my hands finding their home around his neck.

"More recent," he said, pulling back to look at me.

"And what about your new obsession with Bon Jovi? I think I heard a few more of their songs on your playlist. Look at you, adding a newer decade of music to your—"

"Hey, Books?"

"Yeah?"

"Shut up."

His smile was the last thing I saw before he silenced me with the most delicious of kisses.

EPILOGUE

Day 420

The late-afternoon sun poured into Dax's garage. I'd just gotten out for the summer after my first job as a professor at Harvine College. After the twelve-minute ferry ride to the mainland, the community college was only a ten-minute drive. Not bad, if you consider the fact that I got to teach college students, I wasn't stuck behind a computer, and Dax's garage was on the way home from the ferry. Usually, I stuck around for his last half hour or so of work and helped him fill out some invoices, among...other things, if we happened to be the only ones there.

So much had changed in a year. So many of my friends had gotten engaged. Even with all my *indiscretions* last year, my dad had won his campaign. I felt removed from it all. Our relationship had fallen into exactly what I had told him I'd accept. I no longer worked at the cafe, but whenever I saw him on the street, I smiled. Occasionally, he'd call me when he needed something, but I only said yes when I truly wanted to. The need for his approval had all but dissipated and it seemed to make all the difference.

Dax now had a full-time helper by the name of George, who had lost his job early last summer. He hadn't known much about mechanics, but he was hard-working and eager to learn. Bonus: he'd been raised on seventies music, so he fit right in.

Evan, the high schooler Dax had also taken on, turned out to be a natural and had been a great asset to the shop. He was a reluctant convert to the music Dax insisted on playing, but I had no doubt Dax would get him in the end.

He'd gotten me.

I walked into the shop wearing my favorite casual teaching outfit—paperbag coral shorts that hit me mid-thigh and a cream-colored tank top. My students had been out for the summer for two days already, while I had been stuck in meetings and trainings before, finally, being released as well. I smiled when I saw the massive Lego car spinning around in front of the window, a beacon for tourists and locals alike. Making my way back past the empty lobby, I opened the door to the garage and peeked inside.

Dax and Evan were standing on a small fishing boat pulled into the garage on a trailer. Dax was showing Evan something on the motor. His words were patient, easy-going, and kind—all the traits I'd surprisingly discovered about Dax last summer. That secret sweetness he tried to keep locked away, but ultimately couldn't.

After a year of serious dating, light discussions of marriage had been danced around more and more, but Dax had seemed to clam up about it lately. He had come a long way in opening up, but sometimes the closed part of him won out.

But come on...you can't dangle the word marriage in front of a woman for months now, only to get too scared to press forward. I had a whole litter of mini dark-haired, brown-eyed babies I planned to have, and we needed to get cracking.

Dax looked up and saw me standing there. I felt his gaze more than saw it as it trailed down my body, leaving fire in its wake.

"That's enough for today, Evan." Dax looked at me while he spoke. "I'll see you tomorrow."

Evan glanced at me and nodded, clearly understanding some sort of silent man code. He stood and jumped down from the boat.

"Don't forget to clock out."

"You got it, Boss." Evan smiled shyly at me while he ambled toward the old pinup calendar.

"You haven't gotten a new calendar yet?" I laughed.

"Works just fine, doesn't it, Evan?"

Evan shrugged, blushing a bit as he passed me. "I guess."

"Bye, Evan," I called as Dax jumped from the boat and made his way toward me, a panther stalking his prey.

I hoped Evan was gone by the time Dax's hands found me, but I couldn't be sure. Nor could I find it in myself to care.

"Are you mine for the summer now?" he asked as he picked me up, his arms locking around the bottom of my hips. I leaned down, skimming my nose against his, while my hands caressed the stubble on his cheeks.

"Yup."

"How was the last day?"

"Boring, but I'm glad for the summer break."

"Got any plans this summer?" He blew a breath along my neck.

I tightened my hold around his shoulders. "Maybe a few." I moved my forehead down so it pressed against his.

"Good."

"I heard a song the other day that I think you'd like," I said casually, before I lost my nerve. "It's even from your preferred decade."

He put me back down on the ground as I reached in his back pocket for his phone. "So, it's not 'SexyBack'?"

"Not this time, hot stuff."

I looked up the song and pressed play, hiding it away from Dax when he tried to peek over my shoulder. When the music began, I watched Dax's face out of the corner of my eye, growing a bit more hesitant. Each passing second brought more awareness onto Dax's face. A slow, impish smile formed, the kind that always got my heart thumping wildly.

By the time the chorus to "Keep Your Hands to Yourself" by The Georgia Satellites came on, I was itching to leave. I had to move or else I would combust. I had shown too much. Put too much pressure on him. I started a beeline toward the door before Dax was in front of me, his warm body stopping me before he bent down and hoisted me over his shoulder in one swift movement.

"Hey! Dax! I was kidding! We're fine!"

Was I regretting having him listen to a song that basically told him he needed to marry me or I wouldn't be kissing him any more?

Maybe—even though I already knew that would never happen. I was weak and completely head over heels in love with Dax Miller.

His only sign he heard me as he rummaged around a drawer at the counter was a spank on my rear.

"Dax, put me down!"

"This is your own fault, Caroline," he replied as he shoved something in his pocket and strode toward the open garage doors and turned toward the marina.

By this point, I was squealing and feeling really ridiculous that he still had me flung across his shoulder. I reached down and spanked him back.

"Better be careful, I could do this all day," was his only quip before I felt another tap on my butt. I gave up with a secretly delighted huff.

"Put that girl down, Dax Miller!" came a wobbly but screechy voice to our left. "Why don't you come over here and pick up a real woman?!"

Dax breathed out a laugh at the nosy elderly resident sitting on her walker chair on the grass next door. "You're too bossy for me, Virginia!" he shouted back, not breaking his stride. "You know that!"

"You be good to that girl, Trouble."

"Planning on it!"

"Are you?" I asked, my face and stomach flopping against his back as he strode along the boardwalk and onto his boat where the words *Sweet Caroline* had been freshly painted in scrawling red letters.

He walked me gingerly out onto the middle of the boat, where he bent down and gently placed me on solid ground once more. I had been fully prepared to scold him or kiss him or something when I noticed a small table with a white tablecloth in the back of the boat. The same spot we had spent the last Fourth of July watching the fireworks.

It was set for two with napkins and two glass bottles of Coke. "What is this?" Warm arms locked around me from behind, Dax's lips nuzzling against my ear.

"I was going to wait and do this tonight. There were going to be two big burgers on those plates and a mountain of fries. I was going to take you for a drive at sunset and play your song."

I smiled, my entire body bursting with light and happiness, imagining it all happening like he said.

"Can you wait?" the soft voice came again, this time catching my earlobe between his teeth. "Caroline?" Shivers of pleasure ran down my entire central nervous system, feeling warm and safe and loved completely in his arms.

"No," I said softly, shaking my head. "I can't wait."

Dax turned me to face him in his arms, and I immediately erupted in giggles, holding my hands over my mouth. Suddenly, it all felt so overwhelming as I looked at him—looked at the man who showed me every day in words and actions that I was worthy of love, even as imperfect and messy as I ended up being.

Dax bit back a grin and slowly dropped to his knee. When I was able to look at him, I took a breath and found nothing but sweetness in his eyes.

"Caroline Ivy Brooks," he began, "my impatient but irresistible woman, will you marry me?"

I sank to my knees, throwing my arms around his shoulders, kissing him as soon as he had the words out. He was thrown off balance, and we both went backward, where I proceeded to land on his stomach, causing him to groan in discomfort. After laughing for a few long moments, he kissed me again, pulling me closer until no space existed between us.

"I'm going to take that as a yes."

I kissed him again. "Good call."

"I've got one more surprise for you."

"Hmm?" At this point, I was drunk on kisses and high on love when he sat us both up and pointed back toward his shop. It took a minute to find what he was looking at.

On the backside of his shop, on the second story that only people floating on the water would see, was a picture of an open book with a vine of flowers coming out of the spine. It had been spray painted on his building exactly like the temporary tattoo he had given me last year. Underneath the picture, scrawled in bright red, were the words *I love Books*. The word love was a heart.

"I knew you'd be too chicken to tag a building," Dax said.

I laughed, my cheeks aflame as I turned back to him. "So my rebel list is finally complete?"

"You're just getting started."

And then he was kissing me.

THANK you for reading Rebel Summer! Need more of Dax and Ivy? Join my newsletter for a free bonus scene written in Dax's perspective!

Fair warning, there is lots of flirting, banter, almost kisses, and several rolls of toilet paper. Find the link on my website at www.cindysteel.com or click here: https://dl.bookfunnel.com/4mfk11wegm

Looking for more stories in Sunset Harbor? Read the next book in the Falling for Summer Series!

Falling in love is easy. Finding the right guy to spend happily ever after with... that's the hard part.

But I have a foolproof plan. I'm taking the tropes that work in romance books and applying them to my love life.

Only one bed? Never fails.

Caring for someone when they're sick? A classic.

"Who did this to you?" Seals the deal every single time.

So long, loneliness. Don't let the door hit you on the way out.

But the more I try to force romance, the more feelings naturally progress with the one man who's off limits: Walker Collins, the guy I've had a secret crush on since 7th grade, not to mention my best friend's older brother.

Dating Walker crosses BFF lines I swore I'd never cross. Plus, he hates Sunset Harbor, and his pro golf career will take him off the island as fast as he came, sending me back to the land of singlehood, loneliness, and broken hearts.

At the end of the day, I don't want to be the fool in my foolproof plan.

FALLING FOR SUMMER

Summer Ever After by Kortney Keisel
Jane + Walker

Beachy Keen by Kasey Stockton
Cat + Noah

Plotting Summer by Jess Heileman
Capri + Tristan

Summer Tease by Martha Keyes
Gemma + Beau

Beauty and the Beach by Gracie Ruth Mitchell
Holland + Phoenix

One Happy Summer by Becky Monson
Presley + Briggs

Rebel Summer by Cindy Steel
Ivy + Dax

AUTHOR'S NOTES

Thank you for reading Rebel Summer! I hope you've enjoyed your time in Sunset Harbor!

No politicians were harmed in the making of this book. Though I needed Ivy's dad to be a certain way for the purpose of this story, I also recognize that there are many politicians who are great people truly striving to better their communities and serve their country. I mean...there are also many who don't seem that great, but that's for another day.

I tried my best to give the police and court room scenes an authentic feel. That being said—this is still a fictional romantic comedy and I did take some liberties for the purpose of this story. After all—what's a quirky island town without an endearing, matchmaking judge to go with it?

Thank you for reading!

THE PLAYLIST

There were so many moments in this story that played out in my head like a scene from a movie. Dax's seventies music became such a fun part of the book and even I became a semi-converted oldie's fan—but just for SOME of the music. Sorry, Dad!

Here is the link to the Spotify playlist featuring the songs that set the tone and tempo in Dax's shop: https://open.spotify.com/playlist/3wXXMQOzBgEavGlaTRGbdB?si=d6b7f5eac5bd4445

If seventies music isn't your thing, but you're curious about a few of the moments in the book that paired perfectly with the music...here are a few songs that are definitely worth listening to:

"Old Time Rock and Roll" by Bob Segar. This is the song playing when Ivy visited Dax to apologize right after the accident. It was the perfect introduction to Dax. The words and tune seem to transcend all time and became the song I listened to the most while washing dishes and plotting this book.

"You Give Love a Bad Name" by Bon Jovi. This is actually, Ivy's song, but it fits the storyline in a fun way. And it totally seemed like a song Dax would secretly love playing in his shop.

"Bad Moon Rising" by Creedence Clearwater Revival. This

became the perfect song while a despondent Ivy contemplated doing Dax's list.

"I am I said" by Neal Diamond. I didn't name this song in the book, but it was the song about loneliness playing just before Ivy invited Dax to play Volleyball.

"Spirit in the Sky" by Norman Greenbaum. When Ivy discovers Dax has a car on the island, the first ten seconds of this song perfectly captures the mood.

"Sweet Caroline" by Neal Diamond. Neal Diamond is a national treasure. That is all.

"Keep Your Hands to Yourself" by The Georgia Satellites. My dad had me listen to this one, and I knew it would be the perfect, fun song to end the book.

<u>Rebel Summer Playlist</u>

Old Time Rock and Roll - Bob Segar
Witchy Woman - Eagles
Desperado - Eagles
Piano Man - Billy Joel
You Give Love a Bad Name - Bon Jovi
Bad Moon Rising - Creedence Clearwater Revival
I Am...I Said - Neil Diamond
Spirit in the Sky - Norman Greenbaum
Centerfield - John Fogerty
Sweet Caroline - Neil Diamond
Keep Your Hands to Yourself - The Georgia Satellites

ACKNOWLEDGMENTS

Writing a book takes a village. Here are a few people in mine...

First and foremost - James. Thank you for giving me the time and space I needed to write this book. And for all those solo hotel trips when I needed to buckle down and work. You (and Dr. Pepper) are the reason this book got finished. Thank you for supporting my dreams.

To my kids - Thanks for your patience as I figure out how to balance writing with mom life. You three are my favorites.

Lisa - So many ideas come from bouncing them back and forth with you and I appreciate you in my life so much—as a sister, my best friend, and my first reader. I was intensely annoying and needy while crafting this book, but thanks for always picking up the phone.

Dad - Thanks for always having seventies music playing in your shop. I'm sorry for all the crap I used to give you about that. Also, thanks for teaching me what the heck a driveline is and how someone would bolt it to their car.

Mom - Thanks for your help with all the seventies music and for being a great support to me. You're the best.

Kortney, Kasey, Jess, Martha, Gracie, and Becky - This series was a wild ride, but I had a blast working with each of you. I love how we all support and build each other up and I'm so honored to call you all friends.

Karen - You are the first person I want giving feedback on my book. Your thoughts and advice is always spot on, but even more valuable than that is your friendship. I'm so glad this career brought us together.

Karen's lawyer husband, Ben - Thank you for your help and advice for the courtroom scenes!

Hollijo, Whitney, and Karen - Thank you for your support and ideas and being the best critique group ever.

Spencer - Thanks for reading over my manuscript, offering suggestions, and responding to my thousands of texts about police stuff and court proceedings and telling me when it would be okay to fudge a few things for the sake of my story.

Jenelle, Annie, Leah, & Kate - Thanks for helping to babysit on occasion so I could write.

Richard & Caitlin - Thanks for teaching me about the world of academia and answering questions.

Mary Ann - Thanks for your kindness, example, and hours of babysitting.

My beta readers, ARC team, cheer team, and Bookstagrammers - Thank you for reading and taking chance after chance on my books and for all the beautiful pictures, posts, and reviews. You have truly changed my life for the better.

Jana Miller - Thank you for your feedback on the early stages of my book! I'm so grateful for your thoughts and encouragement.

Jenn Lockwood - Thank you for your copyedits! You are amazing and always so great to work with.

Amy Romney - Thank you for the proofread and for your time and talents in helping to make this book sing.

Lindsay Rankin - Thank you for being the last-minute eyes on my book. I appreciate you and all of your help so much!

Melody Jeffries - Your vision for this cover and the entire series was so beautiful! I love working with you!

To my readers - Thank you for reading, all the sweet emails, DM's, comments, posts, shares, and for telling your friends about my books. I see you and I love you. Thank you!

ABOUT THE AUTHOR

Cindy Steel was raised on a dairy farm in Idaho. She grew up singing country songs at the top of her lungs and learning to solve all of life's problems while milking cows and driving tractors—rewriting happy endings every time. She married a cute Idaho boy and is the proud mother of two wild and fun twin boys and a sweet baby girl. She loves making breakfast, baking, photography, reading a good book, and staying up way past her bedtime to craft stories that will hopefully make you smile.

She loves to connect with readers! She is the most active on Instagram @authorcindysteel and her newsletter but she occasionally makes her way to Facebook at Author Cindy Steel and her website at www.cindysteel.com.

Made in the USA
Middletown, DE
08 January 2025

68521480R00215